NOTES
FROM THE
SOUL

January 5, 2024

Dear Kristin,

As a mother of two grown sons, I feel we have a special bond!

I share my story during a time when both my sons had graduated college & were living independently.

I hope some of my story resonates with you.

Thanks again for your trust in reading it!

Enjoy your precious little ones!

Marcella

NOTES FROM THE SOUL

Revised Edition

SPIRITUAL REFLECTIONS ON FINDING THE ESSENCE WITHIN

MARCELLA CARROLL

Charleston, SC
www.PalmettoPublishing.com

Notes From The Soul

First Edition

Hardcover ISBN: 979-8-8229-3089-6
Paperback ISBN: 979-8-8229-2901-2
eBook ISBN: 979-8-8229-2902-9

For The Muskees, you are forever in my heart.
For my future grandchildren, dream big, love big,
and listen to the whispers of your heart.

Wherever you stand,
be the soul of that place.

—RUMI

Table of Contents

SOUL SCHOOL RESOURCES

NOTES

Gratitude

From the bottom of my heart, I am truly grateful for so many people (too many to name) who have made and continue to make my life much better every day by being a part of it. Thank you for choosing to share your lives with me. I appreciate each one of you!

I offer my heartfelt gratitude to the following pivotal people who were with me every step of the way on my journey:

Thank you to God and the soul for never giving up on me and for nudging me on the path of love.

Thank you to my mom and dad for your unconditional love, your commitment to family values, teaching us grit, and demonstrating how to live a life led by the soul.

Thank you to my two amazing sons, the original muskees, for your unwavering love, loyalty, laughter, and many lessons you continue to teach me. You are champions—you keep moving forward, even when times are tough. Your encouragement, support, and love motivated me to take the first step out of my comfort zone. Without you both, I may have never written this book. You continue to amaze me every day and make me want to *Love Big!* "Big things, muskees, big things!"

Thank you to my wonderful daughter-in-law—you are a beacon of light, love, joy, kindness, and laughter.

Thank you to Miss D—your dedication to learning, persistence, grit, kindness, and peaceful presence is inspirational.

Thank you to my nieces for your encouragement, love, support, and hours of chats about manifesting our dreams.

Thank you to my brother and sister-in-law for your continued support, kindness, and unconditional love.

Thank you to my vast extended family—too many of you to name—for your powerful presence and love in my life through the good times and tough times.

Thank you to our soulful pup, Maggie; may your spirit live on forever, and may you rest in peace.

Thank you to Matisse, my writing assistant, who was my faithful companion through many long, arduous, and tedious days and nights.

Thank you to my soulful grandogters, Minnie and Topony, who spread love and joy to everyone they meet, accept everyone, and make me laugh every day!

Thank you to my great-cousin Sister M for introducing me to St. Ignatius and the Spiritual Exercises and for encouraging me on my path of love.

Thank you to my friends for your love, support, and encouragement as we accompany one another on our journeys.

Thank you to the pivotal person who motivated me to pivot. You helped me understand important lessons of friendship, love, and the power of the Holy Spirit.

Thank you to Darcy and Jack for welcoming me into your home and making me feel like family.

Thank you to the Volontario Professionale for the reminder, "It is His work. I am like a little pencil in His hand. That is all. He does the thinking. He does the writing. The pencil has nothing to do with it. The pencil has only to be allowed to be used." (Mother Teresa) And for including me in The Nice Patrol.

Thank you to the many spiritual teachers who shared their journeys about how to let love lead the way.

Thank you to Oprah Winfrey for inspiring me and teaching us how to become the best versions of ourselves. Your Super Soul Sunday podcast helped me learn how to connect within.

Thank you to Kristin and her team at Palmetto Publishing for your patience and kindness every step of the way with me with this book.

Thank you to Bill, Jen, Tracy, Akemi, and the rest of the team at StoryBuilders Press who helped polish the book, and more importantly, helped me believe in my story.

Author's Note

Dear Reader:

You have much more power to create your world than you may realize. At least that's what I discovered on my three-year journey into uncharted territory.

For most of my life, I would categorize myself as a Nervous Nelly—the queen of finding something to worry about. I also had no idea this steady stream of worried thoughts was running my life—until I received a wake-up call.

I packed a few belongings, moved more than seven hundred miles to a place where I knew nobody, and began an adventure way out of my comfort zone. But this isn't a story about a geographical journey; instead, it's a story about a journey within.

It all starts with the mind—learning to detach from the steady stream of (often negative) thoughts to access the peaceful space within. Simply put, it's about becoming observers of those voices in our heads. Our thoughts are powerful—the positive ones can empower us, and the negative ones can defeat us. Through the many books I read and my experiences, I learned we can train our minds with more positive thoughts to keep us focused on our dreams and help us take the action steps necessary toward those dreams, as opposed to allowing the fearful and doubting thoughts to hold us back and keep us stuck.

With the help of more than forty books, a saint from five hundred years ago, Sister M, and hundreds of podcasts, I gradually learned to disengage from my headspace and connect to my soul space. I like to say I was a student in Soul School, my made-up name for this life-changing experience. The school's mission: love for all souls.

How did I get there? I believe I was guided by a higher power of Divine love. I call that power God; you may know it by another name. I discovered this Divine force of love dwells within us and is accessible to us anytime. It is the greatest force in the universe through which we are all connected. I turned to this higher power for signs and direction, which I nicknamed celestial synchronicities. Divine guidance did show up, and I received quite a few of these celestial synchronicities, some of which I will share in this book.

I offer these *Notes from the Soul* with the hope that you may also discover new ways to connect with the essence within you and tune into the desires in your heart, if you feel inclined to do so.

In this book, I share fifty-two simple messages, one message per week for a year. This is designed intentionally to help you take just a few minutes out of your busy week to go inside yourself and hear the whispers of your heart and soul. You may also want to write the message on a note and take it with you for the week as a reminder of the force within.

A toolkit of forty simple practices is included at the back of the book to provide you with some action-oriented steps to help you slow down, enjoy the journey, and discover the treasure within you. Life is a series of peaks and valleys. I use these tools to help me conquer the down times, savor the good ones, and stay focused on my hopes and my dreams from my heart and soul every step of the way. I hope you can too.

Divine love is transformative!

MARCELLA CARROLL
AUGUST 15, 2023

Connect with me at:
amazon.com/author/marcellacarroll
or www.marciecarroll.com

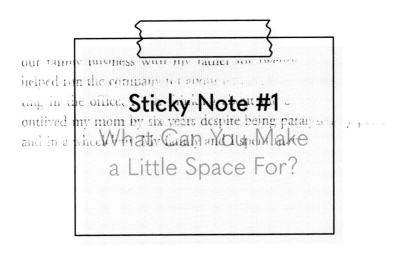

Sticky Note #1

What Can You Make a Little Space For?

"Trusting your heart space is imperative for the growth of a healthy spiritual life."

—WAYNE DYER

Have you ever felt the need for space? Like you suddenly woke up and wondered what you were doing with your life and how you got where you were? Multiply that feeling by twenty. That's how I was feeling. I don't know about you, but I couldn't explain what that feeling really meant and where it came from. It's not as if someone did something to me or something monumental happened. Actually, it was quite the opposite—my life was pretty good. My two sons were healthy, happy, and living independently. I was in the process of transitioning out of the family business where I had worked tenaciously for about twenty years. At that time, I should have been thrilled about the opportunity to relax a bit and unwind, yet I had this gnawing longing for something more.

It all began one morning in October 2019. I awoke with an intense desire and longing for "space." I couldn't explain or describe the feeling in much detail, but it was overwhelming. I kept repeating, "I just need space." I would later learn that "space" is another word for the soul. According to Dr. Wayne Dyer, "The soul yearns for space, expansion, and immensity. It needs to be free to expand."[1]

Father Thomas Keating would help me understand a couple of years later that "space" is a spiritual level of being and the "need for space" is the need for a spiritual journey. And, to some degree, space for my "true self" to emerge. I knew none of this back then.

I realize now that my soul was longing to connect with me and expand. Unfortunately, I had no idea of this when the feelings first arose. I would also learn further on in my journey that the soul speaks through longing. My soul was speaking to me, but I was clueless. I was living a life filled with noise, static, and to some degree, chaos. That would all change soon, and I would begin to awaken to the stirrings within.

On that morning in October 2019, as I was feeling the intense need for space, I had no idea those words were the beginning of my journey to discover my true self. This was also the first of many lessons I would learn over the next few years. My soul was longing to connect with me through stirrings within my heart, gentle nudges, and a yearning for more. I could feel a movement happening inside me.

The truth was I was very much out of touch with my soul for more than fifty years of living. I lived a very active life, as most of us do, and I didn't have time to *tune into the soul* (whatever that meant). I believed in "the soul" but didn't know a lot about it other than I really hoped the soul would continue after death and connect with other souls whom I loved deeply and had passed on.

My life was overflowing with activities and demands. There was no room for any type of soul connection. I had worked in our family business with my father for twenty years and had helped run the company for about ten. If I wasn't physically sitting in the office, I was thinking about the business. My dad outlived my mom by six years despite being paralyzed by polio and in a wheelchair. My family and I spent many years worried about my father's health; my mom was the rock of the family. I spent as much time as I could with my dad during those last six years of his life. My mother passed away suddenly at the young age of seventy-three. Losing my mom so suddenly was a shock for our family. She and my father had been together for almost fifty-five years. My mom took care of my dad. She loved him tremendously and never wanted anyone else to take care of him; she didn't see it as an obligation. After my father passed away, I sold the business. I couldn't imagine working in the company without my dad.

In addition to running the business and spending time with my father, I was blessed with two wonderful sons who graduated from college and, in the case of my oldest son, law school. My sons truly amazed me (and still do). They had to dodge some major curveballs at very young ages, including their parents' marriage crumbling.

My life had some great highs—a loving family, a successful business—and some big lows—the disintegration of a marriage, the sudden death of my mother, who was my best friend, and the death of my father, who was my mentor and business partner.

With my plate overflowing, the gentle soul had been patiently waiting for an opportunity to connect with me when the timing was just right—as I began to come up for some air after a very long time. The feeling of a need for space continued, and I found myself in therapy sessions once a week with a wonderful therapist who seemed to understand what I was saying even though I didn't. She recommended a few books: one on boundaries, which

I found interesting, and another called *The Art of Discernment: Making Good Decisions in Your World of Choices*, by Stefan Kiechle, on discernment—a practice I knew nothing about.

Have you ever read a book and realized there was so much more to it when you read it again months or even years later? It's pretty ironic now, knowing everything I was searching for came in the form of a book from my therapist at the beginning of my journey. But I wasn't tuned in to signs from above that were being sent my way to guide me. I hadn't learned yet to be aware of who or what was coming into my path in the form of people and books or to consider the possible meanings and messages. I wasn't in the right space then, but that was about to change.

CELESTIAL SYNCHRONICITIES

The Art of Discernment was the first of many celestial synchronicities that God would send my way. I would be reintroduced in much greater detail to discernment and the ways of Saint Ignatius later in my spiritual journey. I nicknamed any event, person, or message that was sent my way to confirm I was on the right track or, as in this case, to serve as a preview of what was to come, a celestial synchronicity. I love the magical sound of those two words together.

I devoured *The Art of Discernment*, probably faster than I should have, because I was impatient and in search of answers. Although I wrote notes throughout the book, I still didn't have any answers. I was, however, able to narrow my options for space down to two paths—stay where I was and carve out a little space, or move and create my own space.

I wanted a simple and quick solution for my longing for space. Patience was a virtue I did not possess. What I learned in my speed-reading of *The Art of Discernment* was that it's

important to listen to our hearts and our inner voices, two chan‑
nels I wasn't tuned in to. In terms of making decisions, the book
discussed choosing the path that leads more closely to love, good‑
ness, and God—the way that contributes more to the growth of
love and justice. Praying to the Holy Spirit was recommended,
yet another channel I hadn't subscribed to. Paying attention to
our feelings was also mentioned—a practice that was not part of
my daily routine. Basically, the book was providing tools to help
me reach a decision, but the reality was that I wasn't in touch
with any of the suggestions—the inner voice, my heart, my feel‑
ings, and the Holy Spirit. It was very hard to put any of the
book's suggestions into practice because they were simply words
on a page to me at that time.

As I look back now, it seems as if *The Art of Discernment*
was my introductory course in Soul School (My made-up name
that best describes what I was learning about—the soul). I am
shocked as I sit here today, years later, writing this book and
rereading *The Art of Discernment*. For I am now trying my best
to live my life according to many of the lessons discussed in that
book, which at the beginning of my journey seemed like it had
been written in a foreign language.

The celestial synchronicities were all there back then when I
was sitting at a major crossroads in my life; I just didn't recognize
them, or perhaps I didn't want to.

Soul Searching:

- What does the need for space mean to you?
- Have you ever experienced a need for space?
- What does the need for space feel like for you?
- What are some ways you've created space for yourself?

- Is there something would you like to make a little space for in your life?
- When can you make some space to connect with yourself, tune into your feelings, or connect with your inner self, even for five minutes?
- Perhaps you can ponder how you go about making decisions in your life. Do you listen to your inner voice? What other tools do you use to make big decisions in your life?

Song suggestion:

"Somewhere Over the Rainbow," by Katharine McPhee

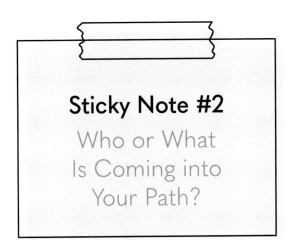

Sticky Note #2
Who or What Is Coming into Your Path?

"God is always trying to get our attention in ways both obvious and subtle."

—KEVIN O'BRIEN, SJ

Have you ever looked back on a chance encounter to realize you were actually destined to be in a certain place at a particular moment in time? Can you recall a time when someone was placed in your path to help you move forward or deliver a message you needed to hear? Have you ever had the feeling of being in the right place at the right time, feeling as if the events of a particular situation were somehow being orchestrated from above? Take a moment to consider your thoughts about destiny and Divine guidance.

I was at a crossroads trying to decide whether to stay where I was and carve out some space or move, so I did what I had done dozens of times when trying to make difficult decisions—I wrote a pros and cons list for each option. Since I couldn't tap into the suggestions from *The Art of Discernment*, a pros and cons list seemed like my only hope. My head was a big fan of using logic and weighing my options for either staying the course in my current situation and finding a little space for myself, or moving out into my own space, wherever that might be (which was a bit horrifying, if I'm being honest).

My heart knew what felt right, but my head didn't agree. When my head was in charge, fear, worry, and the what-ifs took over, and I remained stuck. The soul, however, was longing to travel and expand and was nudging me toward the path of the unknown. I could begin to feel it. My mind thought the idea of living on my own somewhere new sounded crazy. *Where will I live? What will I do with my dogs? What will I do all by myself? I don't know anybody. I won't have anybody close to me.*

The fears and mental static went on and on in my head, while the longing for space from the soul intensified. This became a pattern of longing to take action versus fear of the unknown, like a revolving door with no forward movement. To make matters even more difficult, I had lived in the area I was currently living for most of my life. There was no way the head was going to embrace leaving home for uncharted territory where I knew nobody.

Fear had a tight grasp over me and didn't want to let go, but the stirrings from the soul were becoming more apparent. During this period, I began to notice celestial synchronistic events unfolding in my life, perhaps because I was searching for answers.

Such celestial synchronistic events felt like they had been orchestrated from above and seemed to be a gentle nudging in a certain direction. They were hard to describe in words—more of a feeling. At that time, I was also becoming more aware of the people I was meeting and the conversations I was having with colleagues and friends on business trips. I would later learn to be aware of whom God is putting in my life if I want to know what God is up to in my life. I wasn't aware of the power of those meetings back then. All of these interactions seemed to suggest taking the path to my own space—the unknown.

I remember a few conversations with other women who seemed to be in sync with my desire for space and encouraged me in that direction. But a voice in my head kept repeating, *Stay put. Your life is just fine. You're being dramatic. Everything is fine. Don't rock the boat.* I began to feel the push and pull. Yet the gentle guidance deep within persisted.

As if the growing intensity of my need for space wasn't enough to act on, an event unfolded that jolted me to move forward into the unknown. In what other spiritual teachers have referred to as a "Divine appointment," I received my answer. I hadn't even planned on attending a particular event where I received my answer. I was supposed to be out of town. I remember observing circumstances unfold before me and recognizing that a greater power was in charge guiding me to a "Divine encounter" that would leave a lasting impression on my heart and soul, and give me my answer. It was like watching the pieces of a chess match in my life move forward, but I wasn't moving them. I felt the power from above move me to a meeting; so powerful that I knew it was time to pivot in a new direction. The best way I can describe the feeling is like a surge of energy. It propelled me forward. If I was unsure about the power of Divine intervention and guidance before, this moment was the one that made me a firm believer.

As Kevin O'Brien, SJ, says in his book, *The Ignatian Adventure*, "God has a way of getting our attention and sending the right people to us at the right times."[1] God did just that and, fortunately, got my attention. I was aware now, and I knew the path to take. I no longer had any doubts.

I believe without a doubt God let me know it was time for me to pivot in a new direction. It was time to move away from my past life which was guided mainly by my thoughts and fear, and into the unknown guided by my heart and soul. I wasn't sure why God wanted me to make a move or what would come next, but I knew without a doubt the time was right to move forward. And so, I did. God had my full attention now.

Soul Searching:

- Journal about a time when you felt as if you were being guided by a Higher Power.
  - » Perhaps meeting a certain person felt like it was orchestrated from above?
  - » Or maybe you ended up at an event that you were not supposed to attend and experienced a magical moment?
  - » What did that celestial guidance feel like?
- Write about your thoughts, feelings, and behaviors before and after the event occurred.
- Who or what stands out to you about that time?
- What was your original plan, and how did it change based on the guidance you received?
- What makes it feel like so much more than a coincidence?

Song suggestion:

"The Boss," by Diana Ross

Sticky Note #3
Is It Time to Pivot?

"One must struggle, personally and often in solitude, toward a decision that will never be entirely sure or predictable. One must be prepared to take risks."

—STEFAN KIECHLE

How would you describe what pivoting means to you? I came across an article from the Founder Institute titled, "What Pivoting is, When to Pivot, and How to Pivot Effectively," which does a great job describing what it means to pivot in the business world. "Pivoting requires diligent planning and execution... In business, pivoting is a term that describes the process of changing direction when the current strategy is not delivering the desired result."[1] Although my pivot was not related to the business world, it did require a change in an entirely new direction from the world I knew. Pivoting is hard to do and often requires movement out of one's comfort zone into unknown territory, and taking a risk. The best way I can describe a pivot is a turn toward a new direction—in my case, it was the unknown.

It involves taking a different path than you imagined you would take in your life. The opportunity to pivot often happens when you're at a major crossroads in your life. I've lived through three major pivots in my life and countless minor ones.

On my wedding day more than thirty years ago, I believed my marriage would last forever. I never imagined parting ways. That wasn't the case. I was at a crossroads about fifteen years into the marriage, looking at two potential paths after a major disappointment, deciding whether to stay or pivot. I chose to pivot into the unknown. My decision was driven by a very wounded and broken heart at that time. I didn't need a pros and cons list. I took a turn in a new direction.

My second major pivot was the transition away from our family business. This was a difficult decision but not nearly as difficult as the broken-marriage pivot. To some degree, the business pivot also had some emotional strings attached to it. My father was gone and would no longer be a presence in my daily activities at the office. My dad and I had worked together for twenty years and saw each other every day. I couldn't take the pain of his absence. I pivoted in a new direction, once again, and took a different path than I had initially imagined.

Then there I was, faced with the opportunity to pivot for the third time in my life. This time, however, it was coming from somewhere deep inside me. This was a very different sensation than the other two pivots in my life. It was more of a gentle longing for space. It was a softer pivot and not as much driven by devastation or a broken heart. It felt hopeful, like an invitation to a new world.

And so, I pivoted from a comfortable house and a loving relationship into my own space—a rented small apartment—with our two Labrador retrievers, Maggie and Matisse, and a few suitcases of clothing. I was beginning to release any attachment I had to things and belongings. There simply wasn't any room for a lot of stuff. I was also becoming more aware that I had a lot of unnecessary baggage, and it was time to detach from most of it. That would be my next lesson.

Soul Searching:

- Journal about a time when you felt it was time to pivot or take a road in a new direction.
- How did you know it was time to start a new chapter in your life?
- What or who helped you decide to pivot?
- In which areas of your life are you feeling led to pivot?

Song suggestion:

"Philadelphia Freedom," by Elton John

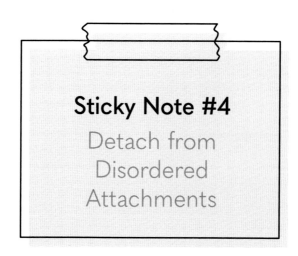

Sticky Note #4
Detach from Disordered Attachments

"When Ignatius says that we should be 'detached,' he's talking about not being tied down by unimportant things. Here's a quick example. What happens if your overriding concern in life is making money? Well, in that case you might not be as open to spending time with people who won't advance your career. You might be less likely to take time off. You might even begin to see other people only as tools—or worse, obstacles—in your quest for upward mobility. Gradually, you might start to see everything as revolving around your job, career, and desire to make money."

—JAMES MARTIN, SJ

Here we go—full disclosure. I'm a bit of a packrat. Not to the degree that I'd make it on the show with all the professional help, but I seriously do not enjoy parting with things, especially when they have anything to do with my boys—well, they're men, currently thirty-one and twenty-nine years old. But if they need any of their artwork from toddlerhood on, or if they'd like to peruse their immunization records or know what they ate every day in their first years, I've got it all.

Knowing my challenge to get rid of things, it should come as no surprise that when my father passed away, I couldn't part with furniture, nor pretty much anything else, from my parents' condominium. I kept it all. My brothers didn't live close by, and the cost of shipping the furniture likely would have exceeded its value. My brothers, family members, and friends kept some things that were meaningful to them, and I stored everything else.

BOUND BY THE MEMORIES

Looking back now, I think keeping all my parents' belongings somehow meant I was keeping them. Their belongings were all I had left of them and, I thought, my only means of preserving their memories.

It's hard losing your loved ones and even harder losing both your parents. I remember shortly after my father's passing looking at each item and reminiscing about how my parents used every piece of furniture.

For example, I remembered my mother sitting on her favorite chair every night when she solved her sudoku puzzles. I remembered countless hours around their dining room table and every holiday meal with family members being filled with love, laughter, and great conversations. I remembered my father sitting at his desk during our business meetings, snuggling with my sons on the couch when they were home for their holiday breaks from college, and our conversations filled with love and laughter there.

I remembered my nieces and other family members relaxing on the couch bringing us up to date with what was happening in their lives, and I remembered my parents' bed, where my father spent most of his final days as our family and friends surrounded him with love. Every single item in their condominium held a special place in my heart and was filled with loving and wonderful memories. I couldn't part with any of it, and I didn't.

The same thing had happened a few years earlier when my sons and I sold the house where the three of us had lived for most of their lives. I put everything into a storage unit. Each item had years of memories, and I couldn't part with any item for the very same reason. Doing so would have somehow meant having to say goodbye to those wonderful and happy memories and years. At least that's how it felt.

It's hard to say goodbye to loved ones who have passed on and to belongings that hold significant sentimental value from years of memories. It's also hard to get rid of belongings from the house your children have called home since they were very little.

WHAT TO KEEP AND WHAT TO LET GO

It's difficult to pivot into new chapters in our lives. At least it was for me. The storage unit was now overflowing with my parents' belongings and the belongings from our house. My entire life, less the contents of a few suitcases, was in a storage unit.

As I look back over so many years, I realize my attachment to things was probably ingrained in me from early childhood. As I grew older, however, the attachment to things was centered more on the sentimental value of the object and the memories associated with it. I wished I could go back in time and freeze those memories somehow.

A physical move from a larger space to a smaller space meant I could only bring essential belongings. It was time to part with the things. That is precisely what I did.

After many months of paying way too much for a rented storage unit, I realized if I had been able to live without those items, I didn't need them. I got rid of everything in the storage unit—furniture, clothing, and most of my other belongings. I cleared it all out, except for things that tugged at my heart, like my sons' art projects, photos, books, and special cards. Those items filled many boxes because I saved every project and card from when they could first write and draw.

The only good thing about being a packrat is I still have every card my parents, my sons, my daughter-in-law, my son's girlfriend, my brothers, my sisters-in-law, my nieces, my aunts, my cousins, and other family members and friends sent me. I have every note my sons wrote to me over the years. My mother was a big fan of sending cards, and I have most of her cards, too. I still read them at times, and I can hear her voice when I do. It helps me feel her presence.

This past year for my fifty-sixth birthday, I read a card she had sent me when I turned thirty years old. I also read cards my sons have sent me over the years when I'm missing them. Reading their loving and kind messages helps me feel connected to them even if we may be geographically apart. I dwindled my entire life down to a couple of suitcases of clothing, a few of my favorite kitchen gadgets (like the coffee maker that got me going each morning), and sentimental items from my sons, parents, and other family members.

BEGINNING TO DETACH

This was the beginning of my detachment from disordered attachments (yet another preview of what was to come). Later in the journey, I would find myself enrolled in the *Spiritual Exercises* of Saint Ignatius. One of the goals of the program is to help participants grow in spiritual freedom and get rid of disordered attachments that keep God out of the center of our lives.

I was beginning to practice what I would later learn. In one of my favorite books from Soul School, *The Ignatian Adventure*, Kevin O'Brien eloquently states,

> Lacking spiritual freedom, we become excessively attached to persons, places, material possessions, titles, occupations, honors, and the acclaim of others. These things are good in themselves when ordered and directed by the love of God. They become disordered attachments or disordered loves when they push God out of the center of our lives and become key to our identity.[2]

Beginning to detach from material possessions was yet another celestial synchronicity serving as a preview of what was to come.

At the time I was clearing out the storage unit, I had no idea who Saint Ignatius was and had never heard of the Spiritual Exercises. This was the beginning of putting into action the lessons I would be learning. I didn't realize any of this at the time.

I noticed I was beginning to feel a little lighter even though I had no idea where I was going. I guess that should make sense because I certainly had less baggage. It's similar to taking only a carry-on bag when flying. Less baggage is less worry. *Things are just things*, I told myself. *It's all about the people, the relationships with those I love and care about.*

GRATITUDE AND HUMOR

Apartment living was a big change, not only for me but for my sweet pups too, with smaller quarters inside and no yard for them to bask in during the day. I knew this was a temporary landing place for us, and we would just be passing through to somewhere—I just wasn't sure where. I was beginning to be open to what would come next because I had no agenda.

I began to also detach from any outcomes. After all, I hadn't planned this journey, so I had no idea where I was even going. A Higher Power was guiding me now, but I didn't know it yet. I also started to look at the positives, instead of the what-ifs, each day.

For example, I remember thinking it was great that the apartment was close to our office building because I could stop home during lunch and visit with my pups. I was looking for the positives everywhere (in all aspects of my new circumstances), and I was finding them. My soul, not fear, was beginning to take over. *How lucky*, I thought, *we even found this apartment.*

My perspective on life was shifting little by little the more my soul took over. Gratitude was becoming a daily practice. I remember at first being concerned my dogs would bark all day when I was at the office and disturb the other residents. After a few days of living in the apartment, I realized there were more dogs in the building than humans.

Laughter, positive thoughts, and gratitude began to quiet the mental noise of worries and fears. I was finding more humor, and less fear, in many situations. I literally had no idea where we would be living and where we were going, but I somehow remained positive, light, and open as much as I could during our stay in the apartment.

I was taking it one day at a time and beginning to be more present in each moment as best as I could. I still look back with fondness on our time in that apartment because it was my first step toward a life guided by love within; away from worry and fear that had been streaming from my thoughts for years. I am truly grateful God sent me a wake-up call and my soul nudged me to pivot from fear toward the unknown. I would later learn in Soul School that experiencing uncertainty and detaching from an outcome are movements on the adventure to the soul. It certainly felt as if I were on an adventure with my soul.

The celestial synchronicities were all around me. I had no idea where I was going and where I would land, but I wasn't attached to any particular outcome other than safety, good health, and love. I remained open, positive, thankful, and aware. I was beginning to let love lead the way. The soul had my attention, and I didn't want to miss anything going forward.

Soul Searching:

- Journal about something or someone you may be overly attached to.
- Make a list of a few possessions you could let go of and those you want to keep.
- What are the objects in your life you can begin to detach from?
- Are there any attachments you may have to things that could be interfering with your relationships with others? Perhaps you could write about one of them.
- Perhaps you can begin to incorporate a little gratitude in your days and write one thing you're grateful for each day.

Song suggestion:

"Shackles (Praise You)," by Mary Mary

Sticky Note #5
Use Your GPS
(God, Please Steer)

*"When we are rooted in prayer and solitude and form part
of a community of faith, certain signs are given to us in
daily life as we struggle for answers to spiritual questions.
The books we read, the nature we enjoy, the people we meet,
and the events we experience contain within themselves
signs of God's presence and guidance. Discernment is a
way to read the signs and recognize Divine messages."*

—MICHAEL J. CHRISTENSEN
AND REBECCA J. LAIRD

During my time in the rented apartment, I noticed a few celestial
synchronicities were suggesting I move down south. At least, it
sure seemed as if I was being steered in that direction. Nothing
was coming together as I looked for places to either rent longer-
term or buy in the Philadelphia area. For more than fifty years
of my life, I had lived in the Philadelphia suburbs, minus a few
years in Maryland and Lancaster, Pennsylvania.

My sons suggested I check out the rental market in the community in South Carolina where we had bought a small piece of
land a few years earlier. I had always dreamed of having a legacy

home someday for our family, and we fell in love with a beautiful and peaceful community in the low country of South Carolina.

FALLING INTO PLACE

I didn't know anyone who lived in the community, but I somehow found myself on a neighborhood site and posted that I was looking for a place to rent. God took over and started bringing people to me. Initially, a few people responded that there weren't any homes available to rent in the community. But when a Higher Power is guiding you, you find yourself in situations that seem to make no logical sense. Somehow, despite being told there were no rental homes, I found myself communicating with someone whose place was available to rent.

Once again, when God wants to get your attention, he will send someone or something to get it. And he sent one of the nicest families in the community. I only saw a few photos of the cottage and had only a general idea of where it was located. This happened within the span of a few days.

Looking back, I can truly see I was being guided from above—Divine guidance was taking over. The idea of renting a place sight unseen in an area where I knew nobody was not something my head would have embraced a month or so earlier, but my soul was leading the way now. Fear was no longer in the driver's seat.

I was allowing my soul and God to give me a little direction for the first time in my life, and the GPS (God, please steer) seemed to take over. For most of my life, I had underestimated the power of guidance from a Higher Power. About one month after my pivot into the unknown, I found myself in the passenger seat of a rented Suburban driven by my son. It was the only vehicle we could rent that would fit all my belongings and our two dogs, Maggie and Matisse. I said goodbye to our little short-term apartment outside of Philadelphia and headed south.

I rented the cottage with no end date in sight. Moving was a bold move for me and way out of my comfort zone. (More than seven hundred miles from my comfort zone, to be precise.) I would later learn in Soul School that a spiritual journey takes you out of your comfort zone, and I had certainly been in my comfort zone for a very long time—yet another celestial synchronicity I wasn't able to see at the time. I was living the lessons before I even learned them.

PANIC AND PEACE

As I tried to remain calm on the drive, I was crumbling inside. The reality of moving far away from home to a place where I knew no one was a tough concept to embrace. I'm moving to a place where I know no one. *What will I do? Have I lost my mind?* I shared my frantic thoughts with my sons, "I'm going to be all by myself. I'm leaving the only place I've ever lived behind."

My loving sons simply smiled at me and said enthusiastically, "You are finally living your life."

Looking back at the beginning of the journey, I still feel the tremendous depth of love my sons were demonstrating as they were encouraging my decision, which was guided by my soul—by Divine love. Some may think my move into the unknown was a courageous one, others a foolish one, but to me, it felt fiercely frightening. I was leaving my comfort zone and safety net behind, but at the same time, I was beginning to notice that a Higher Power was orchestrating and planning this trip. Things were falling into place. It felt as if I was moving with the current of a river.

The cottage in the low country of South Carolina turned out to be a wonderful refuge and an incredibly peaceful place. It was situated on one of the signature holes of the golf course with a view of the expansive May River in the distance. It was breathtaking. My body had found a peaceful space to rest as my soul began to awaken.

YOUR TURN

The best way I can suggest to help you tune into the Divine guidance that is available to you is to begin to observe the people and situations coming into your life. Who are you meeting and having conversations with? What messages are you hearing from others? Are you beginning to notice a pattern of messages coming your way? Perhaps through books, billboards, songs, or people? It begins with openness, awareness, and observance.

Soul Searching:

- When did you feel as if God or a Higher Power was directing you in your life?
- How did it feel to have a power greater than you guiding you?
- Have you ever relocated to a new place where you didn't know anybody? If yes, how did that feel?
- Are you open to the idea of letting God or a Divine power guide you and help you with some of your decisions?
- What GPS device are you using to navigate your life each day?

Song suggestion:

"Carolina in My Mind," by James Taylor

Sticky Note #6
Hit the Pause Button

"When I was a young monk in Vietnam, each village temple had a big bell, like those in Christian churches in Europe and America. Whenever the bell was invited to sound (in Buddhist circles, we never say "hit" or "strike" a bell), all the villagers would stop what they were doing and pause for a few moments to breathe in and out in mindfulness. Our true home is in the present moment."

—THICH NHÂT HANH

Do you ever feel like you're spending your life running on a treadmill, head down, pressing forward, and feeling like if you stopped, you'd fly off the end and into a wall? Can you remember the last time you looked at the sky or spent some time observing nature? Or stopped to smell a flower like my son's and his girl-friend's great dane puppy? Trust me, for fifty-six years, I lived my life on autopilot. I worked myself to exhaustion and collapsed into bed at night thinking of everything I needed to do the next day. The next day was just rinse and repeat.

As I sat with myself alone in a new place, I realized I had no idea who I was anymore or what I was doing with my life. Quiet and space prompt many questions, and "Who am I?"

would be the first of many. I had never paused before in my life to ask myself who I was. If you were to ask me years ago, amid the flurry of activity in my life, I would have probably rattled off roles: mother, businesswoman, daughter, sister, aunt, friend, etc. In his book *Three Magic Words*, U. S. Andersen writes, "What am I? What caused me? Why am I here? Where am I going? These are the questions of the human soul that demand an answer."[1] My soul was awakening and asking some tough questions.

I also had to get comfortable with living alone. For most of my life, I had either lived with someone (family, husband, sons), taken care of someone (children, father, pets), or thrown myself intensely into my career, so I had rarely been alone physically and mentally. There was always a steady flow of constant dialogue streaming through my mind regularly. Very rarely, if ever, could I describe my mind as quiet and still.

FACING THE STILLNESS

The intense quiet brought me face-to-face with myself, but the problem was that I had no idea who I was anymore. Frankly, I don't think I ever knew who I was. I reflected on my life and had many lonely and tearful nights in those early weeks. I felt alone and lonely and doubted if I had done the right thing by moving into the unknown.

Looking back, I realize fear had me in its clutches. A voice in my head kept repeating, *Why are you here all by yourself?* I was starting to recognize the voice of fear when it arose and beginning to feel the difference between a life guided by anxious thoughts and a life guided by the gentle soul.

As I asked myself, *Who am I?* a flood of life's precious and sacred memories surfaced. I reflected on my life. I suppose one does that when they hit the pause button. Not only did I press the pause button, but I also hit the rewind button on my entire life.

I was and still am truly blessed and fortunate to be a mother to two wonderful sons, both happy and living independently. The boxes of photos, my sons' cards, and art projects were the only physical items I had with me as I sat alone in the cottage, and I began to go through all of them. I cherish and love my sons dearly and hold them in my heart always, no matter where they are geographically. We nicknamed ourselves The Muskees (short for The Three Musketeers) when they were in middle school. We still call ourselves that today, and now have included my daughter-in-law, my younger son's girlfriend, and my two "grandogters" in our club. The Muskees have a bond like no other. We have helped each other through life's ups and downs with an unparalleled depth of love.

As I searched through photos, my life flashed before me. I pressed rewind in my mind all the way back to my sons' births—the first steps they took, their birthday parties, all the way through high school and college graduations. Where had the time gone? More than half of my living years have been spent as a mother, a gift I'm truly grateful for.

But now what? As I contemplated my next steps, memories of my parents came flooding back, surrounding me in the stillness.

COOL HAND LUKE

As I've mentioned, I was also blessed to have worked in our family business with my father for almost twenty years of my life. I admired my father and looked up to him. He was a powerful force in a quiet way, as was my mother. Sadly, he passed away in April 2017. Although the loss of my father was devastating, I'm grateful to have had quality time and meaningful conversations with him especially as he approached the end of his life.

Unfortunately, that wasn't the case for my mom. Her passing took place suddenly in September 2010, a week before my birthday. Our family's lives were shattered. I'm not sure which hurts more, the sudden loss of someone you love or knowing that person has a limited number of days left. Both losses were extremely painful, but my father's impending death allowed me to say everything to him I didn't have time to say to my mother. I even asked my dad to say things to my mom when he met her again, which we both hoped would happen.

My parents had been together since they were teenagers—they were high school sweethearts. My father outlived his projected life span of about forty years from his initial prognosis after contracting polio at the young age of twenty-three. At the time of his diagnosis, my parents had a three-year-old son and another son on the way.

My dad lived his life without letting his inability to walk define him and had relentless persistence, courage, a tremendous work ethic, true grit, integrity, and my saintly mother by his side. I can still hear his voice today, "Cool Hand Luke, Marcie," he'd say to try to temper my feisty and fiery spirit in the office. I recalled our many hours together; we spent every working day together during those years. So many feelings and big emotions rose to the surface within the quiet little cottage.

THE POWER OF PAUSING

A tremendous void engulfed me with both of my parents gone. That was hard to get used to. I kept those feelings to myself back then and buried them deep inside. They were beginning to resurface little by little in this new space, now that I had finally paused for the first time in decades.

Frankly, I don't know if I had ever paused before in my life. It was as if I had been swimming laps continually, and never stopping to breathe. Pressing the pause button gave me a chance to come up for some air and reflect on my life in the new space of quiet, guided by the movement of the soul. Hitting the rewind button allowed me the opportunity to savor the many wonderful people and memories and begin to restore and heal my inner space.

I also reflected on my role for twenty years as a businesswoman. Most of my waking hours had been spent either physically or mentally at our family business. I was always thinking about the business and what needed to happen next or what had already happened. I gave my all to our family business. After my father's passing, an opportunity to join forces with another firm and for me to transition out of the business presented itself. I like to think my father was instrumental in bringing our firms together and allowing me to hit the pause button for the first time in my life. I couldn't take the pain of not having him there in the office. It was time. So, after twenty years in our family business, my identity and role as a businesswoman came to a halt.

Now what?

MEETING MY INNER SELF

It began to hit me hard—more than half my life had been spent in roles I no longer performed, although my role as a mother continues forever in my heart. As I sat there in the peaceful cottage asking myself, "Who am I?" I had no answers, only more questions.

I no longer had my core four (mom, dad, and two sons). The four most significant relationships in my life had either ended, in the case of my deceased parents, or shifted, as in the case of my sons.

Questions flooded me: *Who am I? What am I to do next? Am I doing the right thing? Should I even be here in South Carolina? Why did I leave the only place I had ever called home? What the heck am I doing with my life? Am I in the middle of a midlife crisis?*

Brené Brown helped me understand what I was going through in her book, *The Gifts of Imperfection,* "People may call what happens at midlife 'a crisis,' but it's not. It's an unraveling— a time when you feel a desperate pull to live the life you want to live, not the one you're supposed to live."[2] I guess you could say I was beginning to unravel and reflect on how I had been living my life. Was I living the life I wanted to live?

I would soon learn that my soul, not my head, had the answers to these questions. I was also about to learn that who I was had nothing to do with what I did and the roles I performed. For almost fifty years, I had never really paused to ask myself, Who am I? *How could I have gone through fifty years not knowing who I truly was?* But somehow, I had.

Thomas Merton writes, "If I do not know who I am, it is because I think I am the sort of person everyone around me wants to be. Perhaps I have never asked myself whether I really wanted to become what everybody else seems to want to become. Perhaps if I only realized I do not admire what everyone seems to admire, I would really begin to live after all. I would be liberated from the painful duty of saying what I really do not think and acting in a way that betrays God's truth and the integrity of my own soul."[3]

I began to notice that after I asked a question, I would receive an answer; something or someone would appear in my life to provide some clarity in one way or another. For example, in *The Art of Discernment,* the first book I read when I first felt the need for space, Stefan Kiechle writes, "We need to pause to bring about a change of scenery. The moment we enter silence, our inner self comes to life; we become more sensitive and more receptive to subliminal messages revealing the things hidden behind the concerns, impulses, motives, and powers that remain otherwise unnoticed. People who are constantly talking and keeping busy never pause to listen."[4]

This message about the importance of hitting the pause button had been a preview of what was to come next, but I wasn't tuned in the first time I read *The Art of Discernment*. I was beginning to tune in to the subtle messages and insights. It is clear to me now that God was speaking to me through that book and nudging me toward the new path of space for emotions to arise and for my "true self" to emerge.

How had I missed the celestial synchronicities back then? They seemed pretty obvious as I reflected. Hitting the pause button allowed me some space to begin to recognize these Divine signs—celestial synchronicities—I had been receiving and, even more importantly, to begin to look for them going forward so I wouldn't miss them again. I simply needed to hit the pause button, take some space, and sit in the quiet. Then I began to recognize the messages, feel the nudges, and observe the people who intersected my path at critical times.

Now, I was about to embark on the journey of a lifetime, guided by my soul.

YOUR TURN

Allow yourself the opportunity to hit the pause button. I can already hear you saying you don't have the time. But hear me out: all you need is five minutes for one day this week. Find a space where you won't be distracted or disturbed. Set a timer for five minutes, and with your eyes either open or closed, embrace the stillness.

And no, you may not feel very still at first. Your mind may start racing, or you'll notice thoughts and emotions bubbling up you thought you'd pushed away years ago. But trust me, the more you practice five minutes of stillness, the more comfortable you may become with it. And you may notice yourself adding another day, and another until you're taking five minutes (or more) every day.

Soul Searching:

- Allow yourself the time to stop and think about the direction your life has taken.
- Where are the places in your life where it makes sense to figure out who you are or to reexamine some of your roles?
- How can you hit the pause button in your life?
- Perhaps you can journal about a person, event, or thing that you're grateful for in your life. Writing about this person, event, or object will help you savor the person or thing.

Song suggestion:

"How Can You Mend a Broken Heart," by Al Green

Sticky Note #7
Check Your Ego
at the Door

*"As long as the egoic mind is running your life, you cannot truly
be at ease; you cannot be at peace or fulfilled except for brief
intervals when you obtained what you wanted, when a craving
has just been fulfilled. Since the ego is a derived sense of self,
it needs to identify with external things. It needs to be both
defended and fed constantly. The most common ego identifications
have to do with possessions, the work you do, social status and
recognition, knowledge and education, physical appearance,
special abilities, relationships, personal and family history, belief
systems, and often also political, nationalistic, racial, religious,
and other collective identifications. None of these is you."*

—ECKHART TOLLE.

Ah, the ego. Do you think your ego is running your life? Maybe
we should back up for a second here. What does "ego" mean to
you? If you aren't sure, you aren't alone. I always thought people
with an ego were arrogant and full of themselves. Boy, did I need
an education on the ego. I'm so grateful for the spiritual teachers
in Soul School who helped me learn more about what the ego is
and is not and helped me get mine in check.

Now that my soul had my attention, I had quite a few lessons to learn, and the first lesson was about the ego (the false self), which seemed like it had been running my life for a very long time. It's shocking and embarrassing that I had been unaware that the "false self" had been the dominant force in my life for many years.

The ego was mentioned in most of the books I was reading, and Oprah even had a segment devoted entirely to the ego on her podcast. I realized it must be important for me to become better acquainted with the ego and get mine in check. Many of the authors on *Oprah's Super Soul Sunday* podcast were describing the ego and how it showed up in their lives.

Eckhart Tolle describes the ego in *The Power of Now*," As you grow up, you form a mental image of who you are, based on your personal and cultural conditioning. We may call this phantom self the ego. It consists of mind activity and can only be kept going through constant thinking. The term ego means different things to different people, but when I use it here it means a false self, created by unconscious identification with the mind."[1] My mind had been running constantly and somehow I had permitted my thoughts to run my life. I had somehow become one with my thoughts. I had tried hard over the years to stay humble and selfless. I thought I was keeping my ego in check, but at the same time, I did not have a full understanding of the ego.

UNDERSTANDING THE EGO

In his book, *Manifest Your Destiny*, Dr. Wayne Dyer also discusses the ego. He describes the four stages of adult development and writes, "My definition of the ego is the idea that we have of ourselves as important and separate from everyone else."[2] He further states, "This can be an acronym for Earth Guide Only (EGO) since ego represents our exclusive identification with our physical selves in our material world. This ego-dominated stage is full of anxiety and endless comparison of our success."[3]

The ego is self-absorbed. The highest stage of adult development, according to Dyer, is The Spirit. "When you enter this stage of life, regardless of your age or position, you recognize your truest essence, the highest self … you know that nothing dies, that everything is an energy that is constantly changing."[4]

I could relate to Dyer's description of the ego-dominated stage full of anxiety and was slowly beginning to feel the essence within the more I connected to my inner world. I was beginning to feel and live what I was reading. This became a regular pattern of reading about a lesson and experiencing it in daily life. I was also becoming aware that fear and worry were ego-based and, as a worrier, I had been living a life led by the ego for a very long time. That explained why fear and worry were so prevalent in my life.

The lessons began to sink in through what I was reading or situations and events that unfolded. I was becoming an observer, starting to become aware of a much Higher Power that was guiding me, and beginning to connect to that Divine power that seemed to be within me. Letting go and remaining open seemed to be important to connecting to the inner peace within. As I allowed space to enter my life both physically, mentally, and to some degree emotionally, certain spiritual teachers and podcasts were sent my way in various forms, often through recommendations from other people whom I was meeting in the community.

NEW SPIRITUAL TEACHERS

Eckhart Tolle was one of the first spiritual teachers I was introduced to thanks to Oprah Winfrey and her *Super Soul Sunday*
podcast, which I listened to every day on my lunchtime walks
with my pups. Oprah formed a book club on *A New Earth:
Awakening to Your Life's Purpose* and reviewed each chapter with
Eckhart Tolle over a series of several weeks.

This was very helpful because the book was way over my
head, and Oprah has a tremendous gift for putting in simple
terms some of the more advanced concepts of others. This was all
new material for me, and I needed all the help I could get.

I became very intrigued by Eckhart's idea that we are not the
voices in our heads. I devoured his lessons, specifically on the ego.

Eckhart described the ego as thinking, doing, and identifying with form. I replayed Oprah's interview with Eckhart so
many times I could still hear both of their voices in my head
hours later. Eckhart Tolle was one of many spiritual teachers who
taught that we are the observers or watchers of the voices in our
heads and not the thoughts and the voices themselves. That was a
real "Aha!" moment for me because I was beginning to hear those
voices a lot now that I had come up for some air in my life and
embraced some quiet and space. They were not very kind to me
and gave me a hard time about almost everything I did or said.
They were always commenting on what I did wrong or what I
said wrong. They rarely said anything nice about me.

The voices were quite annoying, and I was determined to
detach from them and simply observe them as much as possible,
as the books I was reading were instructing me to do. In order
for me to hear the chatter in my head, I needed some silence. I
started to sit in silence for a few minutes every morning. Further
along in my journey, I would embrace silence and stillness, but
in those beginning days, it was rather difficult. One of the last

things I wanted to do was sit and listen to the negative voices in my head, but I did. How had I lived with this constant chatter for so long and never been aware of it before?

"Our inner purpose is to awaken,"[5] Eckhart reminds us, and that's what seemed to be happening to me. I paused at the "coincidence" that Eckhart had come into my life during the time I was experiencing what he was teaching. What were the odds, I thought, that a spiritual teacher would come into my life and teach me how to put into practice what I was learning during a time when I needed it and was experiencing the very lesson he was teaching? I was given the opportunity to practice what I was reading and learning. Books came into my line of vision when I had questions. People came into my life reinforcing messages I was hearing. I was sensing that there was a Divine force guiding me.

Sitting in silence was a very foreign feeling and unpleasant in those early days. It took some getting used to. It was annoying to hear the negative commentary on my life, but it also felt as if I wasn't doing enough with my days; I was simply being. For a person who had thrived on an overcommitted schedule for most of her life, sitting in silence and doing nothing seemed like a complete waste of time.

I worked through the discomfort, however, and began to embrace little moments of solitude each day. I knew I needed to take baby steps to break down some bad habits and begin to develop some new and healthier ones. I also started to become involved in a few activities within the community to further discover who I was and what I liked to do. After I sat in silence for this period, my extroverted nature needed some stimulation. With a somewhat quieter mind and a soul that was leading the way, I asked myself what I was interested in. It may sound strange, but I hadn't asked myself many questions over the years.

One interest that came to the forefront of my mind was meditation. I had always had an interest in meditation but had never found the time, or rather *made* the time, to incorporate the practice into my life. Ironically, I was sitting in silence for a few minutes every morning, so perhaps that qualified as some type of meditation. As a lover of people, I knew I couldn't sit and meditate alone for hours; I longed for some social interaction. Meditating in a group might satisfy my extroverted needs, I thought. Fortunately, there was a wonderful meditation group within our community that met once a week.

This was the beginning of meeting many kind people and participating in many wonderful events, all orchestrated from above. I signed up for the meditation class, joined some yoga classes, and enjoyed my daily walks in the gorgeous low country with my two pups. I was finally connecting with my inner sanctuary and slowly moving away from the anxious thoughts and voices of the ego. I also found myself reading as many books as I could and listening to as many podcasts as I could find to learn how to connect even more with my soul. It was all new territory for me, and once again, I felt very much out of my comfort zone.

GOD, ARE YOU THERE?

Something else happened when I sat in silence. I began talking with God. I had lost contact with God over the years and hadn't spoken with him for quite some time. Perhaps I began talking with God because I didn't have anyone else to talk with, or maybe God began talking with me and I could finally hear him. I'm not sure who started talking first, but we were talking again.

I started to replace the negative voices in my head with prayers of love and gratitude to God. As soon as I was aware of a negative thought, I would replace it with a simple phrase like, "I choose God" or "I choose love." These simple phrases instantly stopped the thoughts from spiraling down. I also asked God to guide me each day, help me shift from the negative chatter in my head, protect my family, friends, and me, and most importantly, use me to help others. I began to shift my fears and worries to love and gratitude to God. I wasn't asking for certain outcomes; I was simply asking God to guide me where he wanted me to go and bring me to whomever he wanted me to meet. After all, I didn't have an agenda or destination. It wasn't that I was magically cured of my constant worries and fears. I still worried, and my restlessness still persisted with the feeling that I wasn't "doing" enough with my days, that I was just "being."

I began a practice, though, of shifting the worries in my mind immediately over to God to try to derail the train of destructive thoughts as soon as they started. I now had a tool and a place to transfer my worries. That practice became a daily habit. For most of my life, I had only felt at ease with a schedule that was overpacked and a mind that was overstimulated. I had never meditated much before in my life, and I'm pretty sure my mind and thoughts had been running constantly. I realized it would take a good bit of time to undo some bad habits I had been comfortable with for much of my life. I began to remind myself to check my ego at the door and let Divine love lead the way.

Soul Searching:

- How can you take the time to just be?
- Where can you find some time to sit in silence and tune into your inner self?
- What do you notice when you give yourself space to observe your thoughts?

- What can you do to observe if your ego is in the room with you?
- How can you make a conscious effort to check your ego at the door?

SONG SUGGESTION:

"Higher Love," by Steve Winwood

Sticky Note #8
Stay in Your Lane

"Letting go of comparison is not a to-do list item. For most of us, it's something that requires constant awareness. It's so easy to take our eyes off our path to check out what others are doing and if they're ahead or behind us. Creativity, which is the expression of our originality, helps us stay mindful that what we bring to the world is completely original and cannot be compared. And, without comparison, concepts like ahead or behind or best or worst lose their meaning."

—BRENÉ BROWN

Here's a random fact about me—I cannot parallel park. My sons are familiar with my parking issues and have had to ride as passengers for many years during their childhood years. They've often asked how I managed to pass the driver's test. I do prepare others about my parking deficiencies, however, if they're willing to sit next to me in the car. It usually goes something like this—I'll ask them if they're okay walking a good distance to our destination if parallel parking is involved, and I fess up about my parking inadequacy; we either walk or they park. So this "Stay in your lane" message really hits home for me; both on and off the road.

But this chapter isn't about driving. Perhaps I should explain a little more about what "Stay in your lane" means. I started to become aware of some hurtful habits in my life the more I connected to my inner world. After all, I've been out of touch with this space for more than fifty years of my life. One habit I noticed was looking outward at others' lives, watching what they were doing, and being less focused on myself. I was watching others and what they were doing in their lives or lanes and less focused on myself and what was happening in mine.

One of the many lessons I was learning about the ego was that the ego looks outward and loves comparisons to others. That was an important lesson because I was continuing to look outward even as I was becoming aware of this habit. I looked outward where I was living and scolded myself that I should be doing more activities, like most others were in the community. The ego had a tight grip on me.

SO MUCH COMPARISON

I'm not sure when the habit of looking at others' lives first started, but I remember doing it at times in college. I observed what others were studying, what classes they took, what they did during their free time, which friends they hung out with, and where they lived. The list went on and on. Perhaps I was comparing myself with others so that I " blended in" with the group and didn't stand out in any way. I thought my interest in others' lives would subside over time, but it didn't. After college, I observed which jobs others held, who they were dating, and so on. As I reflected on this pattern throughout my life, I noticed the comparison of my life to others' lives seemed to wane quite a bit when I became a mother. I became laser-focused on the two wonderful sons with whom God blessed me.

After my sons graduated college and were living independently as mature men, I switched my focus to our family business and taking care of my elderly father. There was no time to focus on anyone else's life because mine was overflowing. As I write these words, I also recognize my habit of becoming laser-focused on anything besides myself. I seemed to have a pattern of focusing outward rather than inward, which wasn't necessarily a bad thing. I'm a curious person by nature; observing others only became a problem when I became less focused on my own path and began to doubt what I was doing. Simply put, I lost touch with the unique gifts I bring to the world.

I'm not saying observing others is a bad thing to do. Quite the opposite—observing others whom we admire can be inspirational and encouraging; it offers hope. I'm talking more about comparing my life to others' lives in a negative way and allowing the comparison to foster self-criticism which keeps me stuck, rather than inspiring me to press on. Constantly comparing my life with others' lives had become a self-destructive habit that was not giving me any hope. Is comparing your life with others' lives a habit you can relate to?

As I sat alone in my new space, the practice of observing others' actions crept back in.

BECOMING MORE AWARE

In the quiet evenings, the voices in my head scolded me that I should be out with friends for dinner like many others were, not reading one of the many books I had accumulated. As I observed many happily married couples during my days, I thought, *What's wrong with me that I'm not in a loving relationship with a wonderful man?* I reminded myself I had made some choices that had brought me here. The constant comparison to others was beating me down. I was determined to get a grip on this bad habit.

Once more, I was looking at everyone else's lanes, not my own lane. My lane was the slow lane at the moment—a lane I wasn't familiar with. But something interesting began to happen—I was starting to observe my thoughts and catch myself looking at others' lanes when I was actually doing it. I don't think I had any clue I was even comparing my lane to others' lanes over the years. It had become so ingrained in me. Somehow, this habit had become part of my personality.

I was gradually becoming "an observer" of my thoughts and actions, as Wayne Dyer called it. I had another "Aha" moment when I realized no matter where I was—whether Philadelphia or South Carolina or anywhere else, for that matter—I slipped back into the habit of comparing what I was doing with what others were doing. It didn't matter what highway I was on—I still compared my lane to others' lanes.

Changing my geographical location did not change this habit. (The exception was a trip to Italy during which I didn't want to be anywhere else—I was fully present with my sons and open to whatever came to us every day.) I caught myself when I was out of my lane during those early days of the journey and reminded myself, *Stay in your lane.* This short, simple sentence helped to put a halt to my damaging thought patterns and reminded me to observe my own thoughts and actions—to stay focused on my lane.

I was learning the importance of staying connected to my inner voice, not those negative voices in my head. I used to believe that focusing on ourselves was selfish and somewhat narcissistic. What I learned was focusing on ourselves to better understand who we are is not selfish, rather, it's essential for living a life as our best selves. If we don't know who we are, how can we ever let our true essence shine and become the best versions of ourselves?

Even though I reminded myself to stay in my lane, I continued to question God many times about whether I was in the "right" place doing the "right" thing or even in the "right" lane. Doubting God was another bad habit that needed some attention. I'm sure he was getting a little annoyed with me because I sounded like a broken record, constantly asking him for confirmation. I began to feel the loving and gentle reassurance from my soul that I was exactly where I needed to be, in the right lane, doing exactly what I needed to be doing or rather just *being*.

Soul Searching:

- Brené Brown reminds us that creativity helps us stay focused on ourselves and not compare ourselves with others. How can you tap into your creativity to stay in your lane?
- Is there a class that interests you or a hobby you've always wanted to try?
- Can you try something new that gets you out of your comfort zone?
  - » How well are you staying in your lane?
  - » When are you the most present and focused on what you're doing?
  - » When do you notice a tendency to become overly concerned with what everyone else is doing or not doing?

Song suggestion:

"The Light is On," by Christopher Cross

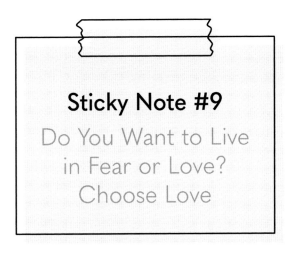

Sticky Note #9
Do You Want to Live in Fear or Love? Choose Love

"Fear is the eternal enemy to living the life we most desire, its voice so powerful we believe it above any other authority. Fear is inverted faith."

—FLORENCE SCOVEL SHINN

Do you worry? Does fear play a part in your everyday life? How would you answer the question—do you live your life in fear or in love or a little of both? I would imagine most of us would hope to answer that we live a life with more love and less fear. It's shocking, though, that my answer would probably have been more fear. I had been living much of my life in fear, and I hadn't even realized it.

Most of the spiritual teachers whose books I read in Soul School agreed that there are two ways to live a life—in fear or love. In *A Return to Love Reflections on the Principles of A Course In Miracles*, Marianne Williamson writes, "But God is love. We were created in His image, or mind, which means that we are extensions of His love. ... A Course in Miracles says that only love is real. The opposite of love is fear, but what is all-encompassing can have no opposite. When we think with love, we are literally co-creating with God. ... The return to love is not the end of life's adventure, but the beginning. It's the return to who you really are."[1] So, we have a choice—to live a life of fear or love. Sounds so simple, doesn't it? Well, it hadn't been that simple for me for about fifty years of living.

Don't get me wrong—I felt a deep love for my sons, my family, and others. It wasn't that I didn't love others, it was that I had a lot of fears and worries spiraling around constantly in my mind. Those fears paralyzed me and blocked me at times from making decisions that could have moved me forward. I also realized oftentimes that what I worried about happening never happened. It was wasted energy. I was shocked at how fear had played such a dominant role in my life when I reread my journal entries over the years.

WAVES OF THOUGHTS

Our minds are powerful and can wreak havoc in our lives if not controlled! Eckhart Tolle's book, *The Power of Now,* and many of the other books I read all had similar messages about the importance of watching our minds, and they explained that much of the fear and worry in our lives stems from our thoughts. The way we live our lives and view our world starts with our thoughts. That deeply resonated with me.

The *what-ifs* were regularly present in my mind. *What if this happens? What if that happens? What if this person is mad at me?* The what-ifs went on and on. I was learning the only way to gain freedom from the worries in my mind was to recognize them, move my attention away from any negative thoughts, focus on my breathing and my inner being, and try to detach from the hurtful thoughts—simply observing them from a detached perspective without judgment. It was important to first acknowledge the thought.

Try it now—if you're worried about something and your mind has been spiraling, acknowledge the thought, shift your attention, focus on your breathing, and try to detach from the thought. Hard to do, right? From my experience, it takes a great deal of practice.

Surprisingly, many of the frenzied thoughts usually subsided after some time. I imagined my thoughts like waves in the ocean—the thoughts would rise and then fall like a wave does. I became an observer, in more ways than one. This simple practice helped me stay grounded in the present moment and not get lost in the what-ifs of past or future moments.

As I looked back on the wonderful memories and loving people from my fifty-six years of living, I also recognized and acknowledged I had been living in a great deal of fear, worry, and anxiety for much of my life.

Worry had become one of my closest friends and a frequent visitor in my thoughts, daily living, and decision-making. I was worried about my sons and others I loved, hoping they would be happy and healthy. I was worried about my job and making sure our business would continue to provide services that would help others. I was worried about finances and whether I would have enough savings to continue to provide for myself and my two sons. I was worried I wasn't giving enough in my relationships with others. I was worried I wasn't doing enough with my life and making enough of a difference in the world. I was worried I should be living a life different than the one I was living. I was worried I hadn't shown enough love to my mother and other family members over the years. I was worried about a lot of things, pretty much every day of my life. I was a master of finding something to worry about. Can you relate to worrying at times in your life?

It became even more apparent to me that worry was consuming my thoughts and running my life when I enrolled in a program in which we journaled our thoughts and feelings. Suffice it to say, worry, fear, and doubt had been the drivers of my life for most of my fifty years, and I had no clue at the time. I felt tremendous love for those in my life, but I seemed to be living internally more in a state of fear and in the arms of perfectionism and procrastination (in my personal life).

THE EGO AND YOUR FEARS

The message of checking my ego at the door seemed to be in sync with the message to choose love, not fear. The ego and fear seemed interconnected. "The ego lives in fear,"[2] Deepak Chopra tells us in *The Seven Spiritual Laws of Success—A Practical Guide to the Fulfillment of Your Dreams*. I needed to watch the ego, for it had been driving my life of fear for many years. My ego, also, was not a good driver and had been causing me to swerve into others' lanes. Chopra continues, "The ego is not who you really are. The ego is your self-image; it is your social mask; it is the role you are playing. Your social mask thrives on approval. It wants to control, and it is sustained by power because it lives in fear."[3] In other words, the ego is our false self, lives in fear, seeking approval from others, and is very self-centered.

So how do we live if we want to avoid living in a constant state of fear with the ego? According to *The Seven Spiritual Laws of Success*, "Your true Self, which is your spirit, your soul, is completely free of self-image, the roles you are playing, and fear. It is immune to criticism, it is unfearful of any challenge, and it feels beneath no one. And yet, it is also humble and feels superior to no one, because it recognizes that everyone else is the same Self, the same spirit in different disguises…. But when your actions are motivated by love, there is no waste of energy."[4] Similarly, Kevin O'Brien, SJ writes, "The writer of the first letter of John assures us, 'There is no fear in love, but perfect love casts out fear' (4:18). Pray to experience such consoling love of God, who deeply desires for us to experience the joy of our creation."[5] Love seemed to be a way to combat the ego. I began to ask myself, *how would love respond*, to steer my thoughts and actions in the direction of love.

SEEKING LOVE AND LIGHT

Understanding that the soul and love constitute the other way to live, I began to feel the difference that came with embracing the soft and gentle soul. Having begun to get a feeling of my soothing soul, I wanted to follow that path and be connected to that space as often as possible. My soul felt like the path to the light and away from fear and darkness. Faith was overtaking fear. I wanted to follow the path of light.

Florence Scovel Shinn was another author who helped me learn more about love in her book, *The Complete Game of Life and How to Play It*. I'd had this book in my library for more than six years and rediscovered the many notes I had written throughout the book when I first read it. I am a big fan of writing a lot of notes in books I read.

As with previous books, when I read this one the second time, I realized how much I missed the first time I read it and was shocked that I had already begun to live some of the lessons it spoke of. Florence speaks of Jesus and Buddha and how many of their principles were similar, though articulated in different languages. I was embracing that concept as well, as I was reading a variety of books, some based on Christianity and others on Buddhism.

She writes, "Fear must be erased from consciousness. Jesus Christ said, 'Why are ye fearful, oh ye of little faith?' (Matt. 8:26). So, we can see we must substitute faith for fear, for fear is only inverted faith; it is faith in evil instead of good."[6] She further writes, "Follow the path of love, and all things are added, for God is love, and God is supply."[7]

When I think of love, I, too, think of God. I imagine God is the biggest force of love there is and every soul flows from this source. 1 Corinthians 14: 1 of *The Message*, Eugene H. Peterson paraphrases, "Go after a life of love as if your life depended on it—because it does."[8]

Further, 1 Corinthians 13 contains the infamous message of love that's often woven into many wedding ceremonies. *The Message* version reads, "Love never gives up. Love cares more for others than for self. Love doesn't want what it doesn't have. Love doesn't strut, doesn't have a swelled head, doesn't force itself on others, isn't always 'me first,' doesn't fly off the handle, doesn't keep score of the sins of others, doesn't revel when others grovel, takes pleasure in the lowering of truth, puts up with anything, trusts God always, always looks for the best, never looks back, but keeps going to the end."[9]

I am a big fan of the simple and direct style of *The Message*. Although I also have a New American Bible my dad read every morning, I prefer the direct and somewhat simple language of Peterson's text. It gets to the point, oftentimes with a little humor. *The Message* and the language of the soul seem to have a lot in common—simple messages, gentle nudges, and a little humor along the way.

FAREWELL AND HELLO

I was not only reading that ego and fear are polar opposites of the soul and love, but I was also beginning to feel the difference. I began to bid farewell to the ego and fear and hello to the soul and love. In his book, *The Untethered Soul,* Michael Singer tells us, "People don't understand that fear is a thing. It's just another object in the universe that you are capable of experiencing. You can do one of two things with fear: you can recognize that you have it and work to release it, or you can keep it and try to hide from it."[10] Singer further writes, "Fear is caused by blockages in the flow of your energy. When your energy is blocked, it can't come up and feed your heart. Fear is the cause of every problem. If you had no fear, you could be perfectly happy living in this world. Nothing would bother you. The purpose of spiritual evolution is to remove the blockages that cause you fear. … Eventually you will understand that there is an ocean of love behind all of this fear and pain."[11] I was dipping my toe in this ocean of love.

Soul Searching:

- How would you answer the question: Are you living your life in fear or in love?
- Perhaps you can notice one thought during the day and ask yourself the question, *is this how love would respond?* This question has helped me recognize jealous or self-serving thoughts that were not how love would respond and act.
- What circumstances make you show up from a place of fear?
- What situations make it easier for you to show up from a place of love?
- Perhaps you can try this:

» Notice if there's a time when you feel afraid this week. Imagine you're an observer of your thoughts—identify the worried thoughts swirling through your mind.

» Try to notice how you feel, and begin to let the thoughts pass through you. Imagine this experience as energy passing through you as Michael Singer suggests in *The Untethered Soul.*

» Relax your shoulders, breathe, and let it move through you. Picture yourself getting behind the negative energy and watching it dissolve. Imagine your spiraling thoughts are like waves of the ocean, observe them rise and fall and slowly dissolve in the air.

Song suggestion:

"Don't You Worry 'bout a Thing," by Stevie Wonder

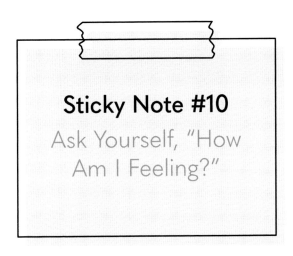

Sticky Note #10
Ask Yourself, "How Am I Feeling?"

"Feelings are a form of information. They're like news reports from inside our psyches, sending messages about what's going on inside the unique person that is each of us in response to whatever internal or external events we're experiencing. We need to access that information and then figure out what it's telling us. That way we can make the most informed decisions."

—DR. MARC BRACKETT

How are you feeling? Why does that one small question create such anxiety in many people? Growing up, my family was more about action and less about feelings, so this wasn't a question that was often asked, and one I'm not able to answer easily. If I asked you right now, would you be able to come up with a feeling other than the surface-level, "I'm fine," kind of response? I truly don't think we ask those closest to us how they're feeling nearly enough, and many of us may not even be able to adequately respond if asked. I would fall into that category.

Thankfully, I was introduced to Dr. Marc Brackett and his book, *Permission to Feel: Unlocking the Power of Emotions to Help Our Kids, Ourselves, and Our Society Thrive*, during Brené

Brown's *Unlocking Us* podcast on one of my lunchtime walks with my pups. As I listened to her interview with him, I became disappointed with myself that I was included with many others who could not list many feelings other than sad, happy, angry, and worried.

According to his studies, I, along with many others, didn't have a very extensive vocabulary when it came to feelings. I bought his book immediately with three goals: to become more educated on feelings and emotions other than happy, sad, angry, and scared; to begin to gain a better understanding of how I was feeling each day; and to shift out of that aforementioned group.

It may sound crazy, but I was very out of touch with how I was feeling each day. When the ego is in charge, there's not much connection to the heart and the soul and feelings go out the window. I don't think I had ever asked myself the question, "How are you feeling?" I was realizing I hadn't asked myself many questions for much of my life. That was about to change, and this would be the first of many questions I would ask myself.

FEELINGS MATTER

Around the same time I ordered *Permission to Feel*, I was learning from other spiritual teachers about the importance of feelings. Another example of Divine guidance from above confirming the significance of this lesson. I was discovering we feel our way into our souls. The soul represents all good and positive feelings filled with love. The ego stores negative thoughts and feelings, including fear. To borrow a word my younger son described his brother's and sister-in-law's puppy during his best man speech to them at their wedding, the ego is a "menace."

I was beginning to understand that connection with the soul may be the death of the ego. I was excited about and committed to leading a soul-based life—a life of love—and was open to any means of getting rid of fear, which was stifling. The practice of quieting the mind to access the peaceful and soothing soul was important. I could also feel the difference between the gentle and soothing soul and the demanding and harsh ego.

Recognizing my feelings was an important lesson and a way to connect to my inner core, *my true self*. I began to write my feelings in a journal each day. I found it easier to write them than to say them out loud. Truthfully, I had a tough time writing my feelings *or* speaking them. I needed a great deal of practice with this lesson, and I imagined I would receive some celestial synchronicities to help me along the way.

I also didn't have anybody to speak my feelings to other than myself, my pups, and God. God seemed like my best option. I began the habit of asking myself at least once a day, *How am I feeling?* At the end of the day, I would often remember I forgot to ask myself that question during the day and would ask it then.

It's hard to create new habits, but with my soul guiding me and my commitment to staying closely connected to it, I received help. I knew how important this one simple question was to keep me connected with my inner being. The question served a dual purpose and also acted as a sensor to help me identify how I was feeling. To better understand why I was feeling a certain way, I went a little deeper and asked myself what was triggering certain emotions. And there was another benefit to this one simple question—it kept me grounded within myself, rather than lost in others' emotions and energies. I began to also ask myself *how am I feeling,* quietly when I was in the presence of others.

A NEW LANGUAGE

Asking myself how I was feeling also began to help me understand patterns in my life and triggers that caused me to feel certain feelings. Tapping into my feelings was like learning a new language for me. I would later discover that feelings seemed to be the language of the soul and God. How had I lived for more than fifty years being so out of touch with how I felt each day? I was shocked at how much I had been lost in my thoughts, disconnected from my heart and soul. The ego had been in charge for a very long time and hadn't been a fan of allowing me to ask myself many questions.

To be clear, it wasn't as if I had never felt any feelings throughout my life. I can remember feeling hurt or sad over the years, but I kept those feelings to myself and pushed them down as soon as I felt them, not quite sure where they went. The habit of keeping my feelings to myself began at a very young age. I wish I had recognized how detrimental it was to one's heart and soul to discard feelings, but I was doing the best I could at the time. Fortunately, Dr. Brackett had come into my path and was offering some tools to help me tune into my feelings and pay better attention to my inner voice going forward.

In his book, he suggests we pause for even a few seconds before answering basic questions from others, like "How are you?" Once again, I was receiving a confirmation about the importance of the pause in the life I was now living. I was hitting the pause button daily, and now it was being recommended in conversations with others.

Now that I had begun to ask myself one simple question about my feelings, another arose: *If I don't understand my feelings, how will I ever understand who I am and what makes me happy?* I was beginning to understand myself a little bit more for the first time in my life. I was the quiet soul, the inner peaceful being who was beginning to observe the self-criticism and negative self-talk from the ego. My thoughts were not very nice to this sweet soul.

Occasionally, I could locate myself inside there, typically in moments of quiet and solitude. I started to learn I was not all the things I did or I thought (thank God), I was not the actions but rather the stillness, the gentle soul who *was*. As time moved on, I looked forward to connecting with my soul in stillness, and meditation became part of my morning routine. I was thoroughly enjoying what I was learning and practicing in Soul School and was excited to share it with my sons and anyone else who seemed interested. At this point in my journey, I imagined myself to be in freshman year.

GOING DEEPER

To others, the idea of sitting in stillness to connect with the soul may sound ridiculous and the last thing they would want to do, but I loved what I was feeling and couldn't get enough of it. Little did I know at this point in the journey that the moments of solitude would soon transform into complete solitude and lockdown for the entire world as the global pandemic made its appearance. Fortunately, I had already begun to embrace a little solitude and quiet, and I was becoming comfortable with it.

The last trip I took before the world shut down for a year was in February 2020. The Muskees traveled to Wyoming to celebrate my oldest son's birthday. Jackson Hole, Wyoming, is one of my sons' favorite places, and his brother and I wanted him to feel extra special on his birthday, since it's a few weeks after Christmas. We had no idea at the time this would be our last trip for a year because of the COVID- 19 pandemic, which was gaining traction.

Accordingly, I would have plenty of time to ponder the question, "Who am I?" with no idea at the time that I'd had the answer all along. I simply had to take time to get in touch with the inner voice of love, tune into my feelings and observe the rhythms in my life. I was slowly beginning to release fear, anxiety, and doubt and welcome stillness, acceptance, and love.

I was also releasing many emotions through my daily letters to God. Now I was crying tears of joy and gratitude, not sorrow. From the space of the soul, my heart was opening, and I was beginning to feel emotions of love, joy, and complete gratitude for the many lessons I was learning. I was also working hard to increase my emotional vocabulary.

Dr. Marc Brackett came to my rescue at a key moment during my journey with his book, *Permission to Feel.* I learned a big part of getting to your *true self* is through vulnerability and understanding your feelings. He helped me see the importance of really listening to myself and validating my feelings on my journey back to my true self.

So, I ask you as he asks readers in his book: *How are you feeling?* It's OK if you struggle to come up with the exact name for your feeling. I still find it challenging to name emotions beyond happy, sad, and scared. And that's OK. The important message is to begin to tune into yourself, and ask yourself some questions.

Soul Searching:

- Ask yourself, "How am I feeling?" at least one time during the day. This one question has helped me stay grounded in my own two feet and not get lost in others' feelings and energy. It's kept me in touch with my inner self. It has also reminded me to stay in my lane.

- Are you able to pause once during the day and do as Dr. Marc Brackett suggests: "Physically stop whatever you're doing, check in with the state of your mind and body, and ask yourself: At this exact moment, what is my emotional state? Am I feeling up or down? Pleasant or unpleasant? Would I like to approach the world or steer clear?"[1]
- Can you identify how your body is feeling during that moment? Dr. Brackett gives some of the following additional questions to ask yourself, "Am I energized or depleted? Is my heart racing, am I clenching my fists, is there a knot in my stomach, or am I feeling balanced, cool, and at ease?" Check in with how your body is feeling.
- Perhaps you can journal about your feelings and some details about the circumstances or people in the moment that may be triggering some of those feelings.

Song suggestion:

"Can't Stop the Feeling," by Justin Timberlake

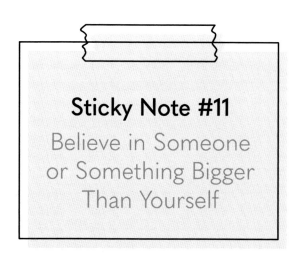

Sticky Note #11
Believe in Someone
or Something Bigger
Than Yourself

*"As with any spiritual journey, I was not the instigator
of the trip … much of this journey involved my
letting go of the need to be somebody else."*

—JAMES MARTIN, SJ

I'm not sure what hurts more—losing someone you love suddenly, or knowing their time on earth is nearing the end. Both losses hurt a lot. Losing each of my parents was very painful. In the case of my mother, she was gone twenty-one hours after being rushed to the emergency room. On the other hand, my father was on hospice care for several months before he passed away. He used his final few months wisely and intentionally. He spent as much time as possible with his family and others who were close to him. My dad spoke individually with some of his children and grandchildren at our last Christmas together. He intentionally met with each one of us individually.

I can still transport myself back to that intimate moment with him as if it were yesterday, walking behind his wheelchair into his bedroom for what was to be our final "chat" after our

Christmas meal. I started crying as soon as I sat on his bed, practically collapsing onto it before he had even uttered a word. I can still see his face and feel the emotions from that moment as I write these words. That was one of those moments in life that was rooted deep within me, that I can bring myself back to and quite often do. I don't have many of those.

In his typical charming way, he smiled and whispered, "You're crying, and I haven't even spoken yet." My father always had a way of bringing humor into difficult conversations. The simplicity of those words made me pause and reflect, as I often did in his presence when he would speak such wise yet simple statements. We spent most of our waking hours together in the office for twenty years, and his humor helped lighten many difficult situations. Perhaps it was his soft and quiet voice that allowed his words to seem even more powerful.

I can't remember every word he said to me that night. I was wishing time could stop and he could be with us forever, and my heart was breaking in two. One phrase stood out, and I will always remember it. He gently whispered, "Believe in someone or something bigger than yourself. You've already proven yourself in business, Marcie. Make a difference in the world in another way."

I knew at that time his reference had something to do with God and helping others. He would often ask me over the years if I went to mass on Sundays, and mentioned many times I would be good at helping the elderly in some way. I think my father was trying to remind me of the importance of having God in my life, daily prayer, regular mass attendance, and helping others in some capacity with his "Believe in someone or something bigger than yourself" statement. I imagine he was also hoping our Catholic beliefs held and that the soul would continue after the body died. He was about to find out.

A TIME FOR REFLECTION

With a lot of space, stillness, and openness, I found myself pondering his message quite often. I asked myself, *Who or what is this force bigger than me? If it's God, who is God, really? Is God male or female? Is God some heavenly judge looking down on me, smiling proudly when I'm good or shaking his or her head in disappointment when I'm off track?*

I was on a roll with asking questions now, thanks to the "How am I feeling?" one from Dr. Brackett. Little did I know at the time, but God would reveal himself to me and show me who he was in my life over the next couple of years. I simply needed to remain open and give God a chance to do so. All I had to do was continue to "show up," as my dad used to always say.

As a Catholic school student for twelve years, I was taught a lot about God both in school and in our home, observing how my mom and dad lived each day. I prayed back then, usually when I was in need of some extra help. When I was younger, I imagined God was a magical force sitting on a throne in Heaven behind golden gates deciding who could enter and who could not and that he was the ultimate judge. I didn't really know how to pray to God or whether I was doing it right. I usually just said a memorized prayer and asked God to help me when I was in a bind.

My mother, on the other hand, seemed to know how to connect with God. She had a stack of prayer cards (which I still carry with me today, even though they are shredded and torn from much use) and would pray every evening before bed. She seemed to be connected to God on a much deeper level. I used to admire her greatly and thought I could never come close to her level of connection with God.

I suppose I subconsciously relied on her prayers to get me through safely in life. I figured she had it covered for me with God. I would also ask her, at times, to pray for me when it came to various things in my life, like doing well on an exam. I think my brothers put in some prayer requests to her too. During my challenging teenage years, I'm sure she was praying not only for me but for herself so she could find the strength to deal with me. Prayer and regular attendance at mass were very important to my mother.

MY ROLE MODELS

If any two people had the right to question someone or something bigger in their lives and doubt the existence of a Higher Power, it would have been my parents. Mom and Dad met in high school and fell in love at a very young age; they were childhood sweethearts. My father had a great deal of competition to win my mother's heart. My mother was a true classic, a diamond in the rough. Believe it or not, my father's biggest competition was God.

My mother had been contemplating a life devoted to God in the convent. I remember hearing stories about this. Apparently my father said, "I can compete with a lot of guys, but I can't compete with the Big Guy." Humor and persistence were two of my father's many gifts.

My dad eventually won my mom's heart, and my parents were married in Hunstanton, England, where my father was stationed during his military service. I imagine back then they were full of young love, excitement, and hope, as most young couples are when they're madly in love. They were probably very excited about their bright future together.

Unfortunately, their lives took a turn in a different direction when my father contracted polio at the young age of twenty-three and was paralyzed from the waist down. He couldn't stand or walk and lived the rest of his life in a wheelchair. That didn't deter my parents, though. They were determined to make the most of everything they had each day, which wasn't much.

After my father finished physical rehabilitation at Magee Rehabilitation Hospital in Philadelphia, he enrolled in night school at Saint Joseph's University to obtain a college degree while working during the day to support my mother and two brothers.

My mother remained steadfast in her faith in God, regular mass attendance, and unconditional love for my father and brothers. That was all she needed. She stayed connected with "the Big Guy." She didn't let anything or anyone interfere with her priorities. She continued to strengthen her faith through prayer and mass, and she remained laser-focused on her family while role modeling exceptional family values for her children.

GRIT

I was born nine years after my oldest brother. I remember sitting around the table at a young age every night, including weekends, for family dinners. Mom and Dad were very present in our lives. My parents did their best to instill the importance of hard work, determination, resilience, persistence, integrity, grit, and faith in God in my two brothers and me. I admired not only my parents, but my two older brothers tremendously—we were a family of hard workers.

After reading Angela Duckworth's book *Grit: The Power of Passion and Perseverance,* I can confidently say my parents had grit. Duckworth writes, "In sum, no matter the domain, the highly successful had a kind of ferocious determination that played out in two ways. First, these exemplars were unusually resilient and hardworking. Second, they knew in a very, very deep way what it was they wanted. They not only had determination, they had *direction*. It was the combination of passion and perseverance that made high achievers special. In a word, they had grit."[1]

My parents valued education and wanted their children to have a much higher level of education than they had received. They made the most of whatever they had (which was not very much in their early days). They continued to work together as a team, and my mother continued to cast her eyes upon God as often as she could during the day and say her prayers every night. She was content with what she had, never wishing for anything different and never longing for more. She knew what it meant to be happy, and she lived every day by being fully present in each moment to the extent she could.

She never complained, and from what I observed, she had every right to complain. She helped my father in and out of the wheelchair every morning before he left for work and every evening when he returned. She made breakfasts, packed lunches, and cooked dinners every day. She kept our little house tidy and clean. I'm not sure when she was able to shop for food because we only had one car, which my father drove to work every day, but somehow, we had food on the table.

My mother always had an eye on my dad, no matter where we were, and if she couldn't see him, she had an extended family of very close friends who could. She helped him with basic tasks such as getting dressed, and he always looked handsome and dapper. The idea of hiring a nurse was out of the question. My mom wouldn't entertain it.

The irony is that as I share their story with you, I realize I never viewed my dad as being disabled. I never told my friends or others that my dad was in a wheelchair. To me, our lives seemed pretty normal; we just had to live in a one-story house because my father was in a wheelchair and not able to walk, but that meant we always had a ramp for his wheelchair, and I could ride my little "krazy car" up and down the ramp for fun.

My father's strong intellect offset any of his physical limitations. He had a sharp mind and a good sense of humor. He drove a normal car that was equipped with hand controls. Most shocking was he also learned to fly planes. What he couldn't do physically, he could do mentally. I can still picture him now being hoisted in a crane and dropped into the small cockpit of his Aircoupe and four-seater plane. I still wear a baseball cap, whose brim is frayed from overwearing it most days, with *Air Carroll* monogrammed on it that we had made in honor of him for his funeral.

I feel his presence with me when wearing the cap and love sharing his story with others when they ask me about the meaning of *Air Carroll*. I've had some interesting conversations with retired pilots and others who share their stories with me about their flying escapades—all from that hat. I'm sure my dad is smiling down during those moments and laughing as I'm leaving out rather important details about the planes he used to fly and some of the flying terms I've heard mentioned but don't know exactly what they mean.

CONNECTING TO A HIGHER POWER

As I was writing this book, I came across notes from a conversation I had with my dad a few years before he passed away. We used to spend weekends together and I would love to listen to his many flying escapades. One of the questions I asked my father was why he liked to fly. He told me, "Some people fly to get from point A to point B. Others fly to fly. For me, it's more of a spiritual journey. I am mesmerized by the scenes and the quiet, calm, and still air. I become taken over by a power greater than myself."

And there it was—the power greater than himself in whom he believed. My father's description of being taken over by a power greater than himself was exactly how I was beginning to feel as I embraced my inner space of quiet and stillness. I, too, was becoming aware of a power much greater than myself, and I was allowing space for that power to come forth and guide me every step of the way from point A to point B. It was yet another celestial synchronicity confirming I was on the right path.

I realize now my father was able to connect to his inner being, soul, or spirit when he flew, just as I could when I quieted my thoughts and connected to my soul. His way was much more adventurous, but I will stay in my lane and embrace my simple way. I don't believe there is only one name for this greater power. I call this Divine power *God*, and I'm hopeful my mom and dad have met him.

Soul Searching:

- What life events have made you consider believing in someone or something bigger than yourself?
- Have you ever experienced feelings of being completely content or at peace?
- When have you ever felt a Divine power in your life?
- Perhaps you can journal how a Divine power feels in your life, and how you connect with it.

Song suggestion:

"Come Fly with Me," by Frank Sinatra

Sticky Note #12
Be an Open Book,
and Stay Alert

*"Open your eyes to see the amazing ways that a higher,
cosmic power has been working in your life."*

—SQUIRE RUSHNELL

As I sat alone in the little cottage, I wasn't able to get my father's message out of my head and heart, "Believe in someone or something bigger than yourself." I was also noticing the more open I remained each day, the more aware I was of the people, activities, messages, and teachers coming to me. I simply needed to remain open, and the people and the paths unfolded.

Remaining open meant not being attached to any specific outcome. I was letting the tide gently guide me. It was hard work to detach from desired outcomes. The teachers, the books, the lessons, and the answers appeared. I began to receive recommendations for books to read thanks to our very wise meditation and yoga teacher.

One of her first recommendations was *The Untethered Soul* by Michael Singer. My fellow meditators and I used to laugh every time our wise instructor would open her bag of goodies. I couldn't control myself and was always looking for a new book to order. Amazon was a frequent visitor and became my go-to library, dropping off a minimum of two books a day. I loved the Amazon library, and there wasn't a due date for any of the books to be returned. That was a good thing because I read many of them several times.

I also couldn't get enough of *Oprah's Super Soul Sunday* podcasts, through which I was introduced to Eckhart Tolle, Gary Zukav, Wayne Dyer, and many other spiritual teachers who became my teachers. In many ways, I was learning remotely through book assignments and podcast interviews with various teachers.

I was like an open book, and I was aware of circumstances unfolding in my life. I was aware, open, and saying yes to whatever came into my path. Awareness and openness seemed to go hand in hand. Since I wasn't attached to an outcome, I was relying more on guidance from above, observing others who were coming into my path, messages I was reading in books, insights that were coming to me, and other signs throughout the day.

After *The Untethered Soul*, I picked up *The Secret* by Rhonda Byrne for the second time. I had read *The Secret* about ten years earlier, and it resurfaced during one of my conversations with my niece. I sent her the book, and we compared our thoughts and had daily phone calls for hours (during the pandemic) discussing the idea of the Law of Attraction and manifesting our dreams.

We encouraged each other to live our dreams. We spent hours on the phone sharing the secrets in our souls. I had written my wishes and desires in the pages of the book ten years ago and was shocked as I shared with her how some of them had actually come true. I became a true believer in the power of manifestation.

"Maybe there is something about visualizing our dreams, the steps toward those dreams, and believing," my niece and I agreed. She shared with me an experience she had that also seemed to confirm the power of manifestation. I remained open to the idea of manifesting my dreams and wishes, especially since it had seemed to work when I had done it many years earlier. Again, I was an open book to ideas and lessons I was learning.

CONTINUING MY SPIRITUAL JOURNEY

Various teachers also intersected my path at critical times to help guide me toward what or who this greater power than myself was. Eckhart Tolle, Wayne Dyer, Michael Singer, Jack Kornfield, Pema Chödrön, Thich Nhât Hanh, Thomas Merton, Thomas Keating, Deepak Chopra, Gary Zukav, James Van Praagh, and even my great cousin, Sister M were some of them. Although these teachers may have had different belief systems and expressed their beliefs using different languages, I was amazed at how similar some of their messages were.

Everything seemed to start with the thoughts in our minds. Mindfulness practices were critical to quieting the mind. Many of them spoke about the importance of stillness and quiet in order to connect with our inner being and soul. They spoke about the power of our thoughts and the importance of becoming aware of our thoughts but not judging them. They seemed to agree that our thoughts are extremely powerful and can be distractions from hearing the voice of our inner being, the soul (I could relate to that). They spoke of the powerful force of love.

My reading list was extensive. I'm amazed as I look back now that many of the authors seemed to agree on the importance of connecting to something deep within ourselves other than our minds and thoughts. They spoke about the transformational power of the heart, soul, spirit—that gentle place deep within us all that they referred to as our true selves. A few of the teachers shared their journeys to their "true selves." Their messages resonated with me and I was beginning to get a glimpse of this "true self" they spoke of.

They called this powerful force of love different names: God, Buddha, the Universe, Divine Spirit among them. But the description of the feeling of that tremendous force of love within us was similar. In some sense, they spoke about the message my father was trying to give me—a Higher Power in our lives, one that lived within us that we could access anytime. The importance of connecting to the soul to access this Higher Power seemed to be a common theme.

Not only was I reading their messages, but I was also putting into practice what they were teaching as I read their books. They stressed the importance of mindfulness, meditation, stillness, and the power of being fully present in each moment in order to connect deep within ourselves. I was beginning most mornings seated in silence, for at least a few minutes, and was beginning to feel the difference in my life, the sensation they had also experienced and written about. I read their books and listened to as many podcasts and interviews with these inspirational teachers as I could find. I also became a regular listener of *Oprah's Super Soul Sunday* podcast. I couldn't get enough of what I was learning in Soul School.

SURROUNDED BY NEW WISDOM

The lessons seemed to appear in a lot of different ways, not just through books and podcasts. In one of my journals I had tucked away, I came across an article in a Philadelphia newspaper I had saved from 1994 that my mother had given me titled, "Openness Keeps Love Alive."

The article was written by Darrell Sifford and talked about how many of us are out of touch with our feelings and thus not able to communicate our needs to our partners. Sifford quoted Barbara DeAngelis's book *How to Make Love All the Time*. DeAngelis wrote, "Many of us never formed a good relationship with the person inside. We need to get to know that person, have a dialogue with that person, listen to the voice of that person…If you can't communicate with yourself, you have no idea what to talk about or ask for when you're with your partner."[1]

DeAngelis further wrote, "When you don't tell the truth about your needs to yourself and to others, you are pushing love out of your life. When you do feel loved and understood, your soul is touched, and your world is brightened."[2] I wish I had understood the importance of remaining open and getting in touch with my feelings and myself decades ago when my mother gave me this article.

But now I was beginning to connect with this place within. I reminded myself of the importance of observing and detaching from my thoughts, feeling my feelings, allowing my thoughts to move through me, rather than allowing my thoughts to control me. This was a much healthier approach than my initial circular pattern of longing and fear before I pivoted into the unknown. I was learning how to train my mind.

God was also sending me opportunities in my life to put into practice what I was reading about and learning. In simple terms, I was beginning to let go and let God and love lead.

I began to understand the importance of openness in order to connect within and access this Higher Power of love, and I was seeing this play out in my life. I was opening my heart slowly and letting God in.

I came across notes I had written in *The Untethered Soul* when I first read the book early in my journey. I wrote, "Just be aware and open. Things will come to me (people to help, a book to write, places to serve, classes to take). It will all flow to me. The dam is open."

I had written those words three years ago and was now living them: the people, books, and classes were coming to me. I was living what I had written early on in the beginning of my journey. I am truly in awe as I write these words that the places, the people, the books, and the classes all came to me once I was open and aware. Everything came to me. I was like an open book.

Soul Searching:

- Where are you able to welcome openness in your life?
- How can you become open to new experiences, people, and ideas that may help you connect more to your inner being—the place of the soul?
- When are you an open book?
- What kind of relationship do you have with the person within you?

Song suggestion:

"Don't Blink," by Kenny Chesney

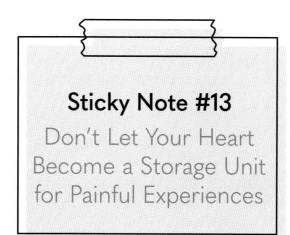

"What is it about the structure of the heart center that permits it to close? What you will find is that the heart closes because it becomes blocked by stored, unfinished energy patterns from your past."

—MICHAEL SINGER

As a former packrat, I was an expert at storing objects in a safe place for later. Have you ever stored your belongings in a storage unit? In my experience, I stored furniture and other belongings and actually forgot what was even in there over time. Apparently, objects weren't the only items I stored away; I had wrapped up and tucked away years of hurtful memories. (I wasn't sure where I was putting those.)

Now that I was embracing openness and beginning to get in touch with my feelings a bit more, it was time to address some past hurts in my life. I began to recognize that my heart stored some really big hurts and wounds and had been closed off for a long time. I suppose it simply couldn't store any more pain. Dr. Wayne Dyer's book, *Manifest Your Destiny—The Nine Spiritual Principles for Getting Everything You Want*, echoed what I was experiencing. Dyer writes, "Most of us in the West have been taught that the center of our wisdom is in our heads. If you ask people where their ability to process thought and experience is, they will generally respond that it is in the brain. Ask consciously spiritual persons the same question and they will indicate the heart."[1] My heart was beginning to open the closer I connected within. I seemed to be on the path toward the *consciously spiritual person* that Dyer spoke of.

One of the first major pings to my heart was the crumbling of my marriage. Although it had been more than twenty years, somehow I had stored the pain, disappointment, hurt, rejection, betrayal, and feeling like a failure deep in my heart.

The next big ping to my heart was the tragic and sudden death of my mother, my best friend. She was my rock, and I admired her like I admired no other woman. She was a huge inspiration for not only me but also many others, and I'm forever grateful she was my mother. That pain was extremely intense, and I stored it deep down in my heart twelve years ago, right on top of my disappointment over the breakup of my marriage.

EMOTIONAL STORAGE

Looking back now, in some ways, my heart had become a storage unit for pain, disappointment, and hurt. Just as the physical storage unit was overflowing with material possessions, my heart storage unit was overflowing with painful emotions. But I kept adding more—the death of my father somehow went into that heart storage space too.

My heart was overflowing with pain, disappointment, betrayal, hurt, devastation, sadness, loss—the emotions went on and on. I was now beginning to see a pattern: I had been storing my pain and sadness deep inside my heart for years. At some point, I needed to open the heart storage unit as I had done with the physical storage unit and clear it all out. But how?

Clearing out a physical storage unit of furniture and belongings had seemed difficult at the time, but nothing compared to the idea of emptying over twenty years' worth of pain and sorrow. I decided that for starters, I needed to better understand why I stored it all deep in my heart—to understand the intention beneath the action. I began asking myself yet another question, "Why?" to somehow get to the core of my heart. The questions I started to ask seemed to be taking me deeper and deeper.

Why did I store the hurt in my heart from a broken marriage of untruths? Why did I store the intense pain of losing my mother so suddenly? Why did I also store the sadness over the death of my father, my mentor? I came up with a few possibilities.

> **The divorce**—I kept my pain inside my heart storage unit because I didn't want to hurt my sons anymore. They were having to deal with their own suffering, and I didn't want to add my pain to their pain. I was determined to be the best mother I could for my wonderful sons. "I will do my best to not let anybody hurt them," I quietly told myself. I worked overtime trying to make sure of that. I tucked all my pain and disappointment deep inside me and tried my hardest to bring as much peace, comfort, and lightness as I could to them. I'm sure I stumbled many times back then, but my intention was to be a pillar of strength and resilience, in many ways like my parents were for me.

> **The sudden passing of my mom**—I did the only thing I could. I stored the pain and heartbreak within. I kept my tears to myself and buried my deep sadness inside my heart storage unit. I wanted to be a pillar of strength for my father,

my sons, and other family members who were also devastated by my mother's death. After all, they were hurting as much as I was, maybe even more. I stored it all deep within my heart.

I can remember reminding myself at my mom's funeral to stand tall with a smile on my face and to keep the service light, like my mom would have wanted. To others, it may have appeared that I was strong and resilient or worse, unemotional. I remember an acquaintance who attended my mom's funeral questioning me later about my lack of tears during the funeral. I was extremely offended that I was being graded on my emotional reaction to losing my mother. I was simply doing the best I could at the time, not only for myself but also for my father, my sons, and the rest of our family. We were all devastated.

The passing of my dad—the storage unit in my heart was really overflowing now. Yet somehow, I made room for the pain and sadness of losing my dad and stored it all in there. The same pattern emerged: I wanted to be a pillar of strength and resilience for my sons and the employees in our company, who were like family. (A few had been with my dad for most of his career. One, in particular, was the main person my mom had relied on to be her second set of eyes on my dad. My mom viewed her like a sister to some degree.) The business had to keep going because others' lives depended on it. Once again, I did my best to be a pillar for my colleagues and was in the office two days after my dad's funeral.

MAKING SPACE

Looking back at those devastating moments in my life, I realized I shoved all my pain and sadness deep within my heart as much as I could. My heart storage unit had no more space. How could I possibly take on any more sadness and pain? I had to begin to clear it out. It was becoming more costly than the physical storage unit.

Reading *The Word Among Us* and journaling my feelings and thoughts now became part of my morning routine, which I looked forward to each day. I was beginning to clear out the sadness in my heart little by little by expressing my feelings and thoughts on paper. I wrote a letter to God each morning as part of the homework assignment for the Spiritual Exercises program I was enrolled in.

As my heart opened a little bit more each day, my feelings poured out in letters to God. I was finally releasing some of the pain I had stored in my heart; it was similar to what I had done months earlier when I cleared the belongings that were overflowing from the storage unit. God was my only hope. I had a lot of pouring out to do. I was releasing emotional attachments I had stored for a long time. God was becoming my pillar of strength on whom I was leaning!

I was also becoming aware of additional hurts I had stored over recent years from a few broken relationships. They were in the storage space, too. I am definitely not an expert in the area of romantic love. As a big believer in the power of love, I believe in soul connections or soul partners. From what others have shared with me about their love stories, the soul connection between soul partners seems like a powerful force of love.

SOUL CONNECTIONS

Have you ever met a couple that seemed like they belonged together? I've met many couples like that who seem as if they just fit like pieces of a puzzle. I have always enjoyed asking them how they met and am still amazed to this day when some partners say they just knew the other was "the one." I used to ask myself, what does that mean—to know a person is *the one*? What does that feel like? I also used to think how lucky they were to have such great love and to have found their soulmate. I seemed to still be searching for mine.

Over the years I have met both men and women with whom I felt a "soul connection" instantaneously upon meeting. Quite a few of those soul connections are good friends today. The connection felt like it was at a much deeper level, and it seemed as if we had known each other our whole lives and possibly from a past life, if that's how it all works. I could feel the difference immediately. It seemed God wanted us to meet for a reason, and our meeting had been orchestrated from above, a "Divine appointment" as Henri Nouwen refers to them. Indeed, I pivoted into the unknown after one such encounter.

There have been other times over my life when my soul was rejected, when another soul didn't seem to want a connection. That hurts and is painful. I imagine many of us have experienced that at some point in our lives. With a more open heart, I recognized the importance of feeling the pain and hurt and not simply storing it anymore in the storage unit in my heart. It was painful to put this lesson to work in my life. Many of the spiritual teachers spoke about observing our feelings, allowing them to flow through us, and detaching from them. That's just what I was trying to do. This was one of the most difficult lessons I learned, and it required a great deal of faith, hope, persistence, and patience. It's one thing to read words in books, and another thing to put the messages into practice. It was hard work.

It's sad and difficult to accept a rejection of love, especially love at the level of the soul. It really hurts. But this was and still is a very important lesson—to accept what is and to not force what isn't part of the grand celestial plan. Acceptance was difficult during this time because my heart was open and feeling every ping quite intensely. Acceptance was critical.

I also learned it's important to recognize, feel, and acknowledge all our feelings, both the happy ones and the sad ones. Recognition and acceptance of my feelings was new for me and something I had not really done much in the past. Many of the books I read in Soul School, however, stressed the importance of doing just that—allowing our feelings to flow through us and being aware of them without judging them as we experience them and feel them in our bodies.

God, once again, was bringing celestial synchronicities my way for me to practice feeling the pain, not storing it deep within, and allowing it to flow through. My heart was finally opening, and I wanted it to remain that way. This was a very painful part of my journey.

HEALING OLD WOUNDS

Each morning during my meditation and prayer time, I would sit in silence and try to connect to God as best as I could. Since I was now in the habit of bringing everything to God, I brought my sadness from past soul meeting rejections. I now had someone to turn to, which was a good thing because storing the sadness in the storage unit in my heart was no longer an option.

One of the insights that came to me during my morning prayer time was, "The Lord is near to the brokenhearted." He must have been really close to me during that time, because my heart felt broken as I relived some painful soul rejections. Having your heart broken can offer some valuable lessons (once you work through the pain), such as acceptance, faith, hope, and surrender. It's hard to remember when it's happening, though.

Another important lesson is even after your heart has been hurt and wounded, it's still very important to keep it open. Life is best lived with an open heart full of love, for out of an open heart comes love. Love seemed to be the fuel of the soul, and I was determined to let love lead the way. I experienced living life with a closed heart for many years, and I have begun to experience living life with an open heart over the past few years. I choose a life with an open heart filled with love going forward. I continue to remind myself of these valuable lessons daily. I am also fortunate and grateful to be surrounded by many wonderful and caring family members and friends whose love I feel strongly every day. Gratitude also helps heal a broken heart. I also reminded myself that growth comes from pain. I hoped I was growing immensely because I was feeling a lot of pain.

I would later discover my "soulmate" had been with me my entire life. I simply had no idea I was searching for something I already had.

Soul Searching:

- Can you start emptying out a few painful emotions from your heart storage unit? Perhaps start with one small emotion at a time. Observe the feeling, allow it to flow through you, and accept it.
- If you feel inclined, you can take out a piece of paper and pen. Sit in a quiet place for a few minutes and see if you are aware of some painful memories you may have stored deep within. Maybe you can start with one and begin to write about it.
- After you've written about it, rip up the paper and throw it in the trash. This action step may help you begin to release some painful memories from the past.

- Visualize the memory disintegrating into space.

Song suggestion:

"Cold Heart (PNAU Remix)," by Elton John, Dua Lipa, and PNAU

Sticky Note #14
Just Show Up

*"Prayer is something that God does within you, so you
don't have to worry so much about your 'doing it.'"*

—JAMES MARTIN, SJ

My history with religion and God was formed through twelve years of Catholic education and my observations of my parents over the years. I believed in God and would occasionally pray to him, usually when I was in need. I didn't know if I was praying the right way, but I tried my best and hoped God would see me trying and cut me a break. I would soon learn that prayer is about what God wants to do. We don't have to do anything. We simply need to show up and let ourselves be loved by God.

For most of my life, my connection with God revolved around rote prayers and asking God for help at times. I learned prayer can simply be a conversation of any length and can be as simple as sitting in silence and feeling the Divine love from the soul. God continued to send celestial synchronicities that allowed me to practice what I was reading and learning. One of the best books on prayer I read was *Learning to Pray* by James Martin, SJ. He writes:

Prayer is for everyone. A few years ago, a man with no formal religious background told me that he had never prayed before. But when we talked about his life, he described a profound experience when he suddenly felt connected to something larger than himself and felt an unmistakable sense of encouragement about his path in life. At the time, he took this as confirmation that he was on the "right path." Before our conversation, my friend hadn't considered the possibility that during this incident God might have been communicating with him. So I encouraged him to think about it not simply as an important insight or a confirmation about his path, but as something greater. Eventually, this recognition—that this was an experience of God, about whom he had wondered all his life—marked the start of an intentional life of faith.[1]

That resonated with me—first, because my father's message to me was to believe in someone or something bigger than myself, and second, because I've experienced what Father Martin said about feeling a sense of encouragement that I was on the right path. I had received signs or celestial synchronicities quite often, which seemed to confirm that I was on the right path. I simply had to remind myself to be aware of them so I wouldn't miss them. It was also a comforting feeling that I wasn't alone anymore; I felt a Divine force of love with me every step of the way.

The Ignatian Adventure includes a wonderful description of prayer by Ruth Burrows, called "Essence of Prayer," that I read daily. I love her description of what prayer is. Reading this helped me understand there wasn't a right or a wrong way to pray, I just needed to show up and allow God to show me what he would like me to do.

"Essence of Prayer," by Ruth Burrows:

> Prayer has far more to do with what God wants to do in us than with our trying to "reach" or "realize," still less "entertain," God in prayer. This truth eliminates anxiety and concern as to the success or unsuccess of our prayer, for we can be quite certain that, if we want to pray and give the time to prayer, God is always successful and that is what matters. …What we think of as our search for God is, in reality, a response to the Divine Lover drawing us to himself. There is never a moment when Divine Love is not at work. … This work is nothing other than a giving of the Divine Self in love. The logical consequence for us must surely be that our part is to let ourselves be loved, let ourselves be given to, let ourselves be worked upon by this great God and made capable of total union with Him.[2]

I began to let myself be loved by this Divine force of Love.

MY FRIEND GOD

I also started talking with God as I would a friend, with gratitude, rather than simply asking for help as I had in previous years of praying. Don't get me wrong—there were many days I fell on my knees and asked God to guide me and come into my situation. He always came through. Little did I know that God was doing his part and it was God who was nudging me back to a relationship with the very one who created me: Him. I simply had to just show up, be open to a relationship with him, quiet my thoughts, listen for insights, and give him some space to enter.

As part of my commitment to praying and believing in something bigger than myself, I began reading *The Word Among Us*, a simple book of daily meditations for Catholics my father had introduced me to a few years earlier. Certain phrases or words caught my attention and seemed to be answers to some of the questions I was asking. It was as if the meditations were echoing thoughts I was having and validating messages. My father read *The Word Among Us* as part of his morning routine in his later years, and I observed him with great admiration as he tried to practice what he read. This book became part of my morning routine also. It made me feel close to my dad in some way as I continued his daily practice on his behalf.

James Martin also wrote about God finding us in prayer and that our responsibility is to simply show up, close our eyes, and let God take over. His book, *Learning to Pray,* has a wonderful chapter titled "Beginning a Friendship with God." Martin reviews some of the important qualities of friendship—spending time with your friend, learning about your friend, being honest with your friend, listening to your friend, allowing your friend to grow, and embracing silence at times with your friend. This analogy of a friendship with God really impacted me, and I began to think of God as my friend. Praying no longer felt unattainable or like a chore. I was also meeting many kind and loving friends and having the opportunity yet again to practice what I was reading.

It was a bit of a relief for me to learn I didn't have to *do* anything a certain way in prayer; I simply had to begin to open my heart to receive love and allow God to show me the way and what he wanted for me. All I had to do was show up in prayer, and God would handle the rest. I could do that.

The best way I can describe what praying felt like is that my body was beginning to relax, and my fists were beginning to unclench. It was as if I had been closed off and tightly wound for most of my life, and as soon as I finally paused and began to let go, God entered, took over, and started sending me messages guiding me through books, conversations with others, podcasts, events, and daily situations. I was experiencing what SQuire Rushnell spoke of in *When God Winks—How The Power of Coincidence Guides Your Life*, "First, you are under the influence of a cosmic guidance system, and every day you receive little nudges to keep you on your chosen path. You can learn to harness the power of coincidences to enrich your future and to strengthen your inner convictions that the life path you've chosen is indeed the right path for you."[3]

God became my pillar of strength (just as I had been trying to be a pillar of strength for others for many years of my life), and I started to lean on him. The old emotions of hurt and sadness were beginning to be released, and new emotions of love, peace, joy, awe, and gratitude were flowing in and out of my heart. I was receiving directions on this new path that both my eyes and my heart could finally see and feel.

My prayer time now often consisted simply of sitting in silence for about ten minutes and asking God to guide me; to show me the way. I figured since I had perfected five minutes, God was worthy of five additional minutes. All I had to do was show up, and God did the rest.

In the words of Saint Augustine from *The Ignatian Adventure*, "True prayer is nothing but love."[4] And to quote Saint John Vianney in *The Ignatian Adventure*, "Prayer is the inner bath of love into which the soul plunges itself."[5]

Soul Searching:

- When can you spare five minutes to sit and receive love?
- How can you just show up?
- What does prayer mean to you? Maybe it's simply connecting with nature.

- Have you ever experienced a time when you felt encouragement that you were on the right path? Perhaps you can journal about your experience.
- Are there any phrases or verses that have resonated with you recently?

Song suggestion:

"Lean On Me," by Bill Withers

Sticky Note #15
Learn the Language
of the Soul

*"For many people God is manifested in a feeling
of calm. As this happens for you, you can start to
recognize what God 'feels' like in prayer."*

—JAMES MARTIN, SJ

What is the most memorable dream you've ever had? Have you ever dreamt about something and then experienced déjà vu in your waking life? According to Oxford Language, "The soul is the spiritual or immaterial part of a human being or animal." It makes sense that tapping into the language of your soul is like finding yourself in another dimension similar to a dream state. I began to notice I was receiving messages in some of my dreams at night.

Now that I had a better understanding of prayer being a conversation with God or simply sitting in silence with God, I was becoming aware of messages I received at other times. Perhaps this was because I was sitting in silence and had begun a habit of observing my thoughts so I could distinguish between the voice of Divine Love within the soul, and the voice of ego in the mind. How would I know which messages were soul-directed and which were more ego-directed?

James Martin, SJ. addressed this subject in *Learning to Pray.* "We are invited to be attentive to all the ways God speaks to us—through relationships, work, reading, nature, and so on—not during time spent in prayer," he writes. "On a more fundamental level, God's voice comes to us through the processes of our minds. Thus, to ask if it's God's voice or my voice begs the question: How else would God speak to us other than through our own consciousness?"[1]

TAPPING INTO CONSCIOUSNESS

Reading the word "consciousness" stopped me in my tracks. Since I was beginning to have quite a few dreams during that time, I had developed a habit of writing each dream down in a journal immediately upon waking. In one of my dreams, an elderly woman visited me with a one-word message: "Consciousness." I remember waking up thinking, *What does that mean?* I started researching the definition of consciousness. I figured if I was receiving messages during the day and in my dreams at night, they were worthy of some attention. Rereading Father Martin's statement now gives *consciousness* an entirely new meaning for me. I now see God was speaking to me in various forms: in conversations with others, in people I was encountering, in nature, and even in my dreams.

At the time I was experiencing different events or dreams, I believed they were coming from a Higher Power and felt they were meant to guide me in some way, but I wasn't entirely sure I was interpreting the messages correctly. They felt like synchronicities from above, hence the name—celestial synchronicities.

Father Martin, SJ goes even deeper on the topic of consciousness and understanding God's voice in his chapter on "Discerning God's Voice," in which he writes, "God's voice will act quietly, gently encouraging you to continue along that good path. Encouragement takes this quiet and gentle form."[2] He describes discouragement as the opposite of the voice of God, which he calls the "evil spirit." He states, "The evil spirit, who wants to lead you away from the good path, will try to disquiet you with 'gnawing anxiety,' 'setting up obstacles' for you and generally act like a 'drop of water on a stone,' which has a noisy and almost violent effect."[3] Father Martin further says, "The evil spirit can be recognized when you feel despair, the good spirit when you feel hope."[4] I was beginning to feel the difference between the anxious and despondent feelings and the peaceful and hopeful ones.

I received another message in a dream during this time. I woke up with the simple message: "Silent hope." As I reread the books, my journal entries, and my love letters, I am in awe that the soul, God, was gently speaking to me in various ways.

LISTENING TO DREAMS

On October 25, 2021, I wrote at the top of one of my journal pages, "I am a messenger intended to share the message of the soul." Then I recorded in my dream journal:

> My aunt visited me in my dream. Her message was that there is no sense of time where she and my parents are. It's all about a connection of souls—those of us still living in physical bodies mainly operate from our egos or false selves. Operating from the soul means being peaceful and wanting for nothing. Awareness or consciousness is soul-based.

Mom's, Dad's, and my aunt's spirits and souls are with me and others always. We simply need to *feel* into their presence. The soul longs and loves. Connecting at the soul level is feeling, not doing.

I further wrote on the page that I am a messenger for speaking about the soul to others. The end of my journal entry stated the publishing company called to see how my book was going as I was writing the above dream in my journal. I hadn't read this journal entry until this moment, as I'm writing these words. This was a dream with a couple of vivid and powerful messages: the language of the soul is feelings, the souls of deceased loved ones are still with us, and continue to write this book. It was all coming together—no wonder I needed a class on feelings. It seems as if we connect with the soul through feelings. I am truly astonished.

Unfortunately, at the time when I wrote the dream in my journal, I didn't take the message as seriously as I wished I had (that seemed to be another bad habit of mine). God and my soul had been speaking to me both through my dreams and celestial synchronicities during the day guiding me. God has had to send me multiple signs to get the messages across.

I'm in awe because just a few months ago, I knelt down and asked God, "to guide me as to whether I should finish this book." I continued, "I don't want this to be a book about me and to be coming from the ego in any way. If you have a message you would like me to get out, God, I'm happy to do that. I'm all ears. I'm not attached to any outcome." Here I was asking God if he had a message for me to deliver and if he wanted me to be a messenger, and I had been told a year earlier in a dream that, "I am a messenger meant to speak about the soul to others." I realize now I am simply a messenger sharing my experiences with the hopes you will also begin to connect with the powerful presence within, learn the language of the soul, and be open to leading a soul-based life.

Soul Searching:

- Record a dream you remember as soon as you wake up.
- Is there a message you can uncover?
- What is your soul trying to say to you?
- Have you ever felt as if you were receiving messages from a Higher Power?
- How did that feel? Have you ever had dreams with inspirational messages?
- Don't give up—the soul is waiting to speak to you. Can you feel it?

Song suggestion:

"Raindrops Keep Fallin' On My Head," by B.J. Thomas (in honor of Mimi)

Sticky Note #16
You've Won the Lottery Just by Being Born

"Since I am a child of God, I am definitely a victor. Have faith in yourself. Have faith, and express this faith in words. Never describe yourself as someone lowly or inconsequential."

—MASAHARU TANIGUCHI

My morning prayer time had evolved from simply sitting for five minutes in silence to reading some short biblical passages, and then journaling about my feelings. This verse from John really resonated with me: "It was not you who chose me, but I who chose you and appointed you to go and bear fruit that will remain," (John 15:16).[1]

This verse touched me because I was beginning to feel the depth of love from a Higher Power, someone much bigger than little me, as I read it. God was gently reminding me I was his child, his beloved, and therefore never alone. He was welcoming me back to him. I was starting to feel the impact of God choosing me and nudging me back to him and to a life led by the soul and Divine Love. I was also being reminded of the significance of my baptism as a baby and that God's spirit is in me, in you, and in everyone.

The feeling of being God's daughter is very impactful. This means I am never alone. The same is true for you: this Divine spirit of love is in you, too. God knows the deepest desires in our hearts; he knows us better than we know ourselves. Those are powerful words, and the significance of them was starting to sink in. As Psalm 139:13-14 says, "Truly you have formed my most being: you knit me in my mother's womb. I give you thanks that I am fearfully, wonderfully made; wonderful are your works."[2] I had never really felt before that power that lives in us. You are fearfully, wonderfully made too. Can you sit with these words for a minute, and feel the impact of the message?

ON THE RIGHT PATH

I was catching on to the celestial synchronistic events and signs that were being sent during the course of my days (and nights) in Soul School, all of which seemed to confirm I was on the right path. I was a big fan of those Divine messages and guidance. The people and the situations continued to appear as I was learning different lessons. These experiences left me with the impression that I should continue to pay attention and that my life was being orchestrated from a celestial world above; I simply had to give them a chance to show me what their plans were and what they needed me to do.

An example of a message confirming I was catching on to lessons happened when I was attending the funeral of my mother's younger sister. This was the same aunt who visited me in my dream to let me know that I was a messenger and she and my parents were close by. For the previous few years, I had been quietly reminiscing about my childhood and looking at different patterns in my life. When a person sits in silence for a few moments a day, thoughts come up that require looking back at patterns in order to see where they originated to better understand them.

I had convinced myself my birth wasn't planned since there are nine years between my oldest brother and me and six years between my middle brother and me. Even though I had read that with God there are no accidents, I was wallowing in a bit of self-pity as I imagined myself an "accident" and only shared my feeling with a couple of family members—this was not something to readily share with others.

After the funeral mass, we gathered for a family luncheon. During one of the conversations with relatives whom I hadn't seen in a very long time, someone mentioned my uncle used to refer to me as "a miracle baby." I looked with shock at this person and was speechless. I had never thought of myself as a "miracle baby."

Her words hit me hard. *I was a miracle baby? How could that be? I wasn't even planned*, I thought to myself. She continued to share with me that my uncle called me that because I was conceived after my father had contracted polio and was paralyzed. I was stunned. I had never thought of myself as "a miracle baby."

I believe without a doubt I was meant to hear that message that day because it reminded me to believe in the message—with God there are no accidents. This Divine force of love is in all of us. We are all miracle babies. You are a miracle baby. I am reminded of the scripture verse, "It was not you who chose me, but I who chose you," (John 15:16).[3]

As was the pattern after I received a lesson, a celestial synchronicity would appear in one way or another to serve as a validation of the lesson, an aid to better understand the lesson, or a prelude of what was to come. In this case, the celestial synchronicity seemed to serve as a validation of the lesson.

MIRACLES

The topic of the miracle of the creation of life arose out of the blue during a family birthday gathering with my sons, my daughter-in-law, and my younger son's girlfriend, who is in her first year of medical school. I've always wished I had gone to medical school and joked with her that she could feel free to share with me what she was learning if it would help her with her studies, as this would be the closest to medical school I would ever get.

She was sharing with us what she was learning in one of her classes about the creation of life and the human fetus. *Interesting timing*, I thought to myself as I was in the middle of writing this chapter and pondering the message that we are all *miracle babies*. Our conversation shifted as she explained the significantly low odds of a conception happening; everything must line up exactly right at the exact right time. That discussion felt like confirmation from above of the importance of this message—we are all miracle babies.

I've often felt the miracle of birth when I've looked at newborn babies in the past but had never truly felt the depth and power of that feeling as I did at that moment. Listening to her describe the science behind the creation of life really hit home for me. Every one of us born on this planet is a miracle. You are a miracle baby, too. "You are fearfully and wonderfully made." And you have Divine presence within you. You have a voice, and it matters. I hope you can deeply feel the power of this message. As her professor put it, "We all won the lottery just by being born!"

Soul Searching:

- Take a few minutes and think about your birthday. Is there a special way you like to celebrate it?

- Write about a favorite birthday celebration if you can remember one:
  - » Who was there?
  - » What kind of cake or dessert did you enjoy?
  - » Where was the celebration?
  - » Did you receive a favorite gift?
- Perhaps you can give thanks for being born and the gift of this day.
- Maybe you can make a wish for one thing this week.
- Perhaps you can savor the gift of each day.

Song suggestion:

"Happy Birthday," by Stevie Wonder

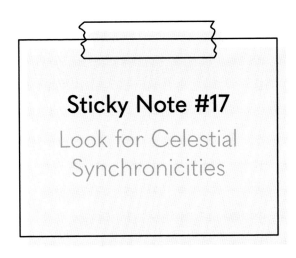

Sticky Note #17
Look for Celestial Synchronicities

"Nouwen believed that God speaks to us all the time and in many ways: through dreams and imagination, friends and people you meet, good books and great ideas, nature's beauty, and critical and current events. But it requires spiritual discernment to hear God's voice, see what God sees, and read the signs of daily life. What he learned from his mentor, Thomas Merton, and passes on in this volume is how to read the signs of God's guidance in books, nature, people, and events."[1]

—MICHAEL J. CHRISTENSEN

By now you may have a sense that I am a big believer in celestial synchronicities! I always have been, but I never had a fancy name for them when I was younger. Ever since I was a little girl, I've loved the idea of receiving a "sign" during the day—some type of reassurance or validation I was on the right track or something good was right around the corner.

When I was younger, many things seemed to fall into the "sign" category. For example, if my daily horoscope was a good one, I would think to myself, *That's a good sign.* Or if I saw a certain animal, like a fox, I would think I was being filled with wisdom. Or if I found a dime, I would see it as a reminder that I was surrounded by angels. I seemed to find signs in many of my daily activities.

My need for a sign rose to an all-time high after my mom and dad passed away. I was counting on them to not only send me signs but also to send clear signs I couldn't miss. Our family had been big believers in signs for a long time. We would often banter with one another over the years that when one of us left this world, we would send a sign to the others who were still here to let them know we had made it (wherever that was).

Since my mom passed away so suddenly, and I didn't have the chance to remind her about sending us a sign, I didn't want to miss the opportunity with my dad. A couple of weeks before my father breathed his final breath, I looked him in the eyes and asked him that all-too-familiar question again: "Can you send me a sign when you get there, wherever there is?" He grinned, looked me straight in the eyes, and quietly whispered, "If it's allowed." His sense of humor remained with him until the very end.

Mom and Dad didn't let us down. Here are a few of the many signs my family and I received from them.

SIGN #1: BUTTERFLIES

A butterfly sighting is now a big sign for my family and me. My sons and I love the idea of receiving signs from my parents (their grandparents) who have passed on to a new dimension. It gives us comfort that they are always with us and guiding us each day. These signs emit feelings of tremendous peace and love.

My mother had received a sign from my great aunt many years ago which she shared in confidence with my son. I was certain if anyone was going to send us a sign after moving to the next dimension, it would be my mom.

Shortly after my mother passed away suddenly, I was among many who were devastated as we were preparing for her funeral. My sister-in-law, a bigger believer in signs than I had been at the time, mentioned the idea of placing images of butterflies on the program, and we all agreed that would be lovely. Later that day that same sister-in-law noticed a butterfly outside our kitchen window, but I was numb and hurting very deeply, so I didn't register the coincidence.

The day of the funeral, a swarm of butterflies flew over my mom's casket as we exited the church. My mom now had my attention: a butterfly was her sign.

But she wasn't finished yet. She knew I was a slow learner. Several days later, as I sat in my father's condominium, devastated from a broken heart after losing her, I glanced outside and noticed a large butterfly positioned on the window flapping its wings. The odds of a butterfly landing on a window several floors from the ground are pretty slim.

I walked out on the balcony to be near the butterfly, wanting to be in her presence. As I stood there, I whispered her name and shared with her how much I missed her. The butterfly stayed there for quite some time, and I simply cherished being in her presence. There was nowhere else I wanted to be. You may think I'm crazy, but I believe my mother was sending a sign that she was surrounded by God and love and was still with us. She was letting me know all was well with her soul! I shared that sign with my sons and family.

It turns out, many family members had also been receiving visits from my mom in the form of a butterfly. Over the years, each of my sons have had butterflies land on their baseball caps at different moments and in different cities and remain on their hats for more than ten minutes. I could go on and on about other butterfly sightings, but I'll spare you the details. I think you get the point. So, every time we see a butterfly, my family and I are reminded of my mother—or as my sons lovingly call her, Mimi—and the feeling that her loving spirit is with us always.

My dad used to get upset when I would share with him the signs I received from mom after she passed away. He would complain, "Why don't I get any signs? Why doesn't she ever visit me?" I reminded him he was blessed to be surrounded by two wonderful nurses who came to us shortly after she passed away. They were like family and deeply cared for my father. Some may see that as luck. I smiled and knew my mother had intervened and brought them into our lives like angels from heaven.

A couple of days after my father passed away in April 2017, I once again noticed a large butterfly on our living room window. I wasn't looking for the butterfly; rather, it found me. This was similar to my sighting of the butterfly after my mother passed away seven years earlier. I sat in its presence, closed my eyes, and felt the enormous love surrounding me. I imagined my father sitting next to me and smiling at me. I believe he was giving me a sign that he was still with me. I took a picture of that butterfly that day, and it sits on my desk as I type these words. I guess he was allowed to send a sign after all.

SIGN #2: A "PRESENCE"

I could write an entire book just on the signs or celestial synchronicities I've received over the past few years but will share only a few extra-special ones. Believe it or not, my father didn't send only one sign; he sent two. Knowing my father, he would have wanted to send his own sign (if it was allowed) and not simply duplicate my mother's sign of a butterfly.

The second sign was extremely powerful and appeared a couple of weeks after he passed away. I remember feeling a presence on my right shoulder. It was very hard to describe and put into words, but I felt it. It was a strong sensation, as if he were next to me. It was on my right shoulder. I knew it was him. Coincidentally, as my father was nearing the end of his life here, he kept looking toward his left shoulder and commented several times that someone was there. Nobody was there—at least no one the human eye could see. This memory came to me as I was feeling his presence.

Whenever I felt this presence, I would gently rest my left hand on my right shoulder. Others wouldn't even notice what I was doing, but I knew, and hopefully he felt it too. Others might have thought I had lost it if I tried to explain I thought my dad was next to me on my right shoulder. I kept that sign to myself.

Oftentimes, I felt his presence when I was in the office in meetings with colleagues. It would make sense that I would feel his presence during those moments because my father and I had worked together for twenty years, and he would have been a part of those meetings. He always wanted to know "the scoop." He was letting me know he was still with me.

I didn't need anyone else to believe or confirm what I felt; I believed, and still believe, we are surrounded every day by those we love who have passed on to a new dimension! Their spirits are still with us; they are just in a different form.

My son shared a dream he had with me shortly after my father passed away. In his dream, Chauncey, as my sons lovingly called their grandfather, came to him and shared with him, "I'm close to you, just in another dimension, and time doesn't exist here. Everything is happening at once." How comforting to believe we are protected by angels, and those we were close to who have moved on to another dimension are still with us. We simply need to be aware, remain open to receiving signs and feeling their presence and their love, and believe. I'm hopeful you will feel it, too.

SIGN #3: ASK AND YOU SHALL RECEIVE

There is a scripture verse from Matthew 7:7-9, "Ask, and you will receive. Seek, and you will find. Knock, and it will be opened to you. For the one who asks, receives. The one who seeks, finds. The one who knocks, enters."[2] I had a powerful experience related to this scripture verse when my father was nearing the end of his time here. I spent every day with my father the last few weeks of his life. I would stop by and visit him and his two caring nurses who had become part of our family and who took wonderful care of him, as if he were their father.

One morning, a couple days before my father took his final breath, I was sitting alone with him in his bedroom. I simply wanted to be in his presence as much as I could, and I suppose in some sad way, I may have been hoping he would wake up and chat with me as he had done every day for most of my adult life. My father and I had grown even closer after the sudden death of my mother six years earlier. I was longing to see the twinkle in his eyes and his mischievous smile again, but his eyes were closed and his face expressionless.

The room was completely quiet; we wanted it to be as peaceful and sacred as possible for him. I was trying to absorb his presence and as many memories of him as I could before he left this world. Suddenly—very much out of the blue—I heard a knock.

It was strange—it seemed to be coming from his bedroom, near where I was sitting. It wasn't on the bedroom door because the door was open, and I was the only one in the condominium with my father at that moment. It wasn't at his front door either. This knock felt and seemed very different, as if it were coming from "above." Without thinking or hesitating, I leaned next to my dad and whispered in his ears, "Ask and it shall be given to you. Seek and you shall find. Knock and it shall be opened to you." I repeated these words over and over, as if it were some kind of a chant.

To this day, I have no idea where those words came from. I had heard that expression over the years as a scripture verse. It was as if my body and my spirit were being guided from above. This was not a normal prayer for me, and I frankly hadn't intended to say any prayers aloud with my father, yet there I stood, repeating it over and over again. I believe without a doubt I was allowing a Higher Power to flow through me.

During that period of my life, I was not very comfortable with reading the Bible and was certainly not one to recite biblical passages, especially out loud. It was as if I were allowing a different dimension to come through me. That's the best way I can describe that spiritual moment—a different dimension flowed through me. I didn't realize at that time I would be lucky enough to receive that same feeling months later on a walk with my son which I share later in the book.

As I share this memory with you now, I am reminded again of the powerful message behind those words, and it still gives me goosebumps today to reminisce about that sacred moment. Ask God for what your heart desires, and believe God grants our desires, especially those desires that elevate us to our highest good and highest selves. I felt the force of a higher being at that moment and have felt it many other times over the past years of my life, usually when I remind myself to be aware, ask for help and guidance from above, believe, and truly let go. I have rarely been let down.

"GOD WINKS"

I received another sign about a year after my mother passed away in 2011. I ran into an old acquaintance in the grocery store whom I hadn't seen since my sons were in elementary school. I shared with her that my mother had passed away suddenly and how I felt such a void, and my heart was shattered. My parents had been regulars at both of my sons' sporting events and pretty much all my sons' activities growing up, and as a result, this woman knew them very well.

As I stood there trying to hold back my tears, this empathetic woman did her best to offer some loving and kind words to try and ease my pain. She said a few of her friends had met people who became very significant in their lives after their mothers passed away. This idea—that my mother could somehow orchestrate meetings for me with loving and kind people—gave me hope. I know it may not sound logical, but matters of the heart often aren't, and I needed a little lift of my spirit at that moment. I walked out of the store that day with my chin held high and a hopeful perspective on life.

Believe it or not, I did in fact have a soulful meeting several months after that conversation in the same spot within the store where she and I had talked! Looking back now, I believe we are all being guided by a force from above. We simply need to ask for signs along the way, from God and even from our deceased loved ones, who have passed on to another dimension.

There's a great book about receiving signs called *When God Winks*, by SQuire Rushnell. It's a book about "God Winks," which Rushnell defines as "little messages to you on your journey through life, nudging you along the grand path that has been designed especially for you."[3] What SQuire Rushnell calls "God Winks," I call celestial synchronicities. The book's main premise is that every day we are under the influence of a cosmic guidance system, and we receive little nudges to keep us on our chosen path. I am a true believer!

When God Winks is a great reminder of the celestial synchronicities and signs we receive along the way if we believe and remain open to seeing them. I first read the book about eighteen years ago when I was navigating my divorce. I picked up the book again in Soul School, as I do with many books that have impacted me in some way through simple yet powerful messages. I smiled as I read some of the notes I had written throughout the book eighteen years ago: "actively look for signs," and "keep a journal of "God Winks,"" which I have done. I have a list of God Winks from twenty years ago.

SQuire Rushnell tells a great story in the book about a woman named Alice who was looking for her soulmate: "If you want me to be married, God, you pick him out. My track record stinks."[4] Alice had just about given up on love after a great deal of heartbreak and prayed to God, "God, if you want me to be single for the rest of my life, that's OK; just put peace in my heart."[5] After she truly surrendered, she began to feel a softening in her heart and remained open to invitations or people who came into her life. She met her soulmate at a church singles group shortly after surrendering. And not only that, but they were both attending the same wedding for their cousins a few weeks later. Alice recognized the "God Winks," or celestial synchronicities, she was receiving, confirming she was on the right path.

After rereading this story, I decided to give Alice's strategy a try. I got down on my knees and said, "God, I surrender my longing to find my soulmate to you. My track record in the area of love with a man stinks." I added a bit of humor and further said, "I would prefer not to go into the convent, though."

As I truly surrendered to God's plan for me, I, like Alice, experienced a softening in my heart. And something else happened—I truly felt a sense of inner peace, of knowing everything would work out however it was meant to be. I felt lighter and more joyful and experienced "silent hope," another message from a dream. I felt a tremendous sense of peace engulf my body; the feeling was similar to the one you get when you know everything will be OK and whatever will be, will be.

I highly recommend turning something over to God. It doesn't have to be a soulmate request. Give it a try now. Is there something you're wanting or a decision you are having trouble making? Turn it over. Surrender and believe. Observe how you feel. It's powerful, at least it was for me.

I continued to receive celestial synchronicities. I believe they were the soul's way of letting me know I was on the right path and I should keep learning and moving forward in the direction I had been going, even though I had no idea what direction that was.

SIGN #4: "PRAY, HOPE, AND DON'T WORRY" (PADRE PIO)

Another celestial synchronicity took place in August 2020. I was visiting the Philadelphia area for a week and had a longing to visit the cemetery where my mom and dad are buried and chat with them. When I sat on the ground next to their tombstone, I noticed it was 12:08. That time represented the month and day when my mom was born—December 8.

As I was sitting there trying to talk aloud to my parents without anyone noticing me for fear they might think I was talking to myself, a butterfly flew right near me and seemed to want my attention. At the exact time I became aware of the butterfly, my brother texted me a picture of a butterfly. He had no idea where I was at that moment. All of this happened as I was asking my mom and dad to please send me a sign letting me know I was on the right track and that they were with me on my journey into the unknown.

The celestial synchronicities continued when a roar of thunder came from the sky as I was walking out of the cemetery.

Thunder would have been normal on a rainy day, but it was a bright, sunny day. And as if those signs were not enough, I heard a voice quietly say, "Sorry I didn't call you back."

I pivoted on my heels quickly, wondering if I was hearing God's voice. A priest who I had only met a couple of times over the years was sitting on a private patio snacking on an apple. I had phoned him many weeks earlier during my "need for space" crisis, but we hadn't connected. The fact he even recognized me was truly a miracle. We hadn't seen each other for a couple of years. We chatted briefly, and I shared with him how I was looking for a sign and asking my parents if I was on the right path. He commented on the thunder, which roared out of nowhere a second time as we were speaking, and said it seemed as if they were letting me know they had heard me and were with me.

Later that day, he sent me the following text: "So I believe in signs. I was sitting there eating my apple and thinking that I'm so behind on things and I'm so bad at getting back to people (which I hate to have in my mind), and there you appear. Wow! God's grace. So good to chat for a few moments. All I can say is TRUST GOD WILL PROVIDE THE PATH!! Or as Padre Pio says: 'Pray, Hope, and Don't worry.' Great to see you. Keep in touch."

I couldn't have received a more dramatic celestial synchronicity than thunder at the cemetery and a priest confirming he, too, believed in signs. I am a true believer in the power of celestial synchronicities. The priest's message was also a reminder to keep channeling my worries to God and to have faith in God's plans for me.

Transferring worry and fear to God in prayer had become a new habit of mine. I wonder if my dad played a part in my crossing paths with the priest at just the right moment so the priest could share with me that he believed in signs and that "signs may be allowed."

DIVINE GUIDANCE

Many times I've been guided by gentle nudges and celestial synchronicities, usually after I've truly surrendered. They all were accompanied by the same feeling; I physically and emotionally let go. I wasn't attached to any specific outcome, I BELIEVED I was heard and would be guided. After I asked and surrendered, my body felt lighter and my spirit freer. I imagined myself loosening my grip around a rope one time, and another time I visualized a cardinal being set free. It was after these moments I received signs and celestial synchronicities.

In addition to receiving very clear signs from my parents, I was receiving very clear signs on a near daily basis, on a much larger scale than a hopeful horoscope reading or a random animal sighting.

Some of the signs I was receiving now I hadn't asked for; rather, they were being sent my way, and I was noticing them. To be clear, I was still asking for signs, but I was trying hard not to ask for too much after the grand signs at the cemetery. That practice had been ingrained in me from a very young age and was a hard one to let go of.

I was also realizing these signs were clearer than the ones I had received in the past. These signs felt much more symbolic than the ones from years ago and seemed to be nods that I was on the right path and to keep going forward. It was as if the celestial beings were nodding their heads and saying, *Keep going. You got it.*

The more celestial synchronicities I received, the more I continued to look for them. I also classified myself as a slow learner who needed some extra signs along the way. I imagine God has a good sense of humor and would smile at this. I asked God to send me celestial synchronicities each day because I was in unknown territory and needed to know if I was on the right track. I was very specific with some of my requests. I was never let down.

For example, I remember I asked God to send me a white feather to let me know he heard me. I asked and then let it go. Later that day, on my morning run, I came across a white feather that seemed to want to be noticed. I was beginning to understand the celestial synchronicities and signs because they seemed to get my attention, not the other way around. They were coming to me. I didn't have to search for them.

As I started to receive more little signs, I started to ask for some larger signs. What truly astonished me, though, was I started receiving them without even asking. For example, someone would mention something that was in alignment with what I had been thinking about or writing about earlier in the day. That seemed to happen very often. I even enrolled in a program to be certified as a professional life coach without much thought; it was as if it just somehow happened. The more I let go and surrendered, the clearer my path and the signs on my path became. The people and the events came to me.

I started to receive signs on a regular basis and began writing them down in a journal. Some were big, and others were small, and I was truly grateful to receive each and every sign, whatever the size. Your prayers will be answered, too. All you have to do is ask, have faith, and stay alert. You, too, will receive celestial synchronicities and nudges along the way.

SIGNS FROM BILLBOARDS: DON'T WORRY, BE HAPPY.

Signs can come in various forms: dreams, people, conversations with others, events, and even billboards. A friend and I were talking the other day about the importance of staying positive. She was asking me how she could teach her children to be positive in a world that is so divided and violent at times. I commented on the T-shirt she was wearing, which read, "I remain mostly positive." I told her her children were observing her positive attitude as evidenced in the shirt she was wearing, on a daily basis.

She shared with me a story about how she and her children were driving in a car down a local road and her mind was completely preoccupied and full of worry and fear. She turned her head to look at a beautiful view of the marshes and the low country and saw a handmade sign that said, "Don't Worry, Be Happy." She said she had never noticed the sign there before and was surprised because this was one of her favorite views when driving (coincidentally, it's one of my favorite views, too, and I've been smiling at that sign for quite some time). She continued to share with me the impact those four words had on her and how they shifted her mindset instantaneously. When she read those words, the simple reminder lifted her spirits and helped her stop the negative chatter in her mind so she could simply savor the present moment.

Signs can also come to us directly on billboards, on buses, on cars, in conversations with others, in books, and amid our busy travels. We simply need to be open, surrender, and be aware.

SIGNS FROM OUR DREAMS

I also received many messages and signs in my dreams, yet I wasn't taking them seriously enough at the time. I'm thankful I kept a journal of the many messages I received in my dreams because I am truly amazed by the power of God when I reread each dream much later.

I remember one dream in particular in which my mother and I were in the lobby of her condominium building with several other women. They were all chatting incessantly while my mom was quiet. When she spoke, she simply said, "Too much talking. I'm going to visit your brother." This was clearly a message about the importance of pausing and listening rather than always talking.

I asked my brother the next day if mom visited him in his dreams. I didn't share with him what she had said to me in my dream. He proceeded to tell me at great length his dream about my mom. He and I were stunned. At that time I remember believing in the power of the messages that come from our dreams, but somehow I wasn't completely convinced yet.

Sue Monk Kidd writes in her book *When the Heart Waits*, "In the Bible, dreams are one of the most significant ways through which God communicates."[6] This was a powerful reminder for me. One of the most powerful dreams I've had contained a very clear message from my father. It was so vivid and so clear that I wrote every detail in my journal when I awoke. I even named the dream "The Chart." Here is my journal entry from December 17, 2020:

"The Message from the Chart"

> Stop worrying and focusing on where I "should be" and what I "should be doing next." JUST BE NOW. In college, I was always searching, rarely content. I wasn't sure if I was in the "right class" or studying the "right material" instead of just being present where I was and focusing where I was (i.e., whatever class I was in or what I was doing at the moment). STOP SEARCHING. JUST BE! Be where I am doing what I'm doing. JUST BE. Here, now, and in every moment. Life is a series of classes. When I'm in one, stop thinking and focusing on the next one. Be in the one I'm in.

In this dream, my father displayed to me a chart representing my life that showed me moving in various ways. It was as if I was moving a lot but going nowhere. It was a simple and very organized chart, almost like a flowchart with different options and arrows pointing in different directions. My father's message was for me to stay focused doing what I'm doing each moment. That's it. Seems like a good way to live our lives—focus on what we are doing in each little moment.

In my experience, and according to many of the books I read in Soul School, messages in dreams can be very important and helpful in navigating daily life. I learned when we sleep, we are able to enter into another dimension more fluidly. It's as if we are tapping into universal consciousness and we are one with all—both living and deceased. If we can tap into that world when we sleep, perhaps we can also do so when we are awake, if we remain open and aware.

Henri Nouwen wrote eloquently about signs in our dreams in his book *Discernment,* stating, "God is always speaking to us—individually and as the people of God—at different times and in many ways. Through dreams and visions, prophets and messengers, scripture and tradition, experience and reason, nature and events. And that discernment is the spiritual practice that accesses and seeks to understand what God is trying to say. Discernment is a way to read the signs and recognize Divine messages."[7] I was learning the practice of discernment by recognizing Divine messages, and trying my best to understand what God was trying to say.

I highly encourage you to ask for a sign, a celestial synchronicity. Perhaps you can say, "Please give me a sign; point the way," and observe what happens. As I wrote these words, a swarm of birds flew around my window wanting to be noticed. Yet another celestial synchronicity?

Soul Searching:

- Can you notice a celestial synchronicity, a sign in your day? Are you hearing a certain message more than once? From various people or sources?
- Who's on your path?
- Perhaps you can ask for a sign about a certain decision you are trying to make, and stay open to receive it.
- Journal about the different celestial synchronicities you've encountered.
- Where was God in your life today? Perhaps you can remind yourself to trust God will provide the path.
- Maybe you can write down any dreams you have when you first wake up. Are there any recurring messages?

Song suggestion:

"Butterflies," by Kacey Musgraves

Sticky Note #18
Let Go and Surrender

"I hope you will never dismiss your little signs, your winks from God, which are being placed along your path for a reason—even if that reason is no more than a gentle jab in the shoulder, a pat on the back, or a dose of humor to lift your spirits. Like a wink from your grandfather, these winks are communicating God's message to you: 'Hey kid, I'm thinking about you—right now.'"

—SQUIRE RUSHNELL

SQuire Rushnell shares a story in his book, *When God Winks* about how Oprah Winfrey let go and the "God Wink" she received. Oprah auditioned for the role of Sofia in the movie *The Color Purple*. According to *When God Winks*, "She had never wanted anything more in her life"[1] than to play that role.

After she auditioned, she heard nothing. She decided to take action. This is a key point that Rushnell stresses—take some kind of action. She enrolled in a workout retreat to lose some weight. She thought perhaps she hadn't gotten the part because of her weight. During one of her workouts, she remembered a spiritual message, "I surrender all," and began singing that over and over as she ran around the track. She let go. Oprah did get that role.

She received a call after she truly let go and surrendered. The message from this "God Wink" story is the following:

> When you wish for something, you also need to take action yourself—to place yourself in the direction that you believe to be in alignment with your destiny. Get on the path. Do everything you can do to be prepared for your maker's reply to your wishes and prayers. Then, like Oprah, let go and wait for the God Wink.[2]

OUT OF ORDER. GOD, TAKE OVER

I was becoming a little more comfortable with letting go and surrendering to a Higher Power, especially when it came to difficult decisions or moments in life. I began to sit in the passenger seat and let God and my soul lead. This lesson was a major turning point for me in my journey into the unknown.

In my journal entry on October 6, 2020, I wrote, "Out of order. God, take over." This phrase had come up during The Spiritual Exercises program I participated in, and it stuck with me, to the point I repeated it quite often.

It worked, too—not only did I transfer my worries and fears to God, but God did take over, and he worked in mysterious ways. I was beginning to feel God's grace when I needed it during various moments in my life, and as I look back, God was (as he still is) very important in my life and my go-to for decisions, doubts, and pretty much everything. God was beginning to heal my inner wounds.

Yoga was a new habit I had incorporated into my weekly schedule during this time. Yoga seemed to be another way to help draw myself within through silence and to connect with my inner self. The final resting pose at the end of a yoga class is known as savasana. The instructor typically asks students to unclench anything on the body they may be holding on to—any tension in their face, their jaw, or anywhere else in their body. Letting go and surrendering to the unknown feels similar to letting go of certain body parts that are tense at the end of a yoga practice.

I've been reminding myself of this important lesson to let go and surrender recently. In fact, just this morning, I got down on my knees and asked God to please send me a sign that I was on the right track as it related to my purpose and helping others. I surrendered to God my desire to help others in some capacity, which I long to do, but I am not sure how. As I write these words, my attention is drawn to a butterfly dancing around in front of my window. I take that as a sign I'm being heard.

Here's what happened later in the day. After I completely surrendered my desires to help others as a counselor or in some other way, I received a call seemingly out of the blue from Sister M simply to say hi. She has a very tight schedule, and any time with her usually needs to be scheduled. She happened to mention during our call that she sees me as somewhat of an "adviser" to others—I like to help others and offer advice.

As soon as I hung up the phone, my son called me, and I shared with him a little bit about my conversation with Sister M. He proceeded to say, "Yes, you would be a great mentor and adviser to others." Two weekends later, I found myself enrolled in a class and became certified as a professional life coach. I had received several signs from loved ones encouraging my quest to help others.

This is one of my top-five favorite messages, so I hope this one sticks with you. It's a game changer—at least it was for me. Any time I truly surrendered and turned it over to God, I would receive an answer. And I mean, *really* turned it over to God. As in, drop to your knees, cast your eyes above, feel it in your heart, and have no attachment to any outcome at all. Perhaps you can give it a try now.

SPREADING LOVE

I began to hear the simple message "Spread love" most mornings during my prayer and journal time shortly after I had surrendered to God to better understand my purpose. I journaled that I wanted to spread love throughout the world through a smile, a kind word, a soft gesture, laughter, listening to others, encouraging others, accepting others, and helping others. I asked God to keep showing me how to spread love to everyone I met and bring others to me who needed to feel loved. He did.

I found myself writing little notes that said, "You are loved" and handing them with a few dollars to people who would come across my path during the day. At this point in my journey, I was living in downtown Nashville for a few months, and sadly many homeless people were coming across my path. I put the notes of love and a few dollars in an envelope and handed them to whomever I felt called. There was one stipulation—I had to look them in the eyes with love and kindness. I was beginning to see the force of love, God, in everyone's eyes. After all, the eyes are the windows to our souls.

This simple message of letting go has been transformative for me. Like pivoting, it's difficult to do, but very valuable in life. I transferred my moments of fear, doubt, and worry, as well as everything else, to God. I released them all. It was amazing how much lighter I felt after turning to God, and in some sense, it snapped me out of my downward spiral of doom and gloom. Letting go and surrendering to God was a major turning point for me in my journey. This is a tool I continue to use on a regular basis in my life. I hope you can too.

Looking back now, I realize as soon as I pivoted toward the unknown in search of space, I began the process of letting go and surrendering to a greater power; I had no idea where I was going and what the outcome would be. That first step was the beginning of letting go and letting God and the soul lead me every step of the way.

The more I surrendered and let go, the more guidance and answers I received.

Soul Searching:

- How can you begin to let go and surrender to a Higher Power?
- Is there a wish or a dream you've had for quite some time?
- Can you spend two minutes and voice your wish to a Higher Power and ask for a sign?
- Then, let go and surrender.
- When was a moment when you felt as if you were being guided from above?
- When did you ever receive an answer to a wish?
- What action step are you ready to take?

Song suggestion:

"When You Wish Upon a Star," by Louis Armstrong

Sticky Note #19

"Look for God Moments Every Day"—Sister M

Love is the energy of the soul. Love is what heals the personality. There is nothing that cannot be healed by love. There is nothing but love.

—GARY ZUKAV

In September 2020 I enrolled in a program that would transform my life to an extent I could have never imagined and introduce me to a new practice—looking for "God Moments" each day— the Spiritual Exercises of Saint Ignatius led by Sister M. I knew nothing about the program prior to enrolling in it, but figured I was lucky to have any chance to be in Sister M's presence. In fact, I really knew very little about any of the programs she had been offering at her retreat prayer house for most of my adult life. I had been too preoccupied with the external world and less focused on the interior world of the soul, Sister M's world.

Sister M is an inspirational woman with a magnificent spirit. When you're in her company, you can't help but feel like you're in God's presence with her peaceful presence and unconditional love. My family was blessed to be in her presence almost daily during my father's last few weeks on this planet. She and my father were cousins and had a close relationship with each other over many years. Sister M and other friends and family would simply be together in my dad's room as he slept. She didn't need to speak any words; her presence and demeanor said it all, and you felt the goodness and purity in her heart and soul. She was, and still is, a tremendous source of comfort and peace for so many people, including me.

THE SPIRITUAL EXERCISES

I vividly remember our conversation when I first asked about the Spiritual Exercises. I was sharing with her my desire to do more and serve others in some way, but I wasn't sure how. I had just received a copy of her newsletter and was amazed at the large number of programs and retreats she led.

I remember asking her about one in particular that interested me: the Spiritual Exercises program that met weekly in New Jersey for thirty-two weeks. It's pretty ironic that the program that interested me the most was the one with the biggest time commitment. I was jumping in full force but didn't realize it at the time. I can still hear her gentle voice when I asked her if I could sign up for the program. She said something along the lines of, "It's a very intense program that meets weekly. That's quite a time commitment. Do you think you're up for that?" Not to mention the fact I was living in South Carolina. My soul was in charge now, and I enthusiastically and confidently replied, "Yes. I'm excited to do it." I had no idea what I was getting myself into.

The best way I can explain the Spiritual Exercises is to defer to Kevin O' Brien, SJ, whose book, *The Ignatian Adventure—Experiencing the Spiritual Exercises of Saint Ignatius in Daily*

Life, served as our guide for the program. Father O'Brien, SJ explains, "The Exercises are a school of prayer. The two primary forms of praying taught in the Exercises are meditation and contemplation. In meditation, we use our intellect to wrestle with basic principles that guide our life. Contemplation is more about feeling than thinking."[1] Tuning into our feelings was at the heart of the Exercises. Another purpose of the Exercises is to help a person discern their personal vocation or mission in life. It's no accident I was drawn to this program—I was still struggling to find my purpose in life and continually asking myself, *Who am I?* and *How can I make a difference in others' lives?* among many other questions.

The Spiritual Exercises help others find the freedom to make good decisions and let go of disordered attachments in their lives. I recognize now this celestial synchronicity as I had just lived through the process of detaching from possessions. Our group met every Tuesday for ninety minutes from September to May. I am forever grateful Sister M allowed me to join remotely from South Carolina.

I had very little knowledge of Saint Ignatius of Loyola and the Spiritual Exercises he created in the early 1500s. Ignatius believed the exercises could help others grow closer to God as they had helped him do, discern God's call in their lives, and learn to live their lives more from the heart rather than the head. I was still working on the latter. The simple premise of the exercises was to help souls. As a student currently enrolled in Soul School, it's no coincidence my soul would enroll in a program whose mission is to help other souls!

One hour of prayer each morning was structured around scripture verses and suggested meditations and conversations with God. This was much different from my Catholic upbringing of memorized and rote prayers. We moved from our intellect through scripture readings and contemplation into our feelings, our emotions, and our desires. The latter was certainly an area I was not very comfortable with. I remember asking our small group in the first few weeks, "How do I shift from the head to the heart?" After asking that question aloud, I realized I clearly needed help in this area.

Sister M and The Spiritual Exercises were like an Advanced Placement class in Soul School. This program would teach me how to connect with my heart and would further enlighten me on my personal mission—yet another celestial synchronicity.

LETTERS TO GOD

The Spiritual Exercises were life-changing for me, to say the least. During the class, Sister M would gently nudge us to look for God's presence every day in acts of love, nature, and throughout our daily activities. She called these moments of love "God Moments." *How wonderful,* I thought, *our homework assignment is to look for God Moments or moments of love every day and write a few down at the end of each day.* That was a dream assignment for me because I was always in search of love in one way or another and seemed to have been doing that naturally in my life for years. I've noticed love in the context of couples, families, and other situations for most of my life, and thanks to Sister M, I have a name for what I've been doing—looking for God Moments.

The Spiritual Exercises were a structured program with a scripture reading each day which we read and contemplated. It was recommended to journal after each prayer time. I took pure delight in the journal writing part since I'd been journaling for the past ten years. Oftentimes, I feel as if I'm not able to fully express the depth of my love for those closest to me verbally, and turn to written words to express the depth of my love. The hopeless romantic part of me surfaced yet again, and I decided to write a love letter to God each morning as my journal entry, for thirty-two weeks. Surely, God would hear me and answer my prayers in the 224 love letters I would write.

I wrote to God each day from September to May. Most letters had some substance, but there were a few letters in which I simply wrote, "God, where are you?" At the end of the thirty-second week, I felt a little lost without Sister M and my Zoom friends, but my son's wedding was less than a week away, so my thoughts, energy, and love were all cast onto my son and his soon-to-be wife's wonderful celebration of love for each other.

What a fantastic opportunity to notice many God Moments at their celebration of love for one another. The God Moments would be overflowing for sure. Reflecting now on the Spiritual Exercises, I recognize looking for these God Moments became a wonderful habit of mine, a practice I still engage in today. It's a positive way to move through the day with love and gratitude. Perhaps you can give it a try and look for a God Moment this week.

In my experience, a God Moment typically causes a feeling of awe and wonder when witnessing something or someone's act of kindness and love, an exchange of love. God Moments tug at my heart. Sometimes, they bring a tear to my eyes, in a good way, like an abundance of love is pouring out from my heart. I've also felt God Moments when my heart is so full of love I have wanted to express it in some way. I'm not talking only about romantic love but rather love for anyone or anything. These moments usually cause me to pause and completely absorb the moment. Sister M suggested we ask ourselves, "Where is the love?" Where there is love, there is God; hence the term *God Moment*. It's about looking for love in all the right places.

LOOKING FOR LOVE

I had a lot of talks with God about love over the years and asked him to help me keep my heart open to love so I could recognize God Moments in my life. *I'm counting on you, God*, I would tell him. To a lesser degree, one could say I've always been looking for love and have given God a really hard time over the years he hasn't sent me my "soul partner." As I write these words, I now understand why this has been such a desire of mine. I'm fascinated by love, both by observing it in others and creatures in nature and by giving love to others. I love the subject of love. It makes complete sense that I would have the desire to meet my soul partner and experience love at a very soulful level.

Friends and family members have given me a hard time about my television and movie preferences over the years because I always prefer a good love story or a movie with a happy ending. Violent movies or horror movies were and still are out of the question for me. Dark movies don't work for me either. Discovering little likes or dislikes about ourselves helps us come to terms with what we're comfortable with. Discoveries like this one also played a big role in helping me answer the question, "Who am I?" There are many moments of love both little and great happening all around us.

The message is simple: it's all about love. I remind myself to be aware of where love is showing up each day and where the opportunities to give love exist. Where there is love, there is God, and where there is God, there is love. I ask myself, *Where was the love?* at the end of each day. I started a habit of writing a few God Moments in my journal at the end of each day.

These moments are all around us and can be little moments or very grand ones. I've found them when I've observed animals in nature, exchanges between people, compliments and nice things others say or do, a song I hear at exactly the right time when I need to hear a message, words in a book or audio program that jump out to me, inspiration to send loving words or messages to another, answers to a challenging situation, a smile to a stranger, looking a homeless person in the eyes with kindness and love, and a multitude of other ways. Divine love is channeled through other people, animals, and many other mediums. The more aware I've become, the more I've noticed them.

Here are some God Moments from my journals over the years that I'll share with you with the hope that you may become aware of a few in your life.

THE BIRD FAMILY

As I write this chapter, I am amazed and in awe of what I've been observing outside my window for the past ten days. My daughter-in-law discovered a bird's nest outside our bathroom window, and since its discovery, I have become slightly obsessed with observing the baby birds and the mother's devotion to her babies. Each day, the mother bird spends hours flying to and from the nest gathering food for her three babies. She begins her feeding early in the morning, and it lasts until dusk. It warms my heart each time I see her dropping food into her babies' mouths as they hold their beaks open. She never lets them down.

Soon after I started my observations, there was a bad storm with gusty winds and heavy rain. That didn't stop the loving and loyal mother. She joined her babies in their tiny nest and kept them dry and safe by spreading her wings on top of them. On the eighth day (I even kept notes on a calendar), after watching their daily activities, I noticed the babies were getting a little restless and moving around quite a bit. This made me so nervous I actually ordered gloves in case one of them fell out of the nest. They had become part of our family now, and I wanted to help the devoted mother as best I could. Fortunately, none of the birds fell out of the nest.

On the ninth day, I came home and went right to the window to check on our little family and noticed there was no activity in the nest, but the mother bird and her male companion were very vocal when I walked outside to look more closely. It was almost as if they were still keeping watch over their babies; however, I had no idea where they were. I was hopeful that the babies, now called fledglings, had relocated to a safer and larger home. I decided if I wanted to spot the fledglings I needed to keep a close eye on Mom and Dad. I watched them both as they chased a squirrel off the property, chirping at him and attacking him with their beaks. I began to chase the squirrels away. I was sure the fledglings were close by.

My heart jumped for joy when I looked out the window in front of my writing desk and noticed a fledgling stumbling out of some shrubs right outside, the feathers on the top of her head disheveled. She hopped to sit on a wood piling, turning her little head to the left and to the right. I could imagine the little bird being amazed at the world outside of her little home. This reminded me of a newborn baby who enters our world of bright lights and loud sounds. Perhaps this little fledgling was feeling similar sensations. I continued to watch this little one as he or she tried to use his or her wings to fly and almost right on cue, the mama bird flew next to her baby and began demonstrating how to fly.

My heart was and still is so full of love for the tenderness and love God created in all creatures. We are more similar than we realize. My studies of our little bird family occupied a great deal of my time. I sat for hours at my writing desk watching and smiling at the love and devotion of the mother for her babies. Even the father was there to help protect them and support the mother. I can relate to the mother bird as I still have very strong maternal instincts to protect my grown children, their spouses, and future offspring (my grandchildren). That unconditional love and devotion never dies.

The following day another fledgling hobbled out, but this one wasn't as curious. He sat at the edge of the shrubs, or what I perceived as the front door to their house, and chirped for his mother. Sure enough, she flew back and continued to drop food into the little one's open beak. I smiled as I watched this shy and nervous one who didn't want to leave the safety of home. I was astonished by the patience and love of the mother, who stood outside of their house opening and closing her wings as if to say, "Come out. You can do it." This shy one came out for a short time but didn't stray very far and hobbled back into the home.

The patience, kindness, devotion, and selflessness displayed by this mother for her three babies represented love at its greatest.

SMALLER GOD MOMENTS

Many of the other God Moments I've noticed have been impactful on a smaller scale. My son's girlfriend gave me a little plaque for Christmas that says, "Today's little moments become tomorrow's special memories." I love that message because it reminds me every day of the importance of spreading love.

These moments of love during the day become the memories I journal about each night. Here are some of the God Moments, or moments of love, from my journal:

- Spending time with my family and feeling the unconditional love between us.
- Spending time with friends as we encourage one another on our journeys, share in the joys of our lives, and truly want the best for each other.

- Quiet walks in nature listening to the sounds of God's creatures and observing beauty.
- Praying for the world as a community at mass.
- During my morning prayer time, I came across the phrase "With God, all things are possible." This message of hope fills my heart with love.
- Sitting next to a young mother and her nine-month-old sweet baby girl on a flight and chatting with the sweet mother. Observing and feeling the tremendous love between the mother and her daughter.
- A kind man who stopped and took the time to help me when I had car trouble during a long trip.

I'll end this chapter with a very grand and powerful God Moment my son and I experienced the morning of the day he proposed to his wonderful wife.

THE OWL AND AWE

This experience was extremely powerful! Looking back on it, my son and I both agreed it felt as if we were in another dimension and very close to the world of spirits of those deceased, which we believe surround us every day. This was the closest I've ever felt to the celestial or Divine dimension.

The two of us decided to go for a walk in a beautiful park in Nashville the morning of the day he was planning to propose to the love of his life. It was a foggy and overcast day, and I was looking forward to having some alone time with him as he was about to embark on an exciting and fantastic new chapter in his life. I left my phone and all my belongings in the car and was completely present with him, as he was with me. We had no agenda other than a simple walk in nature together. There was nobody else around as we walked.

After some time, my son looked up and saw an owl staring at both of us from a tree. We stopped and stared at it. None of us uttered a sound (including the owl). I'm truly not sure how long this exchange lasted, but at some point, our wise and friendly owl spirit flew away. We were both in awe! No words could really explain the majestic and powerful feelings we both felt. That was truly a magical moment.

We continued walking and discussing how rare it was to see an owl during the day and how it seemed as if the owl wanted us to see him and be in our presence. We both had this strong feeling. We continued wandering through the woods onto the edge of a golf course in a state of complete and utter presence, for lack of a better description. There was nowhere else we wanted to be, and our thoughts were right where we were, with each other. It was as if we were connected with each other and everything around us without any words.

After some time, we ended up back at our car. My son reached for his keys, but they weren't in his pocket. Again, neither one of us spoke a word, and we began to walk in different directions in search of his keys. We just moved with silence and oneness. He went one way; I went the other. Had we been thinking logically, we would have realized the odds of us finding his keys were incredibly slim as we couldn't even fully retrace our footsteps through tall grass, a wooded forest, and the perimeter of a golf course. But we were still in another dimension in our ways of being led by a Divine power greater than ourselves.

I'm not sure how long we walked on our own in different directions in search of the car keys because it was as if time didn't exist. Eventually, I stopped and was nudged to turn around to see my son approaching me from a distance. We were both being guided to the same place over the many miles we had walked. I waited for him, and we both stared at the very tall grass in front of us. My son said, "The keys will be here." He pointed down, and there they were.

Anyone reading these words might think this was a mere coincidence. Having experienced what we experienced, I believe we were being guided by God and were in the realm of angels and spirits. He said he felt a similar sensation and that we were indeed in a different dimension of some sort. We had surrendered our thoughts and our minds; we were just being, and we were engulfed in God's love and the angels' and spirits' love. This was one of the most transformational moments of my life, one during which I truly felt Divine power and connected to everything through this Divine power. It came from a state of being; we were simply present where we were. That is the best way I can describe it. It was a feeling that came from the awe we felt in the presence of the owl. That awe continued and overcame our beings. The awe and the owl were powerful forces. Our spiritual natures, our souls, were leading the way. We had transcended the physical and human world and it seemed as if we were experiencing the spiritual world.

I pondered how we could experience this way of being in everyday life. For starters, I suppose we must have a belief and an awareness of a greater dimension and world beyond our physical senses. That world is right here with us; it's just not physical. We can connect to that world anytime through our soul or our spirits.

But how do we let the soul lead us like my son and I did that morning in the forest? It seems to start with awareness and presence. Being truly present in each moment—whatever we are doing and whoever we are with, being right there in that moment with that person and not thinking of other things, a total presence filled with love, gratitude, and acceptance. That seemed to be the state my son and I were in. The feeling of awe was overwhelming.

I was a true believer in the powerful force of a Higher Power and began to look for these God Moments every day. I continued to receive encouragement from God through others to confirm I was on the right path.

Once you believe in the force of love inside of you, and you observe its power guiding you in your life, you will notice that nothing in the course of your daily life is an accident. Divine activity is present every day between both humans and creatures in nature.

Soul Searching:

- Perhaps you can notice a God Moment during the day and jot it down in the evening.
- Did you ever experience the sensation of awe? What was that experience like for you? How did you feel? Write about your experience with awe.
- Spend a few minutes recalling an experience that made you pause and captured your attention wholeheartedly.
- Reach out to someone in your heart and let them know you're thinking of them.

Song suggestions:

" Humble and Kind," by Tim McGraw (the song my son and I danced to at his wedding)

Sticky Note #20
Do Some "Self Searching"

"Our over-identification with our feelings and who we think we are is normally the source of our pain. Once you disidentify with your feelings, you know that you can change them. You are not your feelings. But you have to stay alert. The advantage of a spiritual program like AA is to keep you alert and quick to spot the symptoms of the disease that you now acknowledge."

—THOMAS KEATING

One year later, in September 2021, I found myself in an even more advanced program with Sister M called the Spiritual Direction Program. A spiritual director accompanies others on their paths to seeing God in their lives and growing closer to God. It involves a great deal of listening—something I like to do.

As had been the case with the Spiritual Exercises Program, I knew very little about the details of this program. The Spiritual Director Program had an extensive reading list.

Two of the books we read, *The Big Book—Alcoholics Anonymous* by Bill Wilson *and Divine Therapy and Addiction— Centering Prayer and the Twelve Steps* by Thomas Keating, were books about the Twelve Steps program. I didn't know much about the Twelve Steps, other than the program had been transformative in others' lives and had tremendously helped many people I knew. After gaining a little more understanding of the Twelve Steps, I think it's something that could benefit all of us in different ways, even if we may not struggle with alcohol or drug addiction. Many of us may have other struggles and patterns that need some addressing. I know I certainly did and still do. I struggled with (and still struggle with) negative self-talk and self- doubts.

THE TWELVE STEPS

The Twelve Steps program offers some life-changing principles, including surrendering to a Higher Power, embracing silence, asking for forgiveness, and taking a moral inventory of ourselves to see negative patterns in our personalities. The personal inventory was very insightful and helpful for me. I was able to see my patterns of negative self-talk, comparing what I was doing with what others were doing, and anxious thoughts.

These negative habits, I realized, were actually very self-centered at the level of the ego, and further away from the Higher Power of divine love within the soul. Once I became aware of these emotional patterns, I tried to notice them before they took over, and I worked to detach from them as best as I could. This was another game-changer for me.

The program also encouraged us to let go of attachments to our thoughts. Now that I had gotten rid of attachments to material possessions and released painful emotions from my heart, it was time to change some of the negative tapes in my head. That habit was a difficult one to break. One that I continue to work on today. Many of the spiritual teachers emphasized we are not our thoughts and recommended detaching from our thoughts. It was suggested we recognize and observe the thoughts in our heads but not attach to them. It was easy for me to get lost in my thoughts without even realizing it. I found the practice of observing and detaching from my thoughts difficult to do, but I knew how critical it was in order to connect to the peace within. I compared the personality inventory to a cleansing of my inner spiritual world.

By this point in my journey, I had incorporated the practice of sitting in silence for a few minutes a day and was familiar with the many thoughts swirling in my mind. It took a great deal of discipline and patience to simply observe my thoughts and detach from them, but I recognized the importance of not paying them much attention. I was beginning to understand and feel that the thoughts and the noise were not my central core. There was something much deeper inside of me other than my thoughts, and I longed to connect to that peaceful place as often as I could. My thoughts were also very hard on myself. It was as if I was beginning to train my mind and detach from the critical voices. "Whenever one notices that one is having an experience of self-centeredness or selfishness, one would notice it and immediately drop it,"[1] according to Thomas Keating. I was trying my best to put those words into practice.

A SOUL CLEANSE

Taking a personal inventory is like a cleansing of the soul and can help rid our inner world of unhealthy matter. This practice clears the slate by producing a healthier body, mind, and soul. In many ways, it's similar to a cleansing of the body. Awareness of what tends to send us down pathways of negative thinking patterns also prepares us for times when we may be triggered and allows us to come up with tools to prevent the downward spiral from happening. I was beginning to recognize the importance of having tools to turn to for a healthy soul.

Understanding my self-imposed negative thought patterns and cleansing my soul became two additional habits I incorporated into my days. Thomas Keating helped me understand more about creating new habits:

> Habits can be acquired by our own efforts to some degree, but the best habits and the most effective ones are those that are infused by the Holy Spirit. Once you are on the spiritual journey and established in grace, you have as part of your patrimony the seven-fold gifts of the Holy Spirit. One of the active gifts is the gift of counsel in which the Spirit of God nudges us, not with words, but with attractions and inspirations, what to do in great detail in every moment of our lives, if we are willing. …
>
> In other words, it is the Spirit that suggests the aspirations that you were talking about. It is the Spirit that suggests taking inventory. It is the Spirit that suggests it is time for you to take a retreat. You are perfectly free, but you have a sense that you are being led by a Higher Power and that the best thing you can do is follow that inspiration.[2]

I was feeling those nudges from the Holy Spirit who was helping me become aware of bad habits I wanted to address. I was also sensing a much Higher Power that seemed to be guiding me and encouraging me.

Soul Searching:

- What are some negative thought patterns that if you don't stop them may end up going down the rabbit hole?

- Write about one habit you would like to slowly start to change. Awareness of the habit is the first step.
- Write down what you were thinking before the thoughts spiraled.
- What tapes in your head would you like to change or delete?

Song suggestion:

That's Life," by Frank Sinatra

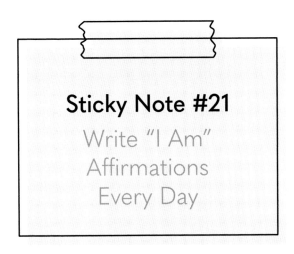

Sticky Note #21
Write "I Am" Affirmations Every Day

"When you say, 'I am,' the words that follow are summoning creation with a mighty force because you are declaring it to be fact. You are stating it with certainty. And so immediately after you say, 'I am tired' or 'I am broke' or 'I am sick' or 'I am late' or 'I am overweight' or 'I am old,' the Genie says, 'Your wish is my command.' Knowing this, wouldn't it be a good idea to begin to use the two most powerful words, I Am, to your advantage? How about, 'I am receiving every good thing. I am happy. I am abundant. I am healthy. I am love. I am always on time. I am eternal youth. I am filled with energy every single day.'"

—RHONDA BYRNE

After doing a little self-searching, I recognized I needed to work on some self-love. I was determined to replace some critical self-talk tapes with new, healthy messages. Pema Chödrön speaks about the importance of loving ourselves in her book, *When Things Fall Apart—Heart Advice for Difficult Times*, when she writes, "It is said that we can't attain enlightenment, let alone feel contentment and joy, without seeing who we are and what we do, without seeing our patterns and our habits. This is called

Maitri-developing loving-kindness and an unconditional friendship with ourselves."[1] It was clear I needed to develop some loving-kindness for myself.

For most of my life, I had recognized the importance of
loving others and reminded myself of that quite often, but I
had somehow forgotten about the importance of loving myself
along the way. I began to hear the comments I would say to
myself about myself, and they weren't very kind. The voices in
my head were kind to others, but not to myself. Brené Brown's
book, *The Gifts of Imperfection*, offered many helpful tools to
learn to live a wholehearted life and increase a sense of worthiness. She writes:

> Wholehearted living is about engaging in our lives from a
> place of worthiness. It's about cultivating the courage, com-
> passion, and connection to wake up in the morning and
> think, *No matter what gets done and how much is left undone,
> I* am enough… It makes sense to me that the gifts of imper-
> fection are courage, compassion, and connection, because
> when I think back to my life before this work, I remember
> often feeling fearful, judgmental, and alone—the opposite
> of the gifts."[2]

The first affirmation I wrote and repeated during the course of
the day was *I am enough*. For much of my life, I ended my days
replaying what I got done and reprimanding myself if I hadn't
accomplished enough. I was a big believer that I was not enough.

It was time to rewire many of my thoughts and my daily
self-narrative. I embraced a new habit—writing positive and uplifting affirmations on sticky notes and speaking the affirmations
aloud to myself every morning. I started each affirmation with "I
am" because it helped bring it closer to me and felt empowering.

These "I am" affirmations also became gratitude affirmations, and many days I simply said, "I am happy and grateful for …" The gratitude affirmations filled pages and pages of my journal, so I decided it was time to devote a separate journal to gratitude.

Here are a few of my regular affirmations in case you feel the desire to replace a few negative tapes in your mind:

- I am enough.
- I am loved.
- I am filled with grace and love.
- I am a gentle soul who shines light onto others.
- I am receiving love.
- I am comfortable in my own skin.
- I am a magnet for pure love.
- I am surrounded by love.
- I am grateful for many blessings.

I thank *The Secret* for introducing me to the "I am" affirmations. I also remember being reminded about the power of God's name, Yahweh, which is translated, "I AM."

As a regular listener to *Oprah's Super Soul Sunday* podcast, I was introduced to many inspirational individuals. One of her guests, Pastor Joel Osteen, devoted an entire show on the power behind the two words "I am." His message was that whatever we place after the words, "I am," we become! Pause and really let that sink in. Whatever you put after "*I am*" you become! I had never realized the powerful force of the affirmations I was saying each day. Once again, God was letting me know I was on the right path through celestial synchronicities and the daily practices I was creating.

INSIGHT AND INSPIRATION

The "I am" lesson appeared quite frequently in various forms, which I again took as *a sign* that it was an important lesson. It appeared as was one of our morning scripture passages in Exodus 3:14, "God replied, 'I am who am. Then he added, 'This is what you shall tell the Israelites: I AM sent me to you.'"[3] This message resonated with me at a very deep level. "I AM" is the name of God, and whatever comes after God's name *is* very powerful. I had not realized the significance behind "I am" when I first began the practice of incorporating affirmations into my morning routine.

The affirmations I wrote and spoke were simple yet powerful messages to retrain my mind to practice self-love, allow me to believe in myself, and co-create the life I desired with the Divine power within. I believe this Divine force of love is within us all and available to us anytime to help us co-create our lives and manifest our desires. Love was the central theme of my life, and I wanted to spread love, receive love, and stay open for love always, for others and for myself.

I began this "I am" practice in April 2020 as the world was shutting down and the pandemic was gaining traction. The affirmations became very important during that time because I spent most of my time with myself and my loving dog, Matisse. It was a lonely time for the world as we spent months in lockdown with very little social interaction. This *I am* practice helped me feel loved despite being physically alone. I hope you are able to incorporate this into your life and feel the power of love. I certainly underestimated the power of the two words—*I am*—when I first began writing and speaking them.

It's quite surprising that during a period of extreme uncertainty and solitude, I somehow felt a little more connected to my inner being, my soul and not completely alone. For most of my life, I had been very busy physically, preoccupied mentally, or focused on others and what they were doing. I was less focused on myself and what I was doing. The world was in a scary place during the pandemic, and fear and anxiety were at a much higher level, yet somehow I was managing my fear with a few new practices. I'm not saying I didn't feel scared, sad, or worried. I did. But I turned to some new practices and tools to begin to calm my anxious brain. I sincerely hope you are able to incorporate some of these practices in your life to help calm your mind if you need to.

Soul School was teaching me about myself and who I really was deep inside, at the level of my soul. I was learning what I liked to do and didn't like to do. I was hearing the unkind words I said to myself quite often. I was learning how I easily tuned into others' feelings and was less focused on my own feelings at times. I was learning how I tried to please others first and myself last. I was learning I never really knew how to just *be*. I was learning that at times I had a hard time saying no to others if I didn't want to do something for fear of hurting their feelings. The many lessons and insights continued to appear.

CONNECTING TO YOUR SOUL

My hope for you, as you read this book, is that you are able to connect with your soul much earlier in your life than I did and begin to lead a life guided by your soul. You may be thinking to yourself, *How do I tap into my inner being and hear the voice of the soul?* This was certainly a practice I was not at all familiar with.

The spiritual teachers whose books I read and interviews I listened to emphasized the importance of stillness and quiet to hear the voice of the soul. The soul speaks softly and gently in whispers and nudges. It is often missed amid loud noise and activity. The sound of the soul is soft. The soul doesn't fight to be heard, doesn't compete, and is not domineering. It seemed as if we *felt* our way into the soul, to God (no wonder understanding our feelings was so important).

My next homework assignment: be still, be quiet, and listen to the longings of my heart. And continue to practice daily "I am" affirmations. This one tool has helped me immensely to replace any negative self-talk. Gradually, I was retraining my mind and replacing any self-critical thoughts with powerful positive ones. It was working. I could feel the difference. I encourage you to say at least one "I am" affirmation twenty times a day. And I hope you begin to feel the power within from this one simple practice.

Soul Searching:

- What are a few "I am" affirmations you can incorporate into your busy day? Perhaps you can start with *I am enough* and repeat it to yourself twenty times.
- Begin to retrain your mind. Choose one negative thought and reframe it into a positive "I am" statement. Repeat it twenty times a day—when you're getting dressed in the morning, in the car, or during a lunch break.
- Journal about your process along the way.

Song suggestion:

"Unforgettable," by Natalie Cole and Nat King Cole

Sticky Note #22
Be Still and Go Inward

"Practicing silence means making a commitment to take a certain amount of time to simply Be. Experiencing silence means periodically withdrawing from the activity of speech. It also means periodically withdrawing from such activities as watching television, listening to the radio, or reading a book. If you never give yourself the opportunity to experience silence, this creates turbulence in your internal dialogue. … What happens when you go into this experience of silence? Initially, your internal dialogue becomes even more turbulent. You feel an intense need to say things…But as they stay with the experience, their internal dialogue begins to quieten. And soon the silence becomes profound. This is because after a while the mind gives up … then, as the internal dialogue quietens, you begin to experience the stillness of the field of pure potentiality."

—DEEPAK CHOPRA

In his book *The Power of Love*, James Van Praagh discusses the importance of stillness and quiet in order to connect to the presence within. He writes, "To embrace the power of love, take the time to be still every day. It is in the silence that you can communicate with your soul's needs and understanding."[1] I was beginning to sense the longings and desires from my soul in the silence and stillness.

The message of stillness and going inward was one of the most important insights I learned. It seemed the way to access the soul was through stillness and feeling our way into our inner world. The soul is about more feelings, and less about actions. Most of the spiritual teachers stressed the importance of stillness and looking inward.

GOING INWARD

The Road Less Traveled, by M. Scott Peck, MD, was a book I read more than twenty years ago when my marriage was falling apart. I was reading the book this time from a more spiritual perspective. The following passage really stuck with me, so much so that it made it into my journal on December 16, 2021: "The ultimate goal of life remains the spiritual growth of the individual, the solitary journey to peaks that can be climbed alone. Marriage and society exist for the basic purpose of nurturing such individual journeys."[2]

M. Scott Peck's words helped me better understand what was happening. I was on a spiritual journey, one that I needed to embark upon on my own—hence my need for space. This also helped to reassure my ego when my mind would nag me that I was spending too much time alone. Too much time alone for an extrovert can lead to a lot of negative talk in the mind—at least it did for me. I had to work very hard to disconnect from those negative voices and ask God to help me realize what I was doing was a good thing and on the path of love. I was slowly healing my wounded heart and soul. I began to feel the peace and serenity the teachers spoke of as I began to disconnect from the swirling thoughts in my mind.

"Your vision will become clear only when you look into your heart. Who looks outside, dreams; who looks inside, awakens."[3] I came across this quote from Carl Jung more than a dozen times on my spiritual journey. Jung's message kept appearing in various books I was reading, in my daily journal as a quote for the day, and it even appeared in literature at a retreat I attended. I was getting the point that a little stillness each day is necessary to connect within. I was being reminded in various ways of the importance of going inward through stillness to awaken and to access the source of love from within.

Matthew Kelly also writes about "The Art of Slowing Down," in his book, *The Rhythm of Life: Living Every Day with Passion & Purpose*. He says, "There is an art to slowing down. In our busy world, it is not easy to master this art, but it is necessary. Slow down. Breathe deeply. Reflect deeply. Pray deeply. Live deeply. Otherwise, you will spend your life feeling like a bulldozer chasing butterflies or a sparrow in a hurricane."[4] I was catching on to the importance of taking some time to sit quietly and simply be with myself and my thoughts.

The message, "Be still," became one I received on a regular basis during the first couple of years in my space of quiet and stillness. "Be still" was written throughout my journal entries and mentioned in many of the books I read. My soul was sending me clues to let me know the importance of stillness—to tune into the essence within, the highest place of love, and notice any insights I received.

LIVING IN STILLNESS

The message of stillness seemed to be everywhere. The first chapter in *Living Buddha, Living Christ,* a book I was reading by Thich Nhât Hanh, is titled "Be Still and Know." The author writes, "Be still means to become peaceful and concentrated."[5]

This message resonated so deeply with me that "stillness" became my one word for 2020. I was living a life of stillness along with the rest of the world during the pandemic shutdown during this time. I was learning and feeling the difference that a quiet, focused prayer time every morning was having in my life. I was also beginning to feel a little more serene, not only during the quiet time, but over the course of the day. This quiet time set the tone for the day. When we sit in silence, the heart speaks. As Rumi said, "Tend to your vital heart, and all that you worry about will be solved."

My heart was beginning to open fully for the first time in my life perhaps because of the connection with my soul. Subtle intuitions and insights came to me, gentle ones like, "Be still." I kept my eyes open and my senses aware as I looked for celestial synchronistic moments in my life, and there continued to be many.

During that time, the message, "be still," came to me in a variety of ways in my morning prayer time. A friend of mine randomly sent me a video from Hong Kong entitled *Be Still*. I had not shared with her the message I had been hearing, so she was unaware of how synchronistic this video was to me. God continued to send signs to make sure I was understanding the messages and lessons I was learning. And "being still" seemed to be a very important one.

One of my favorite scripture verses became, "Be still and know that I am."[6] It was written on the cover of one of my journals, and I hadn't realized the impact of those words there until recently. I was seeing and hearing this message everywhere. I was also continuing to have the opportunity to practice what I was learning. One of the best grades I received in Soul School came from Sister M in a note which said, "You are growing into your beautiful self," encouraging me to continue forward on my journey.

I was beginning to listen and hear gentle messages and answers to some questions I had been asking. I was feeling the difference between the disruptive thoughts from the ego and the peaceful serenity from the soul. Connecting to the soul required moments of quiet and stillness. It was similar to connecting to Wi-Fi to improve cellular service. Connect to your inner being through quiet and stillness to improve soul connection.

THE ART OF SILENCE

Our world is not a world of stillness and quiet; it's quite the opposite. It seems as if the more chaotic, busy, exciting, and noisy, the better. Most of the great spiritual teachers I've read or listened to speak of the power and importance of silence at some point in your day. Many write it is in stillness and quiet that they are able to connect to their inner being, their highest self. I have felt the importance of this principle and experienced its effects. Sitting in silence for five minutes every day had become part of my morning routine and a practice I looked forward to.

Most times after sitting in silence even for a few minutes, I felt my body relax as my thoughts began to slow down as I detached from them. It was similar to shifting a car from fourth gear to first gear. The cumulative effects of short bursts of silence in my days were making a difference. It's not that my anxious thoughts dissipated. My worried thoughts continued, but I now felt I had a way to calm them down and shift to the peace within. The worry didn't spiral out of control. It was as if the soul was soothing my anxious mind.

Sitting in silence is an art. It takes quite a bit of practice to become comfortable with sitting in silence—at least that's how it was for me. When I first began the practice, I told myself I only needed to start with five minutes. And so I began. I set the timer on my phone for five minutes, turned my phone face down, and sat in stillness and quiet. Initially, five minutes felt like a very long time.

I simply cast my eyes downward, breathed, and listened. As thoughts rose to the surface, I would quietly say, "Thinking," in my mind and let them flow like the waves of an ocean. I looked forward to these quiet moments every day and was amazed at the sense of peace I would feel after just a few moments of stillness and quiet. I began to convert my thoughts to conversations with God and started repeating God's name. I would say, "God, are you there?"

After these moments of silence, I journaled my feelings and was amazed at times at how freely my words and feelings flowed. It was in moments of complete silence that I was able to get in touch with how I felt—deep within my soul—and begin to understand who I was and what I wished for as I listened for any insights or nudges God was trying to send. *The Rhythm of Life—Living Every Day with Passion and Purpose* devotes an entire chapter on "The Gentle Voice Within." Kelly writes, "The gentle voice within you is interested in only one thing, helping you become the-best-version-of-yourself."[7] I even had a dream during this time about the importance of silence and listening. God was really trying to get this point across to me. Silence was a practice which helped me reset and connect within to my highest self.

I recently came across one of the many letters I wrote to God during this time; its subject was the art of silence. I asked God in my letter to help me learn the art of silence, listen more than I talk, find awe in nature, and embrace and simply enjoy the quiet. God's voice seemed to be heard in silence. I was experiencing the power of silence and connecting not only to the space within, but to God, too. "It's in stillness that God grows our souls and quiets our hearts," David Arms reminds us. I hoped my soul was expanding and my heart was softening.

There is great power in silence, and many messages and insights have come to me during silent moments. In fact, it's in silence that most insights come to me. I've felt prodded to reach out to certain people in moments of silence. I've felt great love in moments of silence, I've felt relief from anxious thoughts and worries in silence, and I've experienced total serenity. I was beginning to embrace silence, and my soul and my life were beginning to transform in a much healthier fashion.

The Untethered Soul, by Michael Singer, was a perfect introductory book to Soul School because its message was in alignment with my mission to learn as much as I could about how to connect deeply to my inner being, the soul. I filled my days trying to learn how others connected to their inner beings, and when I wasn't reading, I was listening to podcasts on the subject. I was being introduced to books through others confirming the messages I was hearing. One of *The Untethered Soul*'s messages is to lean away from the constant chatter in our minds and become observers. In essence, Singer suggests we drop into stillness. I considered these book recommendations God's way of guiding me in Soul School and on my journey to the soul. God was providing the curriculum—after all, he was my teacher.

The second book I read was *When the Heart Waits,* by Sue Monk Kidd. I was blown away by the opening paragraph: "Overhead a thickening of clouds wreathed everything in grayness. It was February when the earth of South Carolina seemed mired in the dregs of winter."[8] I was reading those words on February 2, 2020, sitting in South Carolina. She further described her "baffling crisis of spirit," something I had been feeling for the previous several months. Looking back, I realize I was being sent celestial synchronicities all throughout the journey; I just wasn't aware enough yet to recognize them.

The message of "being still" was repeated often throughout Sue Monk Kidd's book, as was the message of having patience, a virtue that needed much attention in my life. Being still also meant focusing my attention where I was at each moment and being fully present. I was finding true happiness from going within and allowing the soul to soothe my anxious thoughts. I was also learning that genuine happiness is an inside job and one that involves the soul.

Thomas Keating also wrote about the importance of silence in his book, *Divine Therapy, and Addiction*, "So obviously, the lengthier the time that you can profitably stay in silence and solitude, the more change you expose yourself to because the silence and solitude accompanied by centering prayer or some non-conceptual form of prayer is cumulative in the deep rest that it brings to the psyche and consequently to the body because the two, body and soul, are so closely united that what one does the other always vibrates to."[9]

The practice of stillness and silence during our busy days was encouraged by most of the spiritual teachers. "The only way to discover the deep presence directly was in the practice of silent prayer and solitude. Henri called solitude 'the furnace of transformation,' that dark place in the soul where we shed all distractions and simply wait in trust and faith for the one who calls us the beloved."[10]

Finally, according to Eckhart Tolle in *A New Earth: Awakening to Your Life's Purpose*, "Stillness is another word for space."[11] I now understand that my longing for space, which prompted this journey, was a longing for stillness, silence, and the soul.

Soul Searching:

- Take a few minutes to practice silence. Perhaps you can set a timer for five minutes. Your mind may be racing and filled with a steady stream of thoughts. It's okay. Don't judge your thoughts. Simply be aware and let them flow through.
- Try turning off the radio for a few minutes when driving in the car. Embrace the silence.
- Take a walk in nature and listen to the sounds around you. Stop to smell a flower or pause to take in a beautiful sunset.
- Are you able to sense any needs and desires from your heart and soul in silence?
- Perhaps you can feel your soul soothe some of your anxious thoughts.

Song suggestion:

"The Sound of Silence," by Simon and Garfunkel

Sticky Note #23
Love Big

"May today there be peace within. May you trust that you are exactly where you are meant to be. May you not forget the infinite possibilities that are born of faith in yourself and others. May you use the gifts you have received, and pass on the love that has been given to you. May you be content with yourself just the way you are. Let this knowledge settle into your bones, and allow your soul the freedom to sing, dance, praise, and love. It is there for each and every one of us."

—ST. THÉRÈSE

I have always classified myself as a hopeless romantic. I love the idea of love. Since a young age, I've been fascinated with love and remember playing classic love songs and dancing in the living room of our small house. I dreamed about love and loved watching movies about people falling in love. I just took for granted I was wired for love. I imagined everyone was wired that way.

Here's an example of how much love means to me. At the beginning of 2021, I attended a retreat during which we were asked to name 2021, to set the direction for the year. I chose "The Year of Love." That was to be my spiritual GPS, and it was. Out of all the possibilities, I chose love. The scripture verse I attached to my year of love was "There are in the end three things that last; faith, hope, and love, and the greatest of these is love" (1 Corinthians 13:13).[1]

SPREAD LOVE, SPREAD GOD

Another interesting thing that happened during Soul School was that when I prayed and asked God how I could help others and make a difference in the world, my inner voice repeatedly said, "Spread love." *That's it.* I dismissed this message initially and doubted its significance. "Spread love" seemed too simple. But God was relentless with me when it came to this one. I heard those two words countless times in my thoughts and seemed to see them everywhere. I guess it made sense love would be part of the way I could touch others. I was all about love. But it still seemed too basic and simple. I was still searching for my purpose, and believed it needed to be extraordinary and monumental in some way. (At least that's what my ego thought.)

During Soul School, I was reminded of the scripture passage that "God is love" in 1 John 4:8. Although I had read that verse quite a few times over the years, the impact of its meaning had never really sunk in. I was beginning to understand and feel the power of love, for where there's love, there is God. If I'm spreading love, I'm spreading God.

Love seemed to be the highest state of joy, happiness, and contentment. I journaled specific examples of how I felt loved each day in little ways, such as my sons and other family members calling me to say hi and check in, and my reaching out to others. I called these moments "little moments of love."

In fact, that was my toast to my son and daughter-in-law at their engagement celebration. As I gazed into their eyes with unconditional love and joy, I nervously spoke a few simple statements: "Show each other little moments of love each day throughout your marriage." I continued, "It's those little moments of love that make life so great. Those little acts of love add up to great love."

This message, "spread love," became one I heard daily during my quiet time in the mornings. Those two words became regular journal entries. "Spread love," I wrote on April 26, 2020. "How am I going to spread love when the world is shut down by the pandemic?" I asked myself and God. I received an answer a few days later when I found myself writing notes from my cottage in South Carolina to strangers in a nursing home in Minnesota. Here are a few simple notes I wrote to spread love to others thousands of miles away:

- "You are loved."
- "Sending a smile your way."
- "Wishing the happiest of days to you."
- "Sending warm thoughts of love, hope, and peace your way today."

Each note I wrote, I believe, was a message from the soul and a God Moment. I could feel the power of love taking over. The more notes I wrote, the more I wanted to send, and I started to send them to other people I held close to my heart too. Love built upon love and was gaining traction at the same pace as the pandemic. I was trying my best to spread love during a very sad and difficult time in the world.

I shared the message to "spread love" with my son during one of our many brainstorming sessions about possible titles for the book. He's very kind and patient when I ask for his advice about different ideas I'm contemplating, and he always gives me something to ponder after our discussions. "Do you think a title with love in it is creative enough?" I asked him.

He asked what my main message was. I exclaimed, "Love."

He said, "If you've devoted an entire book to love, why not call it Love Big?"

"That's perfect," I replied. "That's exactly what I'm trying to do—I'm trying to love everyone and everything and that's a big task. I'm trying to love big!"

Although his clever caption didn't appear in the title, it served as a pivotal message in my journey and the title for this chapter. *If my lesson is to spread love, I'm going to love big*, I told myself. I hadn't realized yet that this lesson may also turn out to be my mission and purpose in life. I would discover that months later. I am truly grateful for my son's kindness and patience exploring ideas with me. His patience, kindness, and love gave me the encouragement to continue writing this book!

I tried my best to spread love through little acts of kindness and love. I didn't know what would happen next and where I would go next, but neither did the rest of the world—it was a lonely and very scary time. I began each morning with two questions: "Who can I help today?" and "Who can I love today?" And at the end of every day, I asked, "Who did I help today?" and "Who did I love today?"

As I recognized the importance of spreading love wherever and to whomever I could, I was more aware of the many celestial synchronicities cheering me on. Not only was I hearing the message "spread love" when I sat in silence, but I continued to see the words in other places, too, which reinforced the importance of the message.

In one of my readings, a quote from Saint Teresa of Calcutta appeared: "Spread love everywhere you go. Let no one ever come to you without leaving happier." My journal entries were filled with this message day after day. It was coming during a time when the world was in lockdown and people were not able to spend time with others. Yet, by the grace of God, I was sending messages of love to others across the country with the hope it would make them feel loved, special, and connected. And it was giving me a sense of connection with others too.

Around this same time, our sweet pup, Maggie, passed away in her sleep. I poured out my sadness and grief over losing her to God. My journal entry after she passed away read:

Dear God,

Thank you for the gift of Maggie. Thank you for the love she brought us. Thank you for granting her peace and her peaceful passing back to you. We were so lucky to have her in our lives. Thank You.

I asked God to help me live like Maggie did. She was sweet in an unassuming way. She was kind to everyone she met. She welcomed all into our world—including her younger sister, Matisse. She was patient with Matisse through her puppy years. She was content with little things and simple moments like lying next to her brothers on the floor.

She loved her family unconditionally. She was always there for us and knew what we needed. She loved life and the simple little moments. She loved frolicking on walks in nature and swimming in the rivers. She loved naps in the sunshine. She was never envious of her little sister who received a lot of attention. She loved staying with friends when we traveled.

She gave my sons and me exactly what we needed in our lives—unconditional love. As I read this journal entry now, I can still feel her spirit, as well as her tremendous goodness. The idea of leading a life like Maggie is helping me today, as I write these words. She truly lived with gratitude each day, accepted others, had unconditional love for others, and was happy in each little moment. She needed nothing more.

My childhood dream of love was taking on an entirely new meaning now. I was beginning to feel love from the depth of the soul, a love like none I'd ever felt before, and I wanted to share it as much as I could. Once again, God was reminding me how important we all are to him. His love is never-ending. I believe this divine love is in everyone and everything. What do we need to do with this divine love in us? LOVE BIG.

Soul Searching:

- To love is a decision. Choose to live a life of love.
- Journal about ways you can choose to love yourself and others.
- How can you Love Big during your day?
- Reach out to someone and let them know how much you love them.

Song suggestion:

"What the World Needs Now is Love," by Steve Tyrell, Burt Bacharach, Martina McBride, Rod Stewart, James Taylor, and Dionne Warwick

Sticky Note #24
Make Every Day
Valentine's Day

*"I realized that only one thing separated the men and women
who felt a deep sense of love and belonging from the people who
seem to be struggling for it. That one thing is the belief in their
worthiness. ... If we want to fully experience love and belonging,
we must believe that we are worthy of love and belonging."*

—BRENÉ BROWN

This may surprise you, but even though I am someone who is
all about love, I used to dread Valentine's Day when I wasn't in
a romantic relationship. The stores are always filled with hearts
and loving gifts for those in love to buy for one another. I felt sad
and disappointed that I didn't have a special someone to send
loving messages and gifts to and that I wasn't the recipient of
those messages and gifts.

As I sent loving gifts and messages to my sons and others
who I hold close in my heart this past Valentine's Day, I wondered if I would ever find my soulmate. After all, given the messages from the soul to love big, I guess it's natural that I would
long for a soulmate, especially on Valentine's Day. But what I've
realized is that love comes in many forms. There is love for family

members, love for friends, love for pets, and love for everyone and everything.

LOVE IS EVERYWHERE

I had an epiphany this past Valentine's Day, thanks to a friend of mine. I asked my friend if he ever wished he had a Valentine, someone special in his life. He asked me if that was a trick question. It was not a trick question. I was genuinely curious how he felt about Valentine's Day. He told me he receives loving messages and notes most days and has nice things happen to him quite often.

I pondered his words and reflected on my own life. I, too, receive kind notes from others and have nice things happen to me most days. His response helped me realize every day can be like Valentine's Day. I decided this past Valentine's Day to do just that. I wrote in my journal that I would give and receive love every day—in simple ways—keep my heart open, and when I thought lovingly of others, I would send them a nice note or reach out to them and let them know I was thinking of them.

I also decided to pay close attention to moments when I was the recipient of loving and kind messages from others. I wanted to share love and express love on a daily basis, and I wanted to do it in a big way. Soul School was teaching me that the key was to always keep an open heart. I began to realize an open heart allowed me to feel both loved by others and love for others. When my heart was closed off in the past, I missed these little moments of love. It's not easy to keep an open heart, especially after being hurt, but I realized the importance of it to allow love to flow freely. Also, since I am a person who has lived most of her life in her head, shifting to the heart has taken a great deal of practice and work.

While I was writing this chapter, I received another celestial synchronicity to let me know I was on the right track with this message about every day being Valentine's Day. This took place during a lunch with friends. My friends were sharing how they had met their partners (prompted by me, I suppose). Each couple had been together for at least twenty years. One couple expressed they just "knew the other was the one." Another couple had worked together, and the other couple had dated in college.

Somehow, we started talking about the movie *Love Actually* and its uplifting message about the different types of love. I realized at that moment the movie's message was precisely what I had decided to do this past Valentine's Day—to make every day like Valentine's Day and to spread love to everyone and anyone I met. I could see the daily signs from God, or "God Winks," reassuring me I was on the right track, and it was all about love. My mission in life seemed to be centered around love, in some way, toward all God's creatures—toward humans and animals, those in my presence and those in my thoughts, even those who had passed on to the next dimension.

BE A FORCE OF LOVE

As I was reviewing hundreds of journal entries while writing this book, I came across a birthday card my mom and dad had sent me when I was turning thirty-five. The card's cover read, "Follow Your Heart," and the message inside was, "The days and years rush by, and yet within them there is a sprinkling of joy and simple times that remind us of what is truly important: to live is a gift, and every ordinary moment is filled with beauty when seen through the eyes of the heart. A wish that you may be given time to dream and to share love and laughter."

Imagine a world in which we all opened our hearts and spread love every day—to others and to ourselves. It would be powerfully transformative, an electrical surge of energy for sure. This message sounds so simple, but for someone like me, who lives most of her life in her head, it involves some practice and consistent reminders (especially spreading love to myself). Brené Brown devoted an entire chapter on love in her book, *The Gifts of Imperfection*. She wrote not only of the importance of loving others, but also the necessity of loving ourselves. "We can only love others as much as we love ourselves,"[1] she states.

Self-love took on a whole new meaning for me because I was determined to spread love to as many people as I could. If I wanted to love big for others, I had to show myself some big love. Soul School was helping me learn that the soul is all about feelings and the heart, and I now understood the importance of connecting to my feelings and allowing my soul to expand.

Around this time in my journey, my son and daughter-in-law were about to be married. My simple intention was to do my best to be a force of love for them and every person who made the effort to celebrate with them at their wedding. I wasn't alone in that feeling of tremendous love, and throughout the week-end, it felt like everyone was connected through the same intent of spreading love to the wonderful couple. This force of love is a very difficult feeling to express in words, but it is extremely powerful.

Fortunately for me, my two nieces decided to stay with me for a month after the wedding. I thoroughly loved having them with me and was sad when it was time for them to leave. My soul soon began to remind me I was still in Soul School and had more lessons to learn. I was once again prompted to pick up the two journals that contained the letters to God I had written during the Spiritual Exercises. As I reread the entries, I was transported to the place of peace and love from when they were written.

Having reviewed my journal entries for the past nine months, I was able to see some common themes. I've worked hard reminding myself to turn my worries over to God and deepen my faith in God. I'm still surprised how much I worried; worry and fear were woven into most of my journal entries. Many of the lessons I learned from the Spiritual Exercises were similar to the messages I had been learning in Soul School.

One of my favorite movie scenes about love takes place in the movie *Meet Joe Black* and features a father and his daughter. The father recognizes his youngest daughter is not in love with the man she is dating and she may be settling. In the scene, he gives his daughter the following advice on love:

> I want you to get swept away; I want you to levitate; I want you to be deliriously happy. At least leave yourself open to be. I say, fall head over heels. Find someone you can love like crazy and who will love you the same way back. How do you find him? You forget your head and you listen to your heart. Because the truth is, honey, there's no sense living your life without this. To make the journey and not fall deeply in love, you haven't lived a life at all. But you have to try. Because if you haven't tried, you haven't lived. Stay open. Who knows, lightning could strike.[2]

I love this scene and the message the father, played by Anthony Hopkins, gives to his daughter. Life is about love and keeping our hearts open. When the heart is open, love flows freely and readily. It's not easy to keep an open heart, especially after it's been wounded and broken, but it seems to be the secret to a life filled with big love and happiness. It's all about love!

Recently, I came across a simple card I bought a while ago. I love sending cards (as my mom did) to others, and I spend a good amount of time picking a card I feel best represents the person I'm sending it to.

The card I found was simple but had four words that delivered a powerful message: "Love is the answer." It reminded me of a song by Dan England and John Ford Coley called just that, "Love is the Answer." Once again, God was sending me signs confirming the importance of love, and love was all around me. I started to sing the song in my mind and decided to include a few of the lyrics here:

> And when you feel afraid, love one another.
> And when you've lost your way, love one another.
> And when you're all alone, love one another.
> And when you're far from home, love one another.
> And when you're down and out, love one another.
> And when your hope's run out, love one another.
> And when you need a friend, love one another.
> And when you're near the end, love one another.
> We got to love, we got to love, we got to love one another.
> Love is the answer.
> Shine on us all, set us free.
> Love is the answer.[3]

I was beginning to feel the power of love that was all around me, and I was receiving nudges and celestial synchronicities confirming the message of love big. Love was showing up every day in some way—and in a big way. I began to embrace the signs with gratitude and love. Love seemed to be the fuel for the soul.

Soul Searching:

- Send a card or note today to someone you hold close in your heart.
- How can you implement a small act of self-care to show yourself how much you are loved?
- Was there a time when you were the recipient of a loving message from someone?

Song suggestion:

"Love is The Answer," by Dan England and John Ford Coley

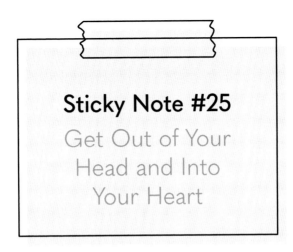

Sticky Note #25
Get Out of Your Head and Into Your Heart

"When I interviewed the participants whom I'd describe as living a Wholehearted life about the same topic, they consistently talked about trying to feel the feelings, staying mindful about numbing behaviors, and trying to lean into the discomfort of hard emotions."

—BRENÉ BROWN

As a student in Soul School, I was recognizing the effects (both joyful and painful) of tuning into my feelings, my heart, and detaching from thoughts in my mind. I wondered, "How can I live each day guided by both my head and my heart?" I realized the significance of tuning into my feelings, but I didn't want to simply allow my feelings to navigate my life aimlessly. I also didn't want to empower the ego and attach to self-destructive thoughts. I was longing to shift any negative thoughts to positive ones and to stay tuned into my feelings in a balanced approach. Was there a way to live each day allowing my heart to radiate loving emotions towards myself and others and tame the critic in my mind?

STAY CONNECTED
WITH YOUR HEART

In his book, *The Seven Spiritual Laws of Success*, Deepak Chopra writes about the importance of staying connected with your heart and allowing it to guide you. Chopra says, "Consciously put your attention in the heart and ask your heart what to do. Then wait for the response—a physical response in the form of a sensation. It may be the faintest level of feeling, but it's there, in your body. Only the heart knows the correct answer. Most people think the heart is mushy and sentimental. But it's not. The heart is intuitive; it's holistic, it's contextual. It's relational."[1] It seemed as if connecting with the heart was an essential component to living as our highest selves, which seemed to be our true selves. Wayne Dyer also discussed the necessity of trusting our hearts, and he emphasized that it's *imperative for the growth of a healthy spiritual life.*

I had spent many months trying to get in better touch with my feelings and to some degree, train my mind, by allowing thoughts to arise, not judging them, detaching from them, and replacing them with positive and loving ones. I didn't want my ego to run my life as it had for most of my life. Gradually, the thoughts dissipated. This practice was very different from how I had lived most of my life. Henri Nouwen describes the ego ideal as, "often made up of self-created expectations and aspirations regarding intelligence, career, physical beauty, moral stature, and so on. The mystery of life, however, is not only that we have a dark side which we want to deny but also that we are better than our ego ideal. Our true identity is found in God, who created us in the divine image."[2]

As a working professional for twenty years, I was very driven by my thoughts, goals, and solutions; more ego-based. I've had to really practice and, quite frankly, work diligently to observe my thoughts and not attach to them, while at the same time, try to get more in touch with my feelings. It was time to shift a little from some of the darker voices in my head to the peaceful voices in my heart and soul.

When I began this journey, I had a limited understanding of feelings. But with Dr. Marc Brackett's help, I had expanded my emotional vocabulary. I began to focus more on my feelings—both the loving feelings and the hurtful ones. I had begun the habit of asking myself throughout the day, "How are you feeling?"

TUNING INTO YOUR HEART

Loving feelings are great and easy to identify. These are moments when my heart is overflowing and wants to send love to others through uplifting messages and giving. It is wonderful when you feel loved by others and happy; it feels like you're walking on sunshine.

I also realized, however, that listening to our hearts means tuning in when it is wounded and hurt, being attentive to those moments when you feel sad because of someone's words or actions. Those are difficult emotions I usually want to pass by quickly, but they seem to linger and get stored deep within. (I was an expert at doing that.)

In the past, I used to think that following my heart meant tuning in to my heart only when it felt overwhelmed with love and joy. I've since learned that it's extremely important to tune in to my heart when it has been wounded and pay even closer attention then. Even the little hurts are important to feel, recognize, and not judge. Simply acknowledge the feelings, but don't attach to them. Connecting to the heart was healing some of the pain I stored deep within. As Henri Nouwen reminds us, "in solitude and meditation the dark and wounded side of us that is still in need of healing also asks for attention and has to be acknowledged as just as much a part of us as our idealized selves."[3]

I've had the misfortune of having my heart wounded many times in my life, as I imagine most of us have. Experiences such as the death of loved ones, broken relationships, and rejection in love are all part of the human experience. But now it is no longer an option to store these feelings away. I've made a pact with myself to continue to keep my heart open, to feel and acknowledge the pain and hurt, and to let it pass through me. It's not pleasant feeling the pain, but it's an important part to acknowledge it and let it flow through.

The Untethered Soul discussed doing just that: acknowledging when your heart feels pain and letting it pass through. It seemed so easy to do when I read those words a couple of years ago, but it's a different story trying to put words from a book into practice when you're feeling the hurt in your heart. I quietly remind myself, "One day at a time," and, "Don't take things personally."

Recognizing patterns from the past has allowed me to chart a different course going forward and rely on some of the lessons I'm learning and tools I've created on my journey. The positive way to look at hurt and rejection is we can learn valuable lessons from the pain as we move forward, and we can remind ourselves, "This too shall pass." And eventually, it does.

I've also incorporated some exercises to help move from my head to my heart. One of my favorite quotes sits on my desk as a reminder to tune into the voice in my heart, "Listen to the voice in your heart before your mind begins to speak," Sri Babaji.

I hope the following questions, which I ask myself, can help you too. (I'm a big fan of asking myself questions now.)

Soul Searching:

Here are three questions to help you listen to the voice in your heart:

- "How am I feeling?" Ask this a few times a day.
- "How does it feel inside of me?"
    - » Describe your feelings—comforted, amazed, sad, or overwhelmed are some examples of feelings deep within you. Journal your feelings.
- "How does it feel in various parts of my body?"
    - » An example is when I hear something that makes me feel happy or something nice someone has done for someone else, I get goosebumps, mainly on my arms. When I feel loved by or for someone close to me, I get a warm feeling in my heart.
    - » Perhaps you can place your attention on your heart and ask your heart for an answer with a decision you may be trying to make.

Happy trails on your journey from the head to the heart and soul.

Song suggestion:

"Heartlight," by Neil Diamond

"God speaks to us all the time and in many ways, but it requires spiritual discernment to hear God's voice, see what God sees, and read the signs in daily life."

—HENRI NOUWEN

I knew very little about discernment when *The Art of Discernment* was first recommended at the beginning of my journey. And, I didn't know much more after I read the book much too quickly the first time in search of an immediate answer to my dilemma. Fortunately, we studied the discernment of spirits in much greater detail as part of the Spiritual Exercises Program.

It continues to amaze me that I was receiving celestial synchronicities early on my journey, almost as a preview of what was to come on my travels to my soul. I was reintroduced to the practice of discernment two years later, after failing the lesson the first time. God was sending me quite a few signs in the early stages of my journey, but I was missing them. I was on high alert now and didn't want to miss any more signs or nudges.

I'll try my best to describe my understanding of discernment. Discernment of Spirits is about learning to recognize the movements of the soul. It's a practice of noticing the interior movements of our hearts, including our thoughts, feelings, desires, attractions, and resistances.

We begin to notice our interior world and desires, and we try to choose the path toward greater faith, love, and hope when making decisions. I also learned that discernment is about finding out who we are and what's right for us. God wants us to be happy. Discernment is a question of identity and finding our true selves. I had no idea I had been practicing a form of discernment on my journey.

GOING DEEPER WITH DISCERNMENT

Michael J. Christensen and Rebecca J. Laird described discernment in The Preface for *Discernment*. It reads, "Discernment is a regular discipline of listening to the still, small voice beneath the rush of the whirlwind, a prayerful practice of reading the subtle signs in daily life ... discernment is a lifelong commitment to "remember God" (memoria Dei), know who you are, and pay close attention to what the Spirit is saying to you."[1]

I remember writing in *The Art of Discernment* by Stefan Kiechle that I believed the move I made toward my own space was a move toward greater faith, hope, and love. I may never have written this book had I stayed in my comfort zone. The practice of discernment of spirits helps by giving us ways to make decisions. I didn't think I was using any of the suggestions from the book to help with my decision at the time, but it turns out I may have been. It sure felt as if my pivot to my own space was a move toward greater faith, hope, and love.

I was also working hard to feel my decisions in my body. For instance, when making a decision, I began to tune into where I felt each decision, the physical sensations. I was beginning to understand which choices felt right to me and which ones did not. Those that felt right gave me a sigh of relief, and those that felt like the wrong decision left a knot in my stomach or left me with a headache.

I discovered when I'm happy and filled with complete joy, I feel a soothing sensation in my heart. Years ago, my son shared with me that he felt a similar calming and warm sensation in his heart when he was in the presence of his grandmother (Mimi) and me. I feel the same feelings in his presence and understood exactly what he was describing. I was learning that the soul is all about feelings, and it is important to know what I am feeling and to feel it in my body. Feelings are the entry point to my soul.

In addition to practicing discernment for decision-making, there are also fourteen rules for discernment to help shift our inner spirits from desolation (when we are down) to consolation (when we feel uplifted and joyful). I rely on these fourteen rules daily to help shift my spirit toward consolation and God and away from desolation and negative forces. Consolation is getting back to who we are, our true identity—what other spiritual teachers refer to as our highest selves. Consolation is an increase in faith, hope, and love.

Desolation is a movement away from faith, hope, and love toward darkness, fear, and negativity. In simple terms, consolation is a pull toward love and light, and desolation is a pull in the opposite direction. I was gaining a better understanding of many of my triggers and negative patterns. For example, I'm prone to excessive fears and worries when I'm physically tired from lack of sleep. Countless times I spiraled into a frenzy of worry and anxiety when not well-rested. I was beginning to feel I had some control, with the help of my soul, some tools, and God, to combat excessive worry and fear. I reminded myself when I was physically fatigued I was susceptible to fear taking over; fatigue became a red flag for me.

I was also feeling the pull of good versus evil in my life, and I wanted to move toward the good, the love, the light, and my soul. I asked God to engulf me in love and protect me from dark and negative thought patterns. I had been given a glimpse of the feelings of love, peace, and light, and wanted to stay there as often as I could. I was also beginning to better understand what brought me consolation versus what brought me desolation. Understanding the patterns of consolation and desolation in my life became very important to help me stay closer to my soul.

In addition to understanding the forces of the negative inner critic and reminding myself to stay in the light of the soul, I relied on the fourteen rules for discernment, which I first learned about from Timothy Gallagher, OMV in his book, *The Discernment of Spirits*. Ignatius of Loyola wrote fourteen rules 450 years ago to help us better understand the spiritual movements in the soul. These rules have allowed me to recognize the voice of the soul (or the Holy Spirit) and separate it from other voices not of the soul, as well as do my best to follow the lead of the soul and let the Spirit guide me.

During The Spiritual Exercises program, we paraphrased the fourteen rules to make them more applicable in our own lives. Putting each rule in my own words helped me to better understand each rule and use it when needed. I apologize to Saint Ignatius for oversimplifying his rules.

My Fourteen Rules for Discernment:

1. Listen for Jiminy Cricket and let my conscience be my guide.

2. Follow Glinda, the good witch, who gives me courage, strength, inspiration, and peace. The wicked witch causes fear, sadness, obstacles, and turmoil.
3. Consolation is love. It is an increase of hope, faith, and charity. It causes a quieting of the soul and brings a peaceful feeling. Write down how I look at the world when I'm in consolation.
4. Desolation is darkness and disturbance of the soul. It causes a feeling of hopelessness and movement away from love. Read what I wrote when in consolation.
5. In times of trouble, Mother Mary comes to me, speaking words of wisdom: "Let it be."[2] Don't change any prior decisions when in desolation.
6. When in doubt, pray it out and help someone. Insist more upon prayer, meditation, and service to others in desolation.
7. Resist persistent darkness by asking for divine help.
8. Be patient. This too shall pass.
9. Be aware of laziness in my prayer; seek God and help others but not in a self-serving way. Remember spiritual consolation is a gift and a grace from God.
10. When I'm in consolation, prepare my toolbox for desolation by writing how consolation feels and how I view myself, others, and the world when in consolation. Read this when I'm in desolation.
11. Always be humble and kind. Thank God for the gift and grace of consolation.
12. Confront negative thoughts firmly and do the opposite of what is being suggested by the evil one. Stand firm and persevere.
13. When in desolation, ask for help. Don't keep negative thoughts a secret.

14. Know where I'm weak, and stay alert for the workings of the evil spirit.

The fourteen rules for discernment became a daily resource to help me become aware of times of desolation and shift to consolation and to be grateful when I was in consolation. Having had a taste of the peace of the soul, I longed to stay there as often as possible.

Soul Searching:

- During times of sadness and despair, call on your discernment to shift to the light, love, and peace of your soul.
- It's important to talk to yourself the way you'd talk to a dear friend.
- Come back to this sticky note for reference, and write your own fourteen rules of discernment.
- Perhaps you can connect with your heart this week. What thoughts, feelings, desires, or insights come to you?

Song suggestion:

"Let It Be," by The Beatles

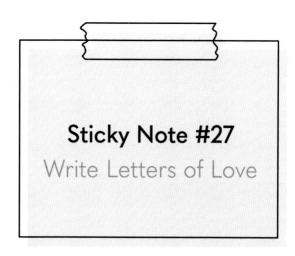

Sticky Note #27
Write Letters of Love

"With his prodigious talent for friendship, Ignatius enjoyed close relationships with a large circle of friends. (That is one reason for his enthusiasm for writing letters.) During his lifetime, he (Ignatius) wrote an astonishing 6,813 letters to a wide array of men and women. He was one of the most prolific letter writers of his age, writing more than Martin Luther and John Calvin combined, and more than Erasmus, one of the great letter writers of the time. Ignatius saw letter writing as an art."

—JAMES MARTIN, SJ

Have you ever been the recipient of a heartfelt letter from someone you love deeply? Did you ever receive a note of encouragement and support during a difficult time? Was there a time when you were touched at your core from the tremendous love and support you felt in a written message? Have you ever received or written a letter of love?

I've been extremely blessed to have been the recipient of years of notes, cards, and letters of love, many from my sons. Their words have often left me speechless. I couldn't seem to capture the right words that would express the depth of my love and gratitude. There weren't any words that could do it. My feelings were too vast and immense to put into words. I would read their notes or cards over and over when I first received them and let each word they wrote sink deeply into my heart.

In today's busy world, receiving a handwritten note of any kind is rare. A handwritten Mother's Day card I received from my son when he was sixteen years old sits on my writing desk as I write these words. My loving son took the time to sit down (at the age of sixteen) and express his love and gratitude for me on three pages of the card. He wrote the card the Christmas after my mom (his Mimi) passed away on her behalf. His loving message of reassurance that she's watching over us and that we should enjoy every moment we spend with those we love is forever etched in my heart.

I carry my sons' loving messages in my heart similar to putting a picture of them in a locket. Not only are their words engraved in my heart, but I continue to read the cards today to feel their love and connection when we are hundreds of miles apart. Their messages continue to fill me with awe, gratitude, love, and encouragement.

Part of the Spiritual Exercises included writing in a journal to become more aware of our interior affective movements, or more simply put, our feelings. God seemed to communicate through feelings. I certainly was sharing my feelings with God in the letters I wrote him each day. It felt like a more natural way to tune in to my feelings.

Upon my completion of the Spiritual Exercises, as I was reviewing my journal entries, it became even more apparent to me I had been consumed with fear and worry for most of my life. My worries included my health and the health of those I loved, not doing enough with my life, being alone, and the happiness of my sons and those I loved, among many others. I began to transfer those worries to God on paper and through my love letters (although not all of the letters were loving). In essence, I was releasing all fears and anxieties to him.

Today, I can honestly say I am no longer living a life consumed by fear and worry. I am living a life of love. To be clear, there are many times when worry and fear appear, but I'm now able to recognize when the anxious feelings begin, and turn to some tools to stop the fear from overtaking me. Journaling my emotions, sitting in silence for a few minutes, or writing a letter to God are some tools to shift my fearful thoughts. This transformation from a life of fear to a life of love could not have happened, I believe, without space, lessons from many spiritual teachers, Soul School, Sister M., support from family and friends, the Spiritual Exercises, celestial synchronicities, and God.

In the letters I wrote to God each morning, I expressed my concerns and doubts and allowed the power of God and the power of love to intercede and take over. I was in Divine therapy for a year every morning with God. I asked him simple questions and listened for any insights or nudges, and I became aware of the people he was sending into my path. I received answers and guidance. God was healing my wounded heart.

Love truly does dispel all fear. I was faithfully surrendering. The more I surrendered, the less powerful my fearful ego became, allowing my soul to continue to expand. I was providing space for the love within me to come forth and help me navigate my daily life. I was also tapping into my inner desires and intuition, and allowing my soul to direct me through my experiences. I was learning each day to follow God's lead and developing more patience to wait and see what would happen. I also understood my initial need for space was really my need for my soul to expand for love. I was feeling the difference between a life of love led from my soul versus a life of ego led mostly from my anxious thoughts.

Upon reflection, I realize writing letters to God became a way for me to channel my worries and fears, and to some degree release them. And that is exactly what happened. I expanded my practice to writing letters of love to others when the soul nudged me and people came into my thoughts. I also wrote a letter to myself from fear as part of an assignment in the midlife retreat I attended. I was saying farewell to negative and stifling emotions that had been with me for a good part of my life.

Writing letters of love to God is cathartic in many ways and has helped me release years of fears and anxieties.

A Few Letters of Love

October 5, 2020

Ephesians 3:17: God's power working in us. "May Christ dwell in your hearts through faith."

Dear God,

Please continue to dwell in my heart. Please help me feel in my heart and get out of my head. Help me find peace and comfort knowing you're with me always. Help me find solace knowing you're with me and I'm surrounded by love.

Please send me a message of love I can deliver at my son's and future daughter-in-law's engagement dinner. Please surround me with love. Help me to "be" in your presence and "receive" your love.

Please send your Divine dynamic presence always, but especially during this time of transition while I wait to see where I'm guided next to help others and to see who will come into my life.

Love, Marcella

*   *   *

October 9, 2020

> "For man it is impossible but not for God. With God all things are possible." Matthew 19:26. When making decisions, ask myself, "What is the most loving choice?"

Dear God,

I feel at peace and full of love and kindness when I'm following you. All my fears and worries subside, and my mind quiets; my life seems to flow. It's also very comforting to feel your presence and to know I am not alone. With God, all things are possible.

Thank you for guiding me and answering me. I feel your gentle nudges and hear your gentle words: "Trust me with your sorrow and disappointment." I feel "at peace" and content when God is in the center of my life. It's a hard feeling to describe on paper, but I feel it in my heart and soul. My mind is quiet; no chatter about anything. I simply "am." I'm here with you; you are in my heart and soul always. When my mind is quiet, I can hear sounds all around me, like the birds chirping. I hear much more with a quiet mind. I see but don't label, attach, or judge. My senses are much more alive.

Thank you for showing me the way and guiding me. Please help me feel this moment deeply and help me return to this state as often as I can. Please always stay in the center of my heart and my life always.

This is the note I wrote to Fear during the midlife retreat I attended. It was time to say goodbye to fear:

Dear Fear,

You've been a big part of my life for a very long time. In some instances, you've done a good job protecting me from harmful situations. I want to thank you, first off, for the many times you've kept me safe. Thank you for caring so much about me and protecting me for fifty-six years. Unfortunately, though, you've also brought your cousin Doubt into my life over the years. This has been way too much for me to handle and process and as a result, has left me frozen and unable to make personal decisions at times. I know that's not what you wanted for me. Can you please do me a favor from this point forward—can you please give me some space to breathe, live, and have fun being my true self? I'm just discovering her, and I like her. Thank you so much for caring about me and truly wanting the best for me!

Love, Marcella

*   *   *

Dear Marcella,

I am truly sorry for being so needy and dominant. Your perceptions are correct; I loved you and still love you so very much, and I didn't want you to get hurt or wounded. I wanted the best for you. You are ready now, and I release you and set you free, like a butterfly. You have your mother's and father's strength, intelligence, sharp mind, and a big heart. You will make good decisions going forward. Live free and have some fun.

Love, Fear

Soul Searching:

- To whom you would like to send a letter of love or thank for being part of your journey?
- Take a few minutes and tell someone how much they mean to you and how much you love them in a letter, email, or text.
- What would you say to yourself in a letter of love? Write it today.
- Choose one habit or part of yourself that you would like to slowly change.
  » Write a letter to that part of yourself. Perhaps it's fear or anger?
  » Imagine you are recognizing this part of yourself without judgment and gently bidding it farewell.
  » You may want to start with something small like getting annoyed in traffic or impatient in lines at stores.
  » Write it today.
- Write a personal letter to a Higher Power and share a habit or personality trait you wish to work on. Ask for help from God.

Song suggestion:

"Call Your Mama," by Seth Ennis (Panu and my song)

Sticky Note #28
You've Got a Friend in Me

"Many people say that during prayer, even though they don't audibly hear God's voice, they feel as if God were speaking with them. ... For example, a friend may say something so insightful that it is almost as if a window into your soul had just been opened: you may feel as if your friend's words are a way that God is communicating with you."

—JAMES MARTIN, SJ

In addition to writing letters of love to God each morning, I also began talking with God much like I would a friend. My morning chats with God seemed to replace the daily morning phone calls I had with my dad for seven years after my mom passed away.

My dad and I had simple conversations—he often wanted to know how I was doing and how his grandsons were. We simply liked connecting. I used to jokingly say to him that he "wanted to know the scoop." He would banter with me, encourage me, and always give me a dose of reality when I needed it (which was often). I really miss those daily phone calls.

Before he and I started our routine of speaking every morning, my mom and I had done so for more than twenty years. My parents and my two sons had been my "core four" for most of my life. We had a solid bond. After my dad was gone, I couldn't help but wonder, *Whom was I going to talk with now? Who would listen to me and put me back on the right path when I was headed in the wrong direction?*

My parents and I had developed a friendship over the years as I had grown older. They had become my best friends. After they passed away, I had nobody else to turn to—any conversation with my dog would be one-sided, and I didn't want to burden my sons or others who were busy with their own lives. I turned to God as my best friend and gave *him* the scoop every morning. Unlike my dog, God seemed to send me insights and celestial synchronicities—something someone said or did would resonate with me or something would happen during the day that would provide an insight for me. These synchronicities seemed to be the language of the soul.

CONVERSATIONS WITH GOD

It may seem strange to picture me talking aloud to God. When I first started talking with him, I checked in with myself quite often to make sure I wasn't *losing it*. Gradually, the more I talked and was reassured that I was aware I was talking aloud, the more comfortable it became. I left nothing out of our conversations, many of which were one-sided. With God, I shared it all. I didn't sugarcoat any of it. I did more talking and less listening during our early conversations. Learning to listen would be a later lesson in Soul School.

At the same time I was beginning a friendship with God, one of the books I was reading devoted an entire chapter to friendship. The celestial synchronicities were in full force, sending me opportunities to again put into practice what I was reading and learning. I also met several new wonderful friends during this time. I read about friendship, was developing a friendship with God, and meeting new friends in the community simultaneously. A few of the friends I met felt as if we had known each other for a long time. I was now tuned in to these significant *divine appointments* as Henri Nouwen refers to them in his book, *Discernment.*

Friendship seemed to be an important lesson. One of my favorite books, *The Jesuit Guide to (Almost) Everything*, by James Martin, includes five traits of a good friendship and compares a friendship with God to friendships with others. I needed some tips on how to be a good friend because for much of my life, my time had been spent raising two wonderful sons as a single mother, running a business, and taking care of my father, and less time had been devoted to cultivating friendships. I also had never imagined I would have a friendship with God. I had always imagined God sitting high in the heavens judging my every move—happy when I was on track and shaking his head when I veered off course.

As I was reading James Martin's words, I was also experiencing new friendships with other people and with God. When your soul guides your life, you begin to notice the people and events in your life are not accidental, at least that's how I felt. I was aware of proddings in a certain direction and lessons I needed to learn through practice. I simply needed to tune in and observe.

I learned the following good traits for a healthy friendship thanks to *The Jesuit Guide to (Almost) Everything*:

1. Spending time with one another. A healthy friendship flourishes when you spend time with one another. Our world can be busy and chaotic. Carving out a little time for a friend is one way to show that you value the other person's friendship.

2. Learning about each other. Discover your friend's hobbies, interests, and what they like to do. Find out what brings them joy and hope.

3. Being honest with one another. Share your authentic self and your true emotions with your friend. Be who you are, not who you think they want you to be.

4. Listening to one another. True listening requires paying attention. Listen carefully, and pay close attention to your friend's emotions and feelings.

5. Allowing space for change and growth. Allow your friend to change as they grow, and cheer them on along the way.[1]

A SOULMATE EPIPHANY

For most of my life, I had prayed for my soulmate, my best friend, to come into my life. My soulmate request seemed to slip into any prayer request I made. I suddenly realized I already had what I was searching for. I'd had my spiritual soulmate and my friend, God, with me the entire time. Once again, the celestial synchronicities were appearing and enlightening me. God sent new people into my life to help me practice the lesson on friendship I was learning. I began to tune in not only to the friendships I was cultivating in the new community, but also to my friendship with God. He seemed to love me more than I loved myself at times, and he did so unconditionally. That sounded like the definition of a spiritual soulmate to me.

I was also awakening to the awe-inspiring idea that God's spirit has been connected to me through my soul from the moment I was born, but I just hadn't been connecting with this spirit! I believe this is true for us all. We can all have a friendship with the very spirit who created us and lives in us through our souls. It would make no sense *not* to have a friendship with this Divine love who lives in us.

Wayne Dyer's words expressed what I was experiencing, "This energy that is you, call it what you will—spirit, soul—can never die and has never died in the past ... the spirit is now. It is in you at this moment, and the energy is not something that you will ultimately come to know but is what you are here and now. ... the energy is within you. If you want to know it, you can tune into it, and when you do, you leave the limitations of this earth plane and enter a dimension of limitless that allows you to create and attract to you whatever it is you want or need on this journey."[2]

I was aware of the powerful energy of love within me. This awareness shifted any doubtful thoughts to the belief that anything is possible. We all have the ability to co-create our dreams and desires with the divine force inside us. This is very empowering. I believe we were all born with this force within us and we all can manifest our dreams. As the main character in the television series, *Ted Lasso* reminds us, "Believe."[3]

The soul sends gentle clues from this center of peace, but they are often missed due to our busy lives. It wasn't until I pivoted into a little space, silence, and stillness that I began to tune in to the whispers and the gentle messages of my soul. In some ways, it reminded me of listening to a radio station that has a lot of static. The static overtakes the words being said, and you try to get a clear connection to better hear the transmission. It's important to get rid of the static in our lives at times.

What a powerful message to have God, my friend and my spiritual soulmate, connected to me through my soul. The same divine force of love is within you too. I truly believe that with God as my friend, anything and everything is possible. We were in this together. This revelation was a turning point for me in Soul School and in my life as a whole.

Soul Searching:

- You've got a friend in you, too. How can you deepen your friendship with your soul? Can you quiet the static for a little bit during your busy day?
- Find time to start a conversation with God, even if it's just five minutes. It can be as simple as *Hi God.* Journal about it.
- Catch up with an old friend you haven't spoken to in a while. Schedule a coffee date.

Song suggestion:

"You've Got a Friend in Me," by Randy Newman

Sticky Note #29
Use Your Filter to Stay Aware

"Become aware of your thoughts and feelings. At the same time, stop judging yourself. If you do get fearful, critical, or upset, don't fight yourself or make matters worse by adding guilt to the other feelings. Release your inner conflict and know that everything in your life is there for a reason, no matter how unpleasant it seems to be at the time."

—JAMES VAN PRAAGH

In addition to the many books I read in Soul School during the day, I continued to receive lessons at night in my dreams as well as regular celestial synchronicities. The more aware I became, the more vividly I was able to remember my dreams and try my best to interpret the messages. The word "awareness" took on an entirely new meaning and feeling. It was as if I started to receive messages in my dreams in addition to in daily life. I would write them down as soon as I awoke, while they were fresh in my mind.

A DREAM MESSAGE

One of the messages I received in a dream was from an elderly woman who simply said, "Consciousness." I wasn't able to identify who the woman was, but her message was impactful. Many of my dreams had only one or two words, and left a lot to my interpretation. That was not an easy task. I remember waking up and *feeling* the message above all else. It left such an impression on me that I started to look for its meaning. What was the woman trying to tell me? Did I need to get to a level of "consciousness?" whatever that meant.

I pondered and reflected on that word and its meaning for months. I paged through many books trying to better understand what consciousness meant. Clearly, I hadn't been practicing it. Many of the books talked about the thoughts in our minds, the ego, and the importance of not identifying with those thoughts. In *A New Earth*, Eckhart Tolle writes that our inner purpose is awareness and being. He suggests allowing consciousness to come through us. In *The Untethered Soul*, Michael Singer writes about observing our thoughts and not attaching to or identifying with them. He recommends we simply become aware of our thoughts, the constant chatter in our minds.

The Untethered Soul was an eye-opener—or rather, a thought-opener—for me. According to *The Untethered Soul*, "Consciousness is the highest word you will ever utter. There is nothing higher or deeper than consciousness. Consciousness is pure awareness of being ... and without awareness of being, or consciousness, there is nothing. ...You live in the seat of consciousness ... now you are in the center of consciousness. You are aware that there are thoughts, emotions, and a world coming in through your senses. But now you're aware that you are aware."[1]

Try this if you wish: imagine your kitchen and picture yourself seated at a table in your kitchen eating breakfast. Were you able to create this image in your mind? Are you aware that you created the picture of your kitchen in your imagination? That awareness is the consciousness Singer speaks about.

EMBRACING CONSCIOUSNESS

Was the elderly woman encouraging me on my path to consciousness or awareness of being? Was she speaking to me from the place of consciousness? Michael Singer's book is about being in the center of consciousness and our roles as observers watching our thoughts, emotions, and senses. That center is the seat of ourselves. It gave me goosebumps when I realized the elderly wise woman's word was one of the most powerful messages I could receive. I also realized the importance of staying aware of my thoughts. This helped me better understand which were coming from my ego and which were from the heart .

I came across a journal entry from September 30, 2021 about consciousness. I had written that consciousness is the goal of evolution. It's acknowledging who we are and turning ourselves over to God. I also wrote that this is hard to do; there are different levels of consciousness throughout our development.

I was so struck by this message that I gave myself a homework assignment—to remain conscious or aware in each moment of each day, or at least to remind myself to stay aware. The assignment turned out to be a fruitful one. I discovered I am very hard on myself, as I imagine many of us are. I also learned I could be a little too concerned with what others were doing in their lives, so I nudged my thoughts back to myself and how I was feeling at any given moment.

It was shocking how often I was not present in the moment I was in. It has become a regular practice for me to remind me to stay inside myself, and connected to the Higher Power of love within. The message here is that the more aware you are of your inner world, the closer you are to living as your highest self.

STAYING PRESENT

I also discovered the importance of being present in each moment. Becoming more aware of thoughts in my mind allowed me to better understand messages that were coming from my soul, as well as more fear-based messages coming from my ego. The more aware I was, the more I was able to discern the difference and continue to follow my soul's words of encouragement toward a peaceful and loving path.

Carl Jung's quote crossed my path again, "Your vision will become clear only when you look into your heart. Who looks outside, dreams. Who looks inside, awakens."[2] I was first introduced to Jung's theory of the collective unconscious at a retreat on personal and spiritual growth in midlife hosted by Sister M.

Jung's philosophy is that humans—both living and deceased—are all connected with each other through a shared set of experiences. The collective unconscious is a layer of our unconscious mind, which we come into this world with, that connects us to the history of thoughts and behaviors of all mankind. Jung became aware of this idea, in part, from his dreams. He noticed his dreams contained things beyond his own knowledge and experiences. I could relate to that.

I was experiencing the same thing in my dreams. A new message, "Believe in the power within," appeared in another dream. The celestial synchronicities continued to appear confirming I was interpreting the lessons correctly. Jung believed we could access the collective unconscious via our dreams and interpret the wisdom we are receiving. For example, my dream of an elderly woman could be a sign to continue to be the observer of my thoughts and that this is an important message for living a soul-based life. I believe we receive direction and messages in many ways through dreams and conversations with others.

The topic of the collective unconscious also came up recently with one of my closest friends at dinner. When I was reintroduced to the topic a second time, I was convinced this was an important message. Once I became aware, I recognized I was being guided by a celestial family which seemed to include God, my mom, my dad, and others who had passed on to the next dimension through messages, dreams, conversations with others, and nudges. "To be aware that you are watching the voice talk is to stand on the threshold of a fantastic inner journey," Michael Singer writes in his book, *The Untethered Soul.* My filter was open, my awareness was becoming much sharper, and I was in the midst of a "fantastic inner journey."

Soul Searching:

- Set an alarm on your phone. When it goes off, take a few minutes to be present in that moment.
- Ask yourself, "Am I aware now?" one time during the day. What do you notice and how do you feel when you ask yourself this question?
- Take notes on how aware you feel.
- Keep a notebook and pen at your bedside to record any messages you may receive from your dreams. Are there any recurring messages?

- Take a five-minute break from social media and sit in silence. Be present with your thoughts as an observer.

Song suggestion:

"The Secret O' Life," by James Taylor

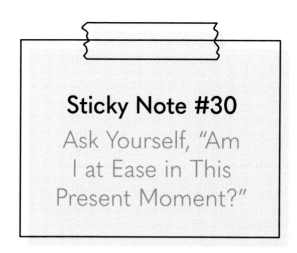

Sticky Note #30

Ask Yourself, "Am I at Ease in This Present Moment?"

"The power for creating a better future is contained in the present moment. You create a good future by creating a good present."

—ECKHART TOLLE

Rhonda Byrnes writes a great deal about the importance of being aware of our thoughts in her book, *The Secret.* "All your power is in your awareness of that power, and through holding that power in your consciousness. ... When you are aware, you are in the present and you know what you are thinking. You have gained control of your thoughts, and that is where all your power is."[1] Awareness and observing our thoughts seemed to be crucial to staying in the present moment. And acceptance of the present moment seemed to be the key to accessing the peace and serenity within the soul.

Since asking myself questions was part of my daily routine, I added another one, "Am I at ease in this present moment?" at different times of the day, in various situations, to bring myself instantly back to the present moment. Give it a try now—ask yourself, "Am I at ease in this present moment?" Do you notice how you are transported immediately to the moment you're in? I was shocked at how often my thoughts drifted to the past through different memories or to the future as I imagined what might or might not happen; I was not in the present moment as often as I thought I was.

Asking a simple question like this one snapped me right back to the present moment and brought me in touch with the thoughts in my mind. This practice helped me to begin to train my mind. Our thoughts are powerful and have the ability to create our world as we see them; changing the thoughts to positive ones was critical and empowering. I viewed training my mind like training a puppy—with a great deal of gentle, positive, and consistent encouragement to learn new healthy and loving habits.

When I was aware that my inner dialogue was not self-loving, I would gently tell myself, "No, we're not going there," and immediately felt the shift in a more positive direction. The irony is that as I write these words, I am taking care of my son's and his girlfriend's five month old great dane puppy, Topo. Rewarding her positive behaviors and helping her learn to repeat those actions seemed to also be a good tactic to use to train my mind to hold more positive thoughts than negative ones.

In *The Power of Now*, Eckhart Tolle talks about the importance of staying connected to our inner being. Having felt the connection to that space which I refer to as, the soul, and the peace and love that come from that space, I wanted to learn how to return there as often as possible during the course of a busy day. The way to connect deep within to the peaceful place seemed to start with shifting from obsessive mental dialogue in the head and placing attention on the soothing place within.

Eckhart discusses directing consciousness into the inner body. He suggests the way to know what's going on in our minds is to feel the emotion in our bodies. An emotion is the body's reaction to the mind. He recommends asking yourself, "What's going on inside me at this moment?"[2]

This is interesting because a big part of the Spiritual Exercises revolves around the importance of getting in touch with our inner beings by asking, "How am I feeling?" several times throughout the day. In both cases, the message is to focus on our emotions within our bodies, not through judgment or analysis, but rather through observation. Become a watcher of your mind and you will become present. Start asking yourself, "Am I at ease in this present moment?"

FINDING THE POWER IN PRESENCE

In *The Power of Now*, Eckhart teaches us to "be the ever-alert guardian of your inner space."[3] He further describes being unconscious as being identified with some mental or emotional pattern in which one can never experience peace. "Once you have understood the basic principle of being present as the watcher of what happens inside you—and you 'understand' it by experiencing it—you have at your disposal the most potent transformational tool. ... Identification with the mind creates a false self (the ego) as a substitute for your true self rooted in Being."[4]

The ego lives in a state of fear and want. I was connecting the dots between messages from various spiritual teachers. Many teachers wrote about the ego as our *false self* and the Higher Power within as our *true self*. The lesson of detaching from our mental and emotional static seemed an important one, and awareness of our mental and emotional activity appeared to be the first step toward that detachment. In other words, do our best to live as watchers of our minds and feelings, and not identify or attach with them—simply observe them. That seems to be the key to being present in each moment. It makes sense because we wouldn't be attached to our thoughts or feelings and would be open to notice what is happening in each moment.

As I reread *The Power of Now*, I realized I had been living in a state of fear recently once again and had been allowing my thoughts to take over. I had lost my connection to my inner being and forgotten this very important and powerful message—to sit as an observer of my thoughts and emotions and not get lost in them. Doing that connects me with the present moment.

I also realized I had been living with a great deal of anxiety about things that hadn't even happened. I was lost in my worried thoughts. I was projecting forward and not accepting and being fully present in each moment. As I write these words, I understand my realizing I haven't been present means I am present at this moment. The importance of watching our thoughts, emotions, and reactions cannot be underestimated! Easy to say, but difficult to do as evidenced in my recent spiral of fear and worry.

The important point is to remind ourselves everyday to continue to be an observer of our thoughts as often as possible. Watching my thoughts on a regular basis brought me away from my frenzied mind into the present moment and closer to the place of peace deep within.

OBSERVER OF YOUR THOUGHTS

Perhaps you can try this now—for a couple of minutes, tell yourself you are going to watch and observe your thoughts, without judging or analyzing them. Notice how often your attention is on past situations or possible future situations. Keep asking yourself, "Am I at ease in this present moment?" to remind yourself your task is to simply observe your thoughts. Attachment to the past and the future are denials of the now, which is all we have. Presence is the key to freedom and peace!

I have made a promise to myself to do my best to monitor my inner state daily by asking myself, "Am I at ease in this present moment?" throughout the day, as Eckhart suggests. This keeps me in touch with what's going on inside me, my internal compass. Writing these words now shifts my attention back to being present, and, quite frankly, lifts a great deal of anxiety I have been feeling over the past couple of months. It's important to be aware of our present moment, accept it with no resistance, and take action to change it if we feel inclined to do so. I feel more at peace in my body when speaking those words aloud as I write them. Eckhart suggests we either change our situation if we can or simply accept it without resisting or judging it. "What we resist persists."[5]

I started practicing Eckhart's recommendation. When I noticed my mind going down a rabbit hole of negativity and what-ifs, I shifted to gratitude and awareness of each present moment and tried my best to ask myself "Am I at ease in this present moment?" to connect to the place of peace deep within. I included a practice of monitoring my emotional and mental states in my daily routine.

It makes sense to check in with our emotional and mental states as we do our physical bodies when exercising or checking our total number of steps for the day. It is all connected—mind, body, and spirit. One of the main points of *Practicing The Power of Now—Essential Teachings, Meditations, and Exercises from The Power of Now,* is to stay in a permanent connectedness with our inner bodies—to feel our inner bodies at all times. Eckhart writes:

> The more consciousness you direct into the inner body, the higher its vibrational frequency becomes, much like a light

that grows brighter as you turn up the dimmer switch and so increase the flow of electricity. At this higher energy level, negativity cannot affect you anymore, and you tend to attract circumstances that reflect this higher frequency. If you keep your attention in the body as much as possible, you will be anchored in the Now. You won't lose yourself in the external world, and you won't lose yourself in your mind. Thoughts and emotions, fears and desires may still be there to some extent, but they won't take you over.[6]

Jon Kabat-Zinn also writes about the importance of being fully present in each moment in his book, *Wherever You Go, There You Are.* He says, "You can easily observe the mind's habit of escaping from the present moment for yourself. Just try to keep your attention focused on any object for even a short period of time. You will find that to cultivate mindfulness, you may have to remember over and over again to be awake and aware. We do this by reminding ourselves to look, to feel, to be. It's that simple … checking in from moment to moment, sustaining awareness across a stretch of timeless moments, being here, now."[7]

FOCUSING INWARD

Perhaps you can try your best to keep your attention within as often as you can each day, and to feel your whole body from within as a single field of energy. Eckhart calls this practice the art of inner-body awareness. As I write these words, I feel my whole body and am aware that I am in a state of peace and contentment, which I attribute to focusing on the present moment with acceptance. There is no resistance. The main principle is to accept each moment fully. That helps us be at ease in the present moment and at ease with ourselves.

Based on my experience, Eckhart's method works. The present moment is all we have, and awareness of our mental and emotional states helps connect us to the present moment and begin to lead a much healthier life. It's similar to checking the exercise activity on our phones—now start checking your mental and emotional activity. How often do you check in with how you're feeling?

It's interesting—other teachers taught similar concepts. For example, Sister M has gently reminded me several times over the past couple of years to stay within myself, connected to my inner being, and to feel my feet planted firmly on the ground, especially in the presence of others. I tend to pick up on others' energy and lose myself in their energy.

Michael Singer also writes about stepping back from the negative chatter in our minds. Eckhart Tolle, Carl Yung, and Michael Singer all write about the importance of staying connected inside our bodies and watching our minds, not attaching to our minds and our thoughts—the same messages, just different language.

WE ARE NOT OUR THOUGHTS

It was transformative for me to discover how lost I had been in my thoughts. I felt empowered with a practice to observe my thoughts and not attach to them or get lost in them. "Be a watcher of our thoughts," Michael Singer reminds us. I still have to remind myself quite often during the day not to spiral down the rabbit hole of negative thought patterns. It requires consistent practice and discipline.

As a watcher, I've noticed in my own life I sometimes assume people are mad at me. My thoughts make up stories and assumptions of what could have happened. I've since come to learn that's not the case at all. Now I simply remind myself this is an assumption with no factual basis. I usually hear from those I originally thought might have been mad at me at some point, and we connect just as closely as before, and all is well. This is an example of how the stories in our minds can lead us down the wrong path and are wasted energy.

The Untethered Soul is about disengaging from our negative thoughts and letting the thoughts flow through. The important lesson is that you are the one who is watching; you are pure consciousness. Soul School doesn't necessarily have grades but rather messages along the way to let you know you are on track and advancing on your journey. I am forever grateful for the elderly and wise woman who gently spoke the word "consciousness" in my dream. I think I understand the message a little more now—we are pure consciousness, pure awareness.

Michael Singer suggests a few additional practices to help us remain centered and aware as watchers of our minds. Every time you get in the car to go somewhere, stop for a moment, and remind yourself not to get caught up in the drama in your mind. This same technique can be used before picking up the phone or opening a door to enter a room. The key is to check in with yourself—your heart, mind, shoulders, and trigger points in your body. Once you are aware, you can feel the tension when it hits and do your best to relax your body and let it pass through.

I'm still working on that exercise of viewing the pain as energy passing through. I am trying my best to keep my heart open. That's a difficult one, but I realize how important it is to live a life of loving big. It's not easy to keep an open heart after you've been hurt and you begin to feel each time the heart is wounded. I believe a person hasn't lived a full life if they've closed their heart because they may be cutting themselves off from love. I wish you a life of acceptance and awareness in each present moment and an open heart every step of the way.

Soul Searching:

- As Eckhart Tolle and Jon Kabat-Zinn suggest, start asking yourself questions to strengthen your self-awareness.
- Am I hearing from my mind or my heart?
- How often do I let my mind wander away from the present moment?
- If I want to settle into the present moment, what is my best first step?
- Check in with yourself once a day—jot down in a small journal what's going on in your mind.
- What are you thinking about?
- Ask yourself, "Am I aware at this moment?"
- Gradually increase the frequency of how often you check in with your mind. You will begin to understand your thoughts, recognize you're not your thoughts, and detach from them.
- Consider this as checking your mental activity as you might check your exercise activity and steps for the day.
- How many times did you check in with your mind and ask yourself, "What am I thinking in this moment?"
- How do you feel within your body after checking in with your feelings?

Song suggestion:

"Peace Train," by Yusuf/Cat Stevens

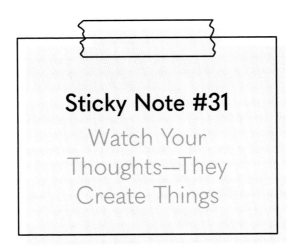

Sticky Note #31
Watch Your Thoughts—They Create Things

"Since thoughts are a form of vibration (word) and, since all things in the universe are made of vibrations, a thought once harbored in the mind will become a seed for creative power. It will sooner or later sprout and exert an influence, not just on our own lives but on all humanity, spreading out over the latter, and becoming a creator with an increasingly more formidable power."

—MASAHARU TANIGUCHI

Not only was I understanding the importance of being an observer of my thoughts, I was also learning that our thoughts are extremely powerful and can create the life we want. In my experience, in order to connect to the peaceful place within, it is necessary to quiet the noise in the mind. I was observing the thoughts in my mind, and I was also feeling the effects of those thoughts in my body. The practice of disengaging from our thoughts, and simply observing them was helping me connect more with what I was feeling and not push the feelings away. It was helping me connect to my inner voice. It was also helping me make decisions in my life by tuning into how it felt in my body with certain decisions. Awareness of my thoughts served many purposes.

And, I was recognizing the tremendous power our thoughts have over not only our bodies, but also the creation of our lives; our thoughts in many ways are how we see the world. I'm a big believer in the idea that each of us has the power to manifest our dreams and create the lives we want. Indeed, I've read *The Secret* so many times that the pages are falling out of the book. I read it one summer when I was in a pool and accidentally fell into the water, but I never let go of the book. I went under the water, but held the book up in the air. When I need a reminder about manifestation and the power of our thoughts, I reach for *The Secret*.

THE LAW OF ATTRACTION

The Secret is about the Law of Attraction and the power our thoughts have to create the lives we want, and it shares stories of others who have done just that. Focusing our minds and thoughts on our desires and holding that focus communicates to the universe what we want and sets it in motion.

The concept of the Law of Attraction can be found in various belief systems, phrased slightly differently. Luke 11: 9-10 says, "And I tell you, ask and you will receive; seek and you will find; knock and the door will be opened to you. For everyone who asks, receives; and the one who seeks, finds; and to the one who knocks, the door will be opened."[1] That was the scripture verse I found myself repeating in my dad's ears shortly before he passed away.

The simple message of the Law of Attraction is we attract what we focus our thoughts and energy on. We are like magnetic energy fields pulling towards us what we think about. If that's true, it's very important to become aware of the images we are holding in our minds!

Rhonda Byrne writes in *The Secret*, "You are a human transmission tower, and you are more powerful than any television tower created on earth. You are the most powerful transmission tower in the Universe. Your transmission creates your life and it creates the world. The frequency you transmit reaches beyond cities, beyond countries, beyond the world. It reverberates throughout the entire Universe. And you are transmitting that frequency with your thoughts."[2] If you want to change something in your life, try changing your thoughts. In my experience, if nothing else happens, at least you shifted your thoughts in a positive and hopeful direction.

Have you ever thought about someone in your mind, and then had that person reach out to you? According to *The Secret*, our thoughts are energy, and we can transmit energy about someone into the universe to be received by the other person. I like to picture myself as a big magnet, as *The Secret* suggests. I visualize and feel my inner heart and soul as one gigantic magnet that radiates love outward and attracts love back with tremendous force.

Just the other day, after I had been thinking about a friend of mine for a couple of days, she called me out of the blue. A coincidence? Perhaps. But why not be open to the possibility that our thoughts hold a lot of power? There's nothing to lose but much to be gained.

Part of my daily practice is to sit quietly in the early mornings and imagine three simple things that would make each day great. These are very simple activities such as going for a run, sending a note to someone I love, or reading a book for twenty minutes. The idea is that this exercise helps me tune into my desires and take small steps in that direction.

Silence allows me to become aware of my thoughts, control them, and make sure they're on the same wavelength as the desires in my heart. This doesn't have to be a long practice; five or ten minutes will allow you to ask, receive, and feel. As *The Secret* also suggests, "To become aware of your thoughts, you can also set the intention, *I am the master of my thoughts.* Say it often, meditate on it, and as you hold to that intention, by the law of attraction you must become that."[2]

In one of my journal entries from December 2020, I wrote about a dream with a simple, clear message: "My thoughts create." I awoke and wrote that message down immediately. My dreams were providing inspirational messages. To quote my dad, "You can't make this stuff up."

You may be reading this and thinking *that hasn't happened in my life. I've thought about a lot of things that never happened.* I can't disagree with you. But consider this, for the rest of your time here on this planet, are you open to the idea you may have a Higher Power within you? If you answered yes or even maybe, wouldn't that mean you possess a power that has the ability to create? Afterall, that power created you. Why not give it a try? What do you have to lose?

For the next week, perhaps you can remind yourself your thoughts are powerful and try your best to choose them wisely. Shift them, as best you can, to what you would like to create in your life; the way you would like your life to be. If nothing else, at least you're spending your time in a positive and healthy way.

Soul Search:

- Take a moment to sit quietly.
- Consider your thoughts in the present moment. Shift any negative thoughts.
- Journal about your greatest wishes and desires.
- Take a few minutes to write three things that would make your day great. Keep it simple and write some

small things you can make happen such as going to bed earlier or making time in your day for a ten-minute walk, or sending someone you love a quick note.

- Remind yourself, "I am the master of my thoughts," when negative thinking shows up. This helps to shift thoughts in a more positive direction.

Song suggestion:

"Hold On (Change is Comin')," by Sounds of Blackness

Sticky Note #32
Have Silent Hope

"It seems to me that one of the greatest gifts that AA offers to its people is hope. Without hope, it is very hard to proceed in any direction…Hope is very closely related to openness to the Higher Power, because we depended on ourselves and our emotional programs for happiness that we got sick in the first place."

—THOMAS KEATING

The messages in my dreams were more frequent, typically only having one or two words, but they sure left an imprint on my heart. Another simple yet powerful dream message I received was, "Have silent hope."

It was interesting. I never received an explanation of the message, just the message itself. I was relying on the power of the celestial synchronicities to help me better understand the messages, since a few words usually weren't enough for me to fully grasp the meaning. I remember when I received this message, I quietly whispered it to myself during the day to feel my way into it.

Perhaps you would like to try it now; whisper to yourself, "Have *silent hope*." How does that phrase make you feel? Do you feel a sense of calm flow through you? Do you feel a sense of excitement and hope? Do you feel a sense of knowing that all will be well? Do you feel at peace with what is? Those are a few of the feelings that the message instills in me. Hope is uplifting and gives us an anchor to hold onto amid our stormy days. *The Word Among Us* encourages us to, "Hold onto hope as an anchor for your soul."[1]

I not only believed in the power of stillness and quiet, but I was committed to practicing it on a daily basis. Having experienced the peaceful presence of the soul, it's hard to go back to the noisy world of the ego. However, the transition takes practice, patience, and work. A few minutes sitting in quiet allows me to tune in to my inner self. Silence allows us to listen to the voices in our hearts. As Father Thomas Keating suggests, "Be silent, but alert." Father Keating also says we should, "Sit down and shut up." Silence and stillness could not be emphasized enough.

PRACTICING PATIENCE

This message seemed to serve as a reminder to be patient and wait on God's timing. Sitting in silence and stillness is hard. I always thought I needed to be doing more; it was hard to simply sit and be. I was impatient most days because I wanted to know what God wanted me to do next and how I could be more helpful in the world. "Have silent hope" was a reminder to sit in silence, be patient, wait, and have hope.

Waiting can be challenging—it was for me. In fact, a friend from my spiritual direction class and I were talking recently about the difference between actively waiting and passively waiting. I like to believe I was *actively waiting* as I reminded myself to stay alert and aware. I was in search of answers as to where I should go and what I could be doing to help others.

"A waiting person is a patient person. ... It is in active waiting in which we live the present moment to the fullest in order to find there the signs of the one we are waiting for."[2] Henri Nouwen's words were encouragement to persevere with patience. Learning to accept and embrace each day and trust in God's timing wasn't always easy. "Waiting patiently in expectation is the foundation of the spiritual life,"[3] Nouwen's contemporary, Simone Weil, tells us.

One of the daily meditations I read in *The Word Among Us— Daily Meditations for Catholics* summed it up perfectly, "While we're waiting, God is doing something in that silence that he couldn't do without that silence. ... The more you recognize the ways God is acting, the more you will realize that he has not abandoned you; he is with you even in your waiting ... even if you've been waiting a long time, don't lose hope."[5] And there it was: *silent hope.*

Soul Searching:

- When can you take five minutes and sit in silence?
- Before you begin, whisper to yourself *I have silent hope* a few times, and then sit in silence.
- How does it feel when you quietly repeat to yourself the words, "silent hope?"
  - » How does your body react to hearing the message, *I have silent hope?*
- Locate some places where you can practice silent hope without distraction, then try them out.

- Is there something you've been waiting for an answer to from God? Are you actively waiting?

Song suggestion:

"Smile," by Nat King Cole

Sticky Note #33
Manifest Your Dreams

"Within you is a divine capacity to manifest and attract all that you need or desire…When you know your highest self, you are on your way to becoming a co-creator of your entire world… you literally become a manifester."

—DR. WAYNE DYER

Okay—let's have some fun. Whether or not you believe in a Higher Power that lives within you, you're here now reading this chapter. Would you rather live embracing the idea that you are a manifester of your dreams or not? For the rest of the time I have here on this planet, I'm going with yes—I believe I'm a manifester of my dreams.

Let me share a story with you. As I was rereading my journal entries, I came across one from August 2015, when I traveled to Italy with my sons to celebrate my younger son's twenty-first birthday and my fiftieth birthday. It was the trip of a lifetime! We spent two weeks together on the Amalfi Coast simply enjoying our time with each other, being fully present with each other, and sharing our dreams with each other. There was no agenda other than quality time together.

Here are a couple of my journal entries from 2015:

- "The secret to life: keep this relaxed state—my whole body is relaxed. My mind is full of creative ideas, not worries, not work, nothing negative. Creativity is flowing. When the mind and body is relaxed, creative ideas flow."
- "I want to transition away from the business by my mid-fifties."

These journal entries had a tremendous impact as I read those words five years later when I was re-reading *The Secret* and realized I was living the words I had written. I was feeling the powerful creative ideas flow with a calm and relaxed mind and body. I also had transitioned from the business in my mid-fifties!

Rhonda Byrne writes, "The Secret is the law of attraction! Everything that's coming into your life you are attracting into your life. And it's attracted to you by virtue of the images you're holding in your mind. ... Whatever is going on in your mind you are attracting to you. ... If you can think about what you want in your mind, and make that your dominant thought, you *will* bring it into your life."[1] Bryne's message was similar to the lesson *Watch your Thoughts—They Create Things* and further confirmed the importance of tuning into our thoughts. Our thoughts have the power to create our lives.

HOW IT FEELS TO MANIFEST

Rereading these journal entries years later was proof for me that it does work to ask, believe, and receive—I was living what I had written in my journal. I reread *The Secret* again to let the simple message fully permeate my body and thoughts and to reinforce the practice of visualizing and manifesting, although somehow I had already done it.

But how had I done it? I had written those words in a very relaxed state and then forgotten about them. I remember when I wrote those words in Italy, I was sitting quietly and simply imagined how I wanted my life to be—my hopes and dreams. I wrote them in my journal, believed, and let them go; I forgot about them. It was similar to when you order something online—there are no doubts and you know it will appear. In fact, I didn't re-read them again until seven years later as I was writing this book.

The process described in *The Secret* to ask, believe, and receive, is similar to the scripture verse from both Matthew 7:7-8 and Luke 11: 9-10 (the same verse I whispered in my father's ear towards the end of his life). This insight empowered me to truly believe in the ability to co-create my life with God. I was feeling this Divine power in my life, becoming aware of insights, and noticing inspirations nudging me in certain directions.

The Secret reminds us, "Inspired action is when you are acting to receive. If you are in action to try and make it happen you have slipped backward. Inspired action is effortless, and it feels wonderful because you are on the frequency of receiving … when you are acting to make something happen it will feel as if you are going against the current of the river. It will feel hard and like a struggle"[2] I could relate to Byrne's description of going against the current with certain situations in my life, and other moments when everything seemed to flow so easily.

As I reflected on our time in Italy, I remembered feeling very relaxed, free from the relentless thoughts and chatter in my mind, and very open to whatever came my way. My sons and I spent a lot of time sharing our wishes and dreams with each other. That state seemed to be the key to connecting to the sacred place within and creating the life of my dreams. Clear the mind, detach from negative thoughts as much as possible, and remain open to whatever happens. Openness could not be underestimated.

CO-CREATING WITH DIVINE LOVE

I believe and have felt we are being guided by a greater power and can access that power at any time. Another one of my journal entries from 2015 reads, "Be a prophet and share the miracle of love." Here I sit, years later, with a burning desire to share my story with you—a story of love, Divine love, and how transformative it is.

It's my belief we all have that Divine love within us and are connected through it. If you believe you have Divine power within you, that's pretty powerful, right? Take a few moments and really ponder that statement. If you believe the Divine power lives within you, that means you can access it anytime. You can also allow it to co-create your dreams with you. Shift from your mind now and try to feel that power deep within you. Try to imagine a bright light deep inside of you shining brightly for all to see.

As I reread *The Secret*, I again visualized the areas of my life I wanted to transform. I felt a desire to spread love. I wrote a list of how I wanted to help others feel loved. One of those ways was writing this book to help others on their journeys to the soul. I imagined a movement of the soul.

I not only imagined these things. I also allowed myself to feel the feelings as if those things already existed in my life. According to *The Secret*, a key part of the manifestation process is to feel the feelings as if you had already received your wishes. I visualized sharing the message with others about the power of this Divine love. I felt joyous and grateful. I imagined Oprah Winfrey reading this book and speaking with her about my journey to my soul. I felt ecstatic and honored to be in her presence. Meeting Oprah Winfrey and thanking her for her commitment to helping others live their best lives has always been a dream of mine, especially because Oprah's *Super Soul Sunday* podcast helped me learn about the ego, the false self, and the soul—the highest self.

After I visualized and felt the feelings of receiving these wishes, I made a vision board of my dreams in other areas of my life: family, relationships, service to others, career, health and wellness, and learning. I visualized each aspect of my life, wrote how I would like it to be, and glued pictures that represented my vision and dreams onto the board. Think of it like you're making wishes for your birthday and blowing out candles on your cake.

I believe what I did next is one of the most critical pieces of this practice. I let my dreams and wishes go. I imagined them as balloons floating into space. I truly surrendered them to God, and I thanked God for the many blessings I had already received. Surrendering and letting go is of the utmost importance in manifesting our dreams. That's what I had done in Italy. I had detached from all outcomes, believed, and truly let go. In truth, I forgot what I had written in the journal once we had returned home and I continued my hectic and active life.

I could see God brings those whom we need and those who need us at precisely the right moments. The many people whom God brought into my life were and still are important souls who taught me valuable lessons, and I hope I helped them in some way, too.

I believed and felt God's presence with me all along as a co-creator of my life. I shed many tears on this journey (of both sadness but also of tremendous gratitude) as I slowly allowed my heart to open and felt the powerful Divine love inside of me that had been there all along. I hadn't recognized it for most of my life because I was too busy looking outward, and not inward.

Sue Monk Kidd also wrote about co-creating our lives with God in her book, *When the Heart Waits*. I began to think that if I combined ideas and practices from *The Secret* with the concept of co-creating my life with God, anything would be possible!

So, how exactly do you manifest your dreams? Here are some practices I've incorporated into my life thanks to *The Secret*:

WRITE IN A JOURNAL

I've been writing in journals for a long time. A few weeks before my birthday each year, I ask myself what some of my wishes are for the upcoming year and I write them down. Every so often, I reread some of my older wishes. I continue to be amazed that many of the wishes I've written have often come true. I'll give you a couple of examples:

- More than ten years ago—I wrote that I wanted to live in a house near the ocean and down south somewhere. I now live in South Carolina on a small body of water a short drive from the ocean.
- Seven years ago—I wrote that I wanted to be a messenger of love. Here I am, sharing the message: Divine Love is Transformative. I don't even remember writing this wish of being a messenger of love.

Having a vision for our lives is similar to setting a navigation system for a destination when driving. It gives our lives direction and a sense of purpose. It also helps us understand ourselves and our desires.

CREATE A VISION BOARD

A vision board is a gathering of pictures and words of what you would like to manifest in your life, glued or taped to a poster board or in a journal or book. It doesn't have to be fancy. You are transferring the desires from your heart into images. Look at magazines and see what captures your attention.

I've also added phrases from magazines to the photos that are in my journal and combined both techniques. This practice has helped me understand what's important to me in my life and what I would like to create. It helps me see what I'm attracted to. The key is to sit down, even if only for five minutes, and to start imagining what you want in all areas of your life. Start dreaming! As you start to imagine and dream, creative ideas may flow from your heart. Imagine yourself in ten years—what do you want to be doing? How do you see yourself? What decisions would you like to see yourself making now?

Looking back, I realize I used the power of visualizing and a different form of vision boarding at work. I remember setting goals to help our clients across the country with project work, and to that end, I purchased a large map of the United States for my office. We tracked each state in which we were working with clients. I also set a goal that we would help a certain number of new clients on a small project over the course of a year. I hung a paper poster board on the wall of my office and wrote the name of every new client that year. I visualized helping new clients and believed we would reach our target. And we did!

I was reminded of the powerful effect of vision boards recently when meeting with a friend. He was telling me about a house he had just bought, which needed quite a bit of work. As he was describing the historic house to me, he said, "Wait a minute. I'll show you."

He came back with a poster that included pictures of every room in the house alongside images and words conveying how he was going to change each room. I smiled and said to him that I loved the idea of a vision board. He shared with me that he had used vision boards in his previous career.

A lightbulb went off in my head—visualizing can be used in many areas of our lives. Dr. Denis Waitley shares the following story about the power of visualization in *The Secret*, "We took Olympic athletes and had them run their event only in their mind, and then hooked them up to sophisticated biofeedback equipment. Incredibly, the same muscles fired in the same sequence when they were running the race in their mind as when they were running it on the track. How could this be? Because the mind can't distinguish whether you're really doing it or whether it's just a practice."[3]

After that visit with my friend, I decided to create a new vision board for the next career phase of my life, which I hoped would be focused on following my passion and desire to help others in some way. Inspired by my friend, I took a small notebook and jotted down ways I could help others.

What typically happens is that when I begin to visualize and plan, a multitude of ideas flow into my mind. I was reminded of a program that had interested me months ago, read the requirements, and began to write categories in my journal—letters of recommendation, essay questions, books I've read, volunteer activities, past professional experiences, résumé, et cetera.

I circled each category and filled in information as it came to me. For example, under the heading "Letters of Recommendation," I thought about past colleagues and wrote down the names of specific people I could reach out to. In the résumé category, I wrote, "Need a plan." I had worked at the same company for most of my life and never had a need for a résumé.

Under that category, I also wrote, "Find someone to help and find templates." I found that this exercise excited me, helped me tune in to my desire to help others in a positive way, and gave me a road map toward achieving my goals.

Here's what happened a few weeks after I created the vision ideas in my notebook:

- I completed an online course and became certified as a professional life coach.
- I came up with a way I might be able to help others.
- I created a name for a company to help others.
- I established a corporation.
- I secured the domain name for the company.
- I wrote up the services I would like to provide.
- I wrote a mission statement.
- I imagined myself helping others.

Things were beginning to fall into place. As if that weren't enough, a friend of mine asked me to speak with her friend who was at a crossroads in her life. My friend said, "I don't know why I'm asking you this, but I feel like the two of you should meet." I hadn't mentioned anything about the program I had completed or the fact that my mission was to work with people at a crossroads in their lives. I was completely blown away.

I had a similar experience when I ran into an acquaintance, and she introduced me as a "person who teaches classes on how to stay positive." I still have no idea where that one came from but I remain open to see what happens next. I remembered a story that Eckhart Tolle shared with Oprah Winfrey that he didn't know what his purpose was until someone introduced him as a spiritual teacher many years ago. Perhaps I will be teaching about staying positive someday? I'll keep you posted.

BELIEVE YOUR DREAMS
WILL BECOME REALITY

After you imagine, write down, and create a vision board of your dreams and desires, let them go and BELIEVE. The main character from the popular television series, Ted Lasso, hung a motivational sign in the football team's locker room that simply said, "Believe." It's not up to you to figure out exactly *how* it will happen or *when*. Just believe. Feel the feelings of having received your desires. Be grateful for receiving them. Simply believe and have faith. And let them go like balloons in the air.

Imagining and envisioning how you want your life may seem overwhelming at first. Where do you even begin?

Keep it simple. Perhaps start with a few basic affirmations of your wishes in life; what are some of your hopes and dreams? Think about different areas of your life—family, relationships, career, living situation, and travel. Being grateful for what you already have now is also key. I felt very grateful for having already received more than enough in my life, and it didn't seem right to ask for anything more.

Looking back now, I realize once I embraced some space in the beginning of my journey and hit the pause button, the people, places, and events came to me; everything flowed easily. It was like a dam had broken open, with the water now flowing naturally and gently. All I had to do was remain open and aware of what was flowing into my life. My pivot into the unknown brought to me the people and things that were meant for me; the teachers, books, and lessons all came to me. I began to realize I already possessed many of the dreams and desires in my heart that were on my vision board.

Soul Searching:

- What do you want to manifest in your life? Imagine some of your desires and things you're attracted to.
- Perhaps you remember some dreams you had when you were younger? What were your dreams when you were twelve or thirteen years old?
- Write down some wishes or find pictures in a magazine of things you would like in your life.
- Picture yourself in five years. What do you see yourself doing?
- Create a vision board to make your desires easily accessible when you need a reminder of those things that are on their way to you.
- What are three birthday wishes you hope for yourself this year? Maybe you can write them down and imagine you've received them. Write how you feel having received them.

Song suggestion:

"Magnet and Steel," by Walter Egan

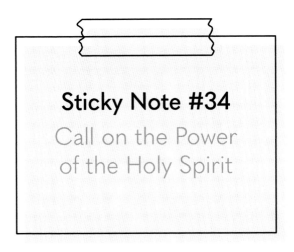

Sticky Note #34

Call on the Power of the Holy Spirit

"Henri believed that the Holy Spirit is an inner presence who is the deep center of our new life in Christ, a center from which discernment blossoms. ... And we need to keep scanning our inner and outer lives to be sure that we are taking everything into account, scanning for signs of the Spirit's presence, noticing its invitations, and listening for what Henri called 'the voice of the beloved.'"

—ROBERT A. JONAS

In Soul School, I began the practice of calling on the Holy Spirit on a regular basis. I had been taught in my Catholic upbringing that the Holy Spirit was the third person of the Trinity (The Father and Son being the first and second), and the Trinity was one God in the Father, the Son, and the Holy Spirit. The Trinity concept was always a difficult concept for me to grasp. I decided to simply imagine the Holy Spirit as God's Spirit. In essence, the Holy Spirit is God's spirit within us. I was counting on the Holy Spirit to help me live as my highest self. Marianne Williamson recommends we ask the Holy Spirit for a miracle when we need one. "The Holy Spirit uses everything to lead us into inner peace,"[1] she writes in *A Return to Love—Reflections on the Principles of A Course in Miracles.*

I now imagined the Holy Spirit as my counselor in Soul School. I began to ask the Holy Spirit for signs of confirmation that I was understanding messages I had received correctly and following the promptings of where to go or what to do next. I asked the Holy Spirit to hover over me.

According to the January 2020 issue of *The Word Among Us*, "Everyone who has been baptized into Christ has received his Holy Spirit. The Holy Spirit is the inner voice of love. He is that still, small voice in the back of your mind urging you to forgive your coworker for what she said about you. He's the tap on your shoulder pointing out a neighbor who seems lonely. He's the quick catch in your throat that arises when you are about to say something inappropriate or hurtful."[2]

I've also experienced the Holy Spirit when certain messages resonated with me or insights came to me. I imagine these as gentle prods of the Holy Spirit, nudging us on the path to peace and love. Have you ever received insights and guidance in various forms? From something someone said, or a central message that seemed to keep repeating itself in your life?

I was sensing these nudges or gentle prods in my life. The Holy Spirit seemed to dwell in the peaceful place which seemed to be my soul. Here I was, someone who had been baptized as an infant and received the Holy Spirit, yet I'd had little contact with this Divine spirit for most of my life. As a Christian, I do believe God lives in us through his Holy Spirit, which is the spirit of God. I respect what others believe, and I don't believe there is only one way to access this Higher Power.

In my humble opinion, it's all about love, and I believe we are all connected through this Divine love which answers to many names. We all have the ability to ask this Spirit or Higher

Power to open our hearts in new and unexpected ways. It's a matter of following the inner voice of love, the Divine Spirit, within your soul.

FOLLOW THE DIVINE LEADER

How do you sense this Higher Power and follow the Spirit's lead? Listen to that still, small voice in the back of your mind nudging you to help someone, or that gentle prod to reach out to someone who you may not have spoken to in a while. Be open. The Higher Power seems to instill feelings of peace, serenity, gratitude, and love.

Every time you act out of love for someone, you are strengthening the foundation of peace and confidence in the Divine Spirit who lives in you and all of us. I believe all souls are connected—both living and deceased—and we are all one through this Higher Power of Divine love. That feels very comforting because it means we are still surrounded by other souls who may have passed on. I include my mom and dad in that category.

Trust this Divine love for you and in you. Let this love fill you. You are a child of Divine love. Once you feel the impact of this, your life will be forever changed. You will begin to live a life from the heart, radiating love to all.

I like how *The Message* describes what the power of the Holy Spirit feels like in Ezekiel 36:26. It reads, "I'll give you a new heart, put a new spirit in you. I'll remove the stone heart from your body and replace it with a heart that's God-willed, not self-willed."[2] I came across a journal entry from November 2020 in which I had written about this passage. My journal entry talked about replacing any negative thoughts with love. I asked God in my letter that day for a new heart filled with goodness and love, and I could feel the new spirit of love and light coming forth.

I begin each prayer time every morning quietly repeating, "Come, Holy Spirit, come." Over the past few years, I have definitely relied on the power of the Holy Spirit to guide me every day toward the path of light and love.

You have Divine presence in you. So, perhaps you can anchor your hopes on this Divine grace and love. This love is always with you and will always be with you through moments of joy and difficult situations. You have a powerful force of Divine power within you waiting for you. Call on this love, this force within you. It will be with you through whatever challenges you may encounter. Perhaps you can say, "Come, Holy Spirit, come." Give it a try.

Soul Searching:

- How can you call on the power of the Holy Spirit? What words will you use?
- When do you feel a Divine spirit in your life?
- Journal about your experiences as you put this into practice!
- What did you say when you called on the Holy Spirit?
- What celestial synchronicities appeared?
- When you received an answer, what happened?
- How does it feel to imagine you may be connected with those you loved who are deceased?

Song suggestion:

"Love's Divine," by Seal

Sticky Note #35
Schedule a Divine Therapy Session

"You turn yourself over to a Higher Power who you believe
can heal you and work with you in the long journey
of dismantling the emotional programs for happiness.
They are the root causes of all our problems."

—THOMAS KEATING

In his book *Divine Therapy and Addiction,* Father Thomas Keating speaks about the human need for happiness. He describes our early childhood needs for "survival and security, affection and esteem and approval, and power and control. ... [E]veryone, of course, is deprived in some degree because no parents are perfect, and, even if they are, they can't control the environment, teachers, and important others that enter the child's life."[1] His statement really resonated with me as I reflected on my early childhood.

Perhaps you can take a minute and reflect on your younger years—was there an area where your needs may not have been met? Maybe a lack of affection or not receiving enough positive feedback? Awareness of an emotional area that may not have been met as a child, as painful as it may be, offers the possibility of recognizing how that unmet need may still be playing out in your life today.

Father Keating's book also introduced me to another practice in Soul School—daily therapy sessions with God. In many ways, God was acting like a therapist. I took everything to him and left nothing out. Thanks to Father Keating, I asked God to help me recognize unmet emotional needs in my life. I pondered and reflected on myself as a child and how my need for esteem and approval played out in my life today. Were those needs met? Was this perhaps the reason I was looking for others' approval at times? The more I asked, the more insights I received, along with help and guidance to address some negative habits from a few unmet needs.

What happened was amazing—I recalled a few childhood incidents that left a negative imprint on my heart. Thankfully, the incidents were minor, but they still left an imprint on that shy and quiet little girl. In my many letters to God, I asked God to help me continue to be aware of childhood wounds, release them, and focus on spreading love and kindness to everyone. I asked for help with my negative self-talk and tendency to compare myself to others. I asked to speak only loving and kind words not only to others, but also to myself. I gave thanks for my many blessings, including loving relationships with my sons and other family members and friends. I asked for help making decisions that would lead me closer to God. The more I asked, the more my heart opened up and the deeper I started to feel.

SURRENDER AND SIMPLICITY

There were even a few times I cried tears of joy and sincere gratitude—feelings of overflowing love, thanks, and awe for the gift of life and the many lessons of love I was learning. My heart was overflowing with love for others. I truly felt the force greater than myself working through me each day. God was my go-to person for everything. I wasn't trying to force anything or change the outcome in any way. God was in charge, and I was leaning on him. I kept asking God to help me lead a simple life made up of many little moments of love and to guide me to others whom I could help. I was trying to live as best I could from what I read from Galatians 5:6, "Faith which expresses itself through love."[2]

I began to start living my life guided by God and love. And I really *believed* in this Higher Power! Once I started asking, God started answering. I felt his grace and love each day. Don't get me wrong. There were many days I had my doubts, but when those moments appeared, I handed them back over to God. I was relentless in relying on him and tried my hardest to begin surrendering to this Higher Power and detaching from any outcome I wanted.

After I brought something to God, I would look for a celestial synchronicity confirming a decision, to see if I was being led in a different direction. I prayed a lot, did my best to follow the promptings of the Holy Spirit, and felt the power of that Divine love. Now that my heart had been cleared out from past hurt, it was more open to giving and receiving love.

Here is a letter I wrote to God to help me stop worrying:

September 22, 2020

Luke 12:22:" Which of you by worrying can add a moment to your life-span? Stop worrying. Do not live in fear."

Dear God,

I realize that I worry a lot, more than I ever knew. I also have a lot of doubts—I journaled quite a lot about my doubts this past week. I have doubts about where I am, what I'm doing, and where I'm headed. Yesterday's journal entry had the word doubt in it eight times. I do believe that you guide us and send us signs, yet I doubt the signs (were they really signs?). I continue to pray that you will strengthen my faith each day. Show me and teach me how to place my trust in you.

Love, Marcella

As my heart was opening, my feelings were all going to God. And he was there. I can't explain it, but he got me through everything. I started remembering pivotal moments when God was there. For example, Maggie, our soulful yellow Lab, passed away peacefully when I was with my sons and family in Nashville celebrating my son's engagement. I remember I had gotten down on my knees a week earlier before I left her and asked God to, "help me help her." I distinctly remember using those exact words. As I write these words, I realize he did help me help her. She passed away peacefully in her sleep without any pain or discomfort.

I visualized God holding his hands out for my heart and soul, which were opening up to him.

Soul Searching:

- When can you schedule a therapy session with God?
- Perhaps you can visualize a Higher Power of love reaching out their hands for you to share with them any hurt you're experiencing or help you may need.
- Describe a time when you felt a Divine force of love or a higher presence in your life.

- Maybe you can write your own letter to God and see what shows up on paper. What insights appear from certain areas in your life where you need help that you weren't aware of?

Song suggestion:

"Have a Talk with God," by Stevie Wonder

Sticky Note #36

Ask Yourself, "Is What I'm About to Do or Say Going to Bring Me Peace?"

"Your mind can be like a runaway steam train if you let it. It can take you off to thoughts of the past, and then take you off to thoughts of the future by taking past bad events and projecting those into your future. Those out-of-control thoughts are creating too. When you are aware, you are in the present and you know what you are thinking. You have gained control of your thoughts, and that is where all your power is."

—RHONDA BYRNE

My daily therapy sessions with God were beginning to make a difference. I was connecting more to the sacred space within me and tuning into guidance from a Higher Power as often as I could. I was committed to leading a life guided by my soul and to continuing to learn how to lead such a life. The sacred space within, the soul, was all about peace and love. Through the various teachings, I was gathering tools to help me stay connected to the place of peace as often as possible. One of the tools I leaned on was asking myself questions during the course of each day. I added another question to the list: "Is what I'm about to do or say going to bring me peace?" This question accomplished two things: it placed me instantly into the present moment, and it reminded me that my desire was to live a soul-based life of peace as often as possible.

BENEFITS OF ASKING YOURSELF QUESTIONS

When you allow yourself to ask yourself certain questions, it brings you into the present moment. Try it now—ask yourself, *"Is what I'm about to do or say going to bring me peace?"* Do you feel a shift to the moment you're in? Did you feel any train of thoughts stop momentarily to answer the question you posed? Asking myself questions helps me stay grounded in the present moment and derails any negative thoughts that may be heading out of control.

Checking in with yourself also helps you to better understand your intentions behind the choices you're about to make, and tune into how you're feeling throughout the day. Having tools to help you make decisions from a place of consciousness, seems to be a more peaceful way of living.

I was asking myself a handful of questions that became helpful tools to keep me stay connected to my inner self even when I was interacting with others, and doing so reminded me to live my life authentically being true to me (now that I had a better understanding of who that was). Asking myself questions helped me feel my feet planted on the ground and not get swept away in others' energy.

As James Van Praagh reminds us, "Regardless of how people and circumstances present themselves to you, when you follow the voice within, you will feel a sense of peace."[1] I was beginning to give the voice within a chance to speak. This helped me make choices that were aligned with my highest self, my soul. I was determined to become more intentional in my daily actions and conversations. Asking myself, *Is what I'm about to do or say going to bring me peace?* reminded me of my intent to be kind to others and emit a peaceful feeling to those I'm with.

This simple question has helped me to pause before delivering messages I might regret, stay focused in the present moment, and stay connected to my soul—the space of peace. It has also helped me make decisions that move me forward toward the direction of love and peace.

Soul Searching:

- Ask yourself the following question when you're speaking with others, "Is what I'm about to do or say going to bring me peace?"
- If the answer is "no," take a moment to pause, reframe it or refrain from saying anything until you find the right words.
- If you find yourself moving away from the peaceful feeling, close your eyes and take three slow breaths in and out, reminding yourself you can always choose peace.
- Try it now: ask yourself, "Is what I'm about to do or say going to bring me peace?" Did that stop any previous thoughts that may have gotten out of control?

Song suggestion:

"Shower The People," by James Taylor

Sticky Note #37
What's Your Mantra?

"Each of us has a mission in life. ... Sometimes the way
to know where you are called to be is to go where you feel
you need to go and be present in that place. Soon you
will know if that place is where God wants you."

—HENRI NOUWEN

If you had to sum up your life's philosophy in one sentence, could you do it? Could you describe how you would like to live your life in one statement? I know I couldn't come up with a short and simple description of how I wanted to live my life each day.

I remember the first few weeks of sitting in my new "space" of silence asking myself a flood of questions like, *Who am I? What am I doing with my life? What's my purpose in life?* I couldn't even answer those simple questions!

I was disappointed with myself that I didn't have a mission or a mantra. I scolded myself with thoughts such as, *Your business had a mission,* and *Other companies and organizations have missions.* Yet I didn't have a personal mission for my life.

Eckhart Tolle reminds us, "Your inner purpose is to awaken. It is as simple as that. You share that purpose with every other person on the planet because it is the purpose of humanity ... Your outer purpose can change over time. It varies greatly from person to person. Finding and living in alignment with the inner purpose is the foundation for fulfilling your outer purpose. It is the basis for true success."[1] Eckhart's words were reassuring, to some extent, because I seemed to be beginning to awaken with the multitude of questions I was asking myself.

CREATING A PERSONAL MANTRA

I'd always had a strong urge and longing to help others and make a difference in the world, to the extent I could, but I didn't know how that would happen. My dad's message to "believe in something bigger than myself" had become ingrained in me now. I remember the early days in the cottage in South Carolina, praying to God and asking to know my purpose. I agree with Henri Nouwen and other spiritual teachers that each of us has a mission. *How could I not know mine?*

I remember thinking to myself that I wanted to come up with a few words to summarize how I hoped to live each day—a short and simple sentence. Maybe if I could come up with a few words as to how I hoped to live my life each day that would at least be a start. Love, kindness, and hope were a few of the words that came from my heart.

Why had I devoted more time on a corporate mission, and no time on a personal one? On one of her *Super Soul Sunday* podcast episodes, Oprah Winfrey shared how she asked God to use her to help others. I decided to do the same. I got down on my knees, closed my eyes and whispered, "God, please use me to help others. Please let me see what you need me to do and go where you need me to go."

My impatience and frustration were rising because I didn't seem to be getting any answers about my mission and purpose in those early days. My inner voice would simply say "Just keep doing what you're doing." In my opinion, I wasn't doing anything. I was simply sitting in silence and talking with God. Many of my journal entries for the first few months of my journey questioned whether I was being selfish by simply being with myself. I received the insight that "any time spent trying to connect with God or a higher being is time well spent." Yet, I still wondered if I was wasting my time, and I had no clue what my purpose, mission or mantra were. Rather than start with a large mission statement, I decided to go for a shorter version, a mantra.

Coming up with a personal mantra—a summary of how you would like to live your life each day—is a big deal and requires a great amount of reflection, silence, knowledge of oneself, and some serious soul connection. At least it did for me. I asked myself, "What's important to me each day?" For me, it was important to live each moment of each day true to my principles and values. But that's not a mantra. So I asked myself again, "What's my mantra?" and, "How do I even come up with a mantra?"

After rereading years of journal entries, writing fifty-two notes from the soul for this book, many brainstorming discussions with my son, and becoming more in touch with my feelings, I think I have my mantra—"Love big." It seems as if this phrase from my son best sums up how I hope to live each day of my life.

I had written, "Spread love," all throughout my journal over the course of ten months of that program. Those words were everywhere in my journal. I remember wondering back then if this was some type of assignment for me, but it seemed fairly trivial. I told myself, "Everyone should love. That's nothing new."

Here I was, receiving insights into my purpose in life, and I was dismissing them because I didn't believe love was significant enough or unique in any way. Me, the very person who noticed love and felt love most days of my life.

Don't worry if you have no idea what your mantra is. It has taken me more than fifty years, more than forty books, hundreds of podcasts on the soul, the Spiritual Exercises Program, hours in prayer, hours in stillness and quiet, hours listening for answers, years of practicing patience, and many conversations with my son to finally reach a better understanding of mine. Thank you, P, for helping me discover my mantra!

The desire to spread love has been with me most of my life, but I thought it was too basic and simple to be considered a purpose or a mission in life. I thought love was too elementary, too simple. I had been trying to live my entire life according to those two simple words for years.

SMALL, BUT MIGHTY

It has taken me fifty-six years to figure out my mission in life and simplify it to a mantra. When I was younger, I thought a person's mission had to be grand and hugely impactful at a global level. I thought a mission was something that would change the world and save lives. After spending the past few years in Soul School, I've come to the realization that a person's purpose in life can in fact be quite small, yet very impactful.

Matthew Kelly reminds us that," you were born to become the best-version-of-yourself."[2] He further writes that when he focuses on being the best-version-of-himself, he is very happy. So the desire to be the best-version-of-ourselves is a good mission in life too.

Part of Soul School's reading list included a simple book entitled *Discovering Your Personal Vocation*, by Herbert Alphonso, SJ. This short book, similar to my purpose in life, is small yet very impactful and is best read very slowly. I believe that thanks to this book, I have come a little closer to understanding my mantra "Love big"—to spread love to everyone and everything. As I write these words, that message still seems small, but its impact resonates with me deeply, and hopefully practicing it can make others' lives a little brighter.

The first time I read Alphonso's little book, nothing happened. I finished the book thinking it was a nice read, but I still had no idea what my purpose or mission in life was. About a year later—with the help of a celestial synchronicity—somehow the book reappeared in my life, thanks to Sister M, who suggested I read it a second time. I dug the book out of my library and again began to read it. This time, however, I read it very slowly, one word at a time. I let each word sink in deeply. I wasn't in a rush. After all, I'd been waiting fifty-six years to discover my mission. What was another couple of weeks? Alphonso's book helped me reflect on times when I felt my heart was uplifted and, to some degree, almost in union with God.

One morning, I sat and pondered this question: During which moments did I feel most connected with God? As I remembered various moments, I realized they were usually moments when I was with people whom I loved deeply, especially my two sons, the loves of their lives, and other family members and friends. The moments typically involved being fully present with the other person and my heart feeling like it was overflowing with love; there was no other place I wanted to be than with them at that moment. I simply wanted to be in their presence—find out how they were feeling and listen to what was new in their lives. I realized the special moments always involved a feeling of love at a very deep level. The love I felt so strongly was hard to put into words, but it was the best feeling.

FOCUS ON LOVE

I have always liked to talk about love, give love, and receive love. I have frequently asked couples over the years to share their "love story" with me. I feel the love between my sons and the loves of their lives. My heart goes out to strangers as well who have shared their stories with me during the course of my days.

For example, just the other day a young woman shared with me how sad she was that her grandmother had passed away. We had an exchange of deep love at the check out area of a grocery store. I listened to her share her story about how close she was to her grandmother and how hard it is going to be for her to move forward without her. I felt her love for her grandmother and her pain from losing her.

When I'm not talking about love, I'm reading about love or listening to podcasts about love and healthy relationships, or I'm watching a movie about love. I recalled the Ignatian Spiritual Exercises and the recurring message I received to "spread love." My journal entries had those two words all through the pages during the course of a year! I also began to see that message reinforced in moments throughout the day.

That feeling of deep love for another and wanting only the best for them always made me happy. I also learned, thanks to Herbert Alphonso, SJ, that one's personal vocation typically has been with one throughout one's life, in different ways. Love certainly has been with me as far back as I can remember.

Once again, I pondered my simple yet impactful mantra, "Love big." I thought back and recognized that I have been interested in the feeling of love since I was very little. I remember at a very young age dancing to love ballads in the living room of our little family house and feeling tremendous joy and happiness.

I remember being fascinated with others' relationships during high school and college and longing to fall in love. I remember feeling such love for my mother. I would call her from a pay-phone (cell phones didn't exist back then) daily from college to hear her voice and chat with her. I just loved spending time with her and simply being in her presence.

I remember a love for my two sons like I'd never experienced the moments they were born; it is still present today and even stronger today as I write these words. I feel the love for my parents, grandparents, brothers, sisters-in-law, nieces, aunts, uncles, cousins, and other family members and friends. I feel deep love for our dog, Matisse, my grandogters—Minnie and Topey, and Maggie (may she rest in peace). I could go on and on. I think you get the picture.

I carry those I love deeply in my heart throughout the day. They are always in my thoughts, my heart, and my soul. Love is a difficult feeling to put into words, but it seemed to be a central theme running through my life. I highly recommend looking back at patterns and feelings in your life at some point. Doing so may help you discover and understand the most important thing in your life.

OUTWARD AND INWARD

The life of looking outward involves doing and movement; the life of looking inward involves being and stillness. It's no wonder I was never able to figure out who I was and what I was meant to do since I was always looking outward. To figure out who you are and what you are meant to do, you must look within. Matthew Kelly writes about his journey to discover his purpose, "Discovering my essential purpose has caused me to realize that happiness is an inside-out job."[3]

I wonder if most people move through life focused outward like I was, not in touch with their inner worlds. I was always focused on others and what they were or were not doing, where I was going next, and what I should be doing next. I had no idea there was a whole world within, and that was the place most deserving of my focus. Do you have a mission statement or mantra?

As I pondered my mantra, which still felt simple and somewhat basic, I came across the following quote from Martin Luther King, Jr. at the top of my daily journal, "We must discover the power of love, the redemptive power of love. And when we discover that, we will be able to make of this old world a new world. Love is the only way."[4] And there it was. Love big.

Soul Searching:

- Time to create your own mantra.
  » Has there been something in your life you've always been passionate about?
  » What excites and motivates you?
  » Has there been a central theme running through your life?
- It's taken me a long time to find mine, so don't worry if yours doesn't come to you immediately. Just keep pondering and stay open. It will come when you are ready.

Song selection:

"I've Got Love On My Mind," by Natalie Cole

Sticky Note #38
Thank Someone

"Adopting an 'attitude of gratitude' can be a practical strategy to get through a tough time. But the kind of gratitude Ignatius was talking about when he tells us to 'give thanks to God our Lord for the favors received' is something deeper and stronger. It's the heart of prayer. Such gratitude is a window into the deepest truth about ourselves—that we are caught up in a relationship with a loving God who is generous beyond our imagining."

—JIM MANNEY

In life, there are no guarantees we'll always be supremely happy as we dance in fields of daisies on days filled with sunshine and rainbows. We all have moments of sadness when we feel down—sadness is a normal part of the human experience. Part of the human condition is all about experiencing ups and downs in the course of our days. And although we have those typical ups and downs, I've found the practice of thanking others helps to shift my perspective and raise my spirits when I'm having a down day. And the best part? It creates a thank-you momentum, putting us on a path of finding many ways to thank others and feel uplifted while doing it.

In his book, *The Jesuit Guide to (Almost) Everything,* James Martin speaks of gratitude: "When you refuse to take things, or people, for granted, and when you are able to take stock of your blessings, your gratitude increases."[1]

With a heart that was more open and practicing awareness of my feelings, the feeling of tremendous gratitude began to take over some of my journal entries. Earlier in my journey, I had begun a practice of replacing fearful thoughts with thoughts of gratitude. Every time I felt worried, I would give thanks for a blessing in my life. Gratitude was flowing naturally and freely. My heart was overflowing with gratitude for the people in my life, the lessons I was learning, and the love I was feeling.

WRITING THANK-YOU NOTES

After my dad passed away, I discovered an index card in his wallet with five questions on it. The fifth question read, "How am I going to show my gratitude to someone else?" I came across the following short letter of gratitude I wrote to God in November 2020, when I decided to replace fear with gratitude:

Dear God,

I choose today and every day to replace each fear with gratitude to you. Every time I start to become afraid, I will thank you for all of my many blessings. I'm converting my past ways of thinking and am reprogramming my thoughts and words.

Love, Marcella

That pact I made to myself and God became a part of me, and the gratitude I felt grew even deeper than I could have imagined. When I've been hurt by others, journaling has allowed me to process the hurt and pain and become aware of any part I may have played in the relationship. It's brought clarity and has allowed me to "accept what is," as Eckhart Tolle suggests we do. Journaling has also allowed me to get in touch with my feelings.

My journal morphed into a gratitude journal in which I give thanks each day for the many blessings I've received. Each day, I write at least three things I am grateful for. Most of my gratitude entries involve relationships with others. Some examples include:

- Writing a book to share some of the lessons I've learned with others
- Learning about the soul
- Spending time with family and friends
- The gift of a new day
- A peaceful night's sleep
- Beautiful nature that surrounds me
- Spreading love to others
- My sweet pup

In addition to writing letters to God, talking with God, and writing in a gratitude journal, I also learned gratitude is expressed in service, not only words. I felt the importance of that lesson when I reached out to others in loving ways, especially during times when I was feeling down. I could feel my spirit lift after calling someone, sending someone a note, and offering to help others in some way. Serving others, however big or small, helped me shift from times of desolation to times of consolation.

Most of the spiritual teachers whose books I read also emphasized the importance of gratitude. I had always been a fan of gratitude and had written in quite a few gratitude journals over the years. Gratitude was also helping me to shift from negative thought patterns when they occurred.

The interesting thing is, once I started to say thank you, I kept going on and on. Have you ever experienced that? Try saying thank you to someone during your day and observe if that one thank you doesn't encourage you to look for another person to thank. It's like a domino effect of gratitude. My soul was beginning to calm my mind, and the voices of kindness, love, and gratitude were speaking up.

Our minds can be filled with negative and disruptive thoughts, and one of the best ways to tame those thoughts is with bursts of gratitude. *The Ignatian Adventure* speaks a great deal about gratitude: "For Ignatius, gratitude is the first, most important step on the spiritual journey. An attitude of gratitude, practiced often enough, helps us find God in all things and can transform the way we look at our life and at other people."[2] I've experienced that immensely.

Here are a couple of letters of love I wrote to God that were filled with gratitude:

September 18, 2020

> *Psalm 23: The Lord is my shepherd. "Beside restful waters he leads me. He refreshes my soul."*

Dear God,

Thank you for guiding me here—by restful waters. You are refreshing my soul every day. Thank you for my family and the many new people you are bringing into my life. Thank you for teaching me about love and showing me how to live life truly from the heart.

Love, Marcella

*   *   *

September 29, 2020

Excerpt from "Messenger" by Mary Oliver,
Thirst: Poems by Mary Oliver

"Let me keep my mind on what matters,
which is my work,
which is mostly standing still and learning to be astonished."

*   *   *

October 8, 2020

"For nothing is impossible with God."

Dear God,

Thank you for showing me how to follow you in the following examples, my need for space, guiding me to the cottage here, teaching me to feel in my heart, and the new and wonderful friends you've introduced me to. "I am your child. Let it be done to me according to your will." Thank you for always teaching me and guiding me.

Love, Marcella

Soul Searching:

- Choose one person to thank every day and be an observer of the experience.
- Thanking someone has a domino effect.
- Try to thank people and be open to following the thank-you momentum train!

Song suggestion:

"Make Someone Happy," by Jimmy Durante

Sticky Note #39
Examine Your Day in Five Minutes

"The examen is a method of reviewing your day in the presence of God. It's actually an attitude more than a method, a time set aside for thankful reflection on where God is in your everyday life. … Real prayer is about change, and change is never easy."

—JIM MANNEY

Soul School didn't take place only during the day. There was one little prayer that was about ten minutes in the evening: the Examen.

A few minutes is spent reviewing the day with God, giving thanks for many blessings, asking to see where we might have strayed away from God during the day, and asking for a grace for the following day.

Examen is a practice Saint Ignatius used 500 years ago and is a very integral part of the Spiritual Exercises. According to Mark E. Thibodeaux, writing in *Reimagining the Ignatian Examen*, "Saint Ignatius of Loyola created the Examen to be a very short prayer. In the Examen, we review our recent past to find God and God's blessings in daily life. Examen is like a thoughtful reflection at the end of each day."[1] It's a five-step routine that can be done in a few minutes:

1. Start with gratitude. Ask God to help you look over your day with a grateful heart. Ask God to help you see how the Spirit was working through you and others.
2. Review the day's events and name the blessings during the day. Savor the special moments of the day. Where was the love?
3. What is stirring in your soul? Pray over feelings that arise as you review your day. Ask God to show you any feelings you may be holding on to. Did the feelings bring you closer to God (happy, joyful, hopeful) or move you away from God (self-doubt, jealousy, anxious)?
4. Give thanks for the gift and grace of awareness even if you're uncomfortable with what you've discovered. Awareness is the first step towards healing a wounded heart.
5. Ask for the grace you need the next day and set an intention for the following day. What do you need from God tomorrow? Some examples may be hope or a deepening of your faith.

These ten minutes have helped me better understand patterns in my life and where I'm closer to God and where I have a tendency to drift from God. It's also helped me better understand who I am and stay true to myself. And, it's helped me trust and have hope during challenging times. If the questions above seem too much, you can simply ask yourself, "What were the highs of your day?" and, "What were the lows of the day?"

Sleeping with Bread by Dennis Linn, Sheila Fabricant Linn, and Matthew Linn suggest you "spend the next month focusing each day on what gave life and what drained life." They also wrote, "Insignificant moments when looked at each day become significant because they form a pattern that often points the way to how God wants to give us more life."[2]

Reflecting on the day has allowed me to see where God was present in my day and where I may have drifted, and it has helped me set an intention for the following day. This is a practice that has allowed me to stay connected to my soul or reconnect to it if I drifted away.

It's as if you can feel the peace and grace of God restoring your soul during this time. In many ways, I view this time as an opportunity to see where I may have lost connection with my soul and a chance to do it over better the following day. It also has helped move me into a peaceful state and set the tone for a restful night's sleep.

Soul Searching:

- Save ten minutes to review your day at night before going to sleep.
  - » What was one thing that happened that you are thankful for?
  - » Who made you feel special and loved?
- Perhaps you can set an intention for the next day.
  - » What is your wish for tomorrow?

Song suggestion:

"Yah Mo B There," by James Ingram, Michael McDonald

Sticky Note #40
I Got You

"God desires to communicate with you all the time, but when you intentionally open yourself to God's voice, you can often hear it more clearly. To use the metaphor of friendship, it is similar to saying to a friend, 'You have my undivided attention.' Ignatian contemplation enables us to hear more easily, or differently, and to recognize something that might otherwise be overlooked."

—JAMES MARTIN, SJ

During my time in the Spiritual Exercises program, I asked Sister M for guidance on how to handle some upcoming difficult situations in my life. She smiled and confidently said, "God will give you the grace when you need it." The combination of that message and her gentle yet reassuring words made me believe that would happen. And it did. I was amazed when I reported back to her that I had handled the difficult situation and God had given me the grace when I needed it.

It reminded me of the phrase people say when they're helping one another with something: "I got you." I always feel a sense of relief and great appreciation when I hear it from others. I feel like someone has my back, and it takes the weight off my shoulders a bit. I was feeling like God was saying that to me, not in words, but through my feelings and the people he was bringing into my life. I would simply say *God, I need a hug and some reassurance that things will be okay* during times when I felt anxious, and God would deliver. He somehow gave me the grace when I needed it.

All you need to do is ask: ask for help, ask for grace, ask for what your heart desires. God will deliver and won't let you down. The Holy Spirit will provide. The message to ask, believe, and receive seemed to be a recurring message.

I was also beginning to understand from *The Jesuit Guide to (Almost) Everything* and the Spiritual Exercises that God meets us where we are. During my journey, I could feel the presence of Divine love in different moments—when I was uncertain if I made the right decision for space, when I felt sad and lonely, and when I was unsure of my future. There were many other times I felt God's love around me, especially when I was doubtful and uncertain of where I was headed. I could somehow feel a peacefulness within (when I quieted my worried mind).

I also felt God's love through the people he was bringing into my life, and the joy I was feeling in little moments throughout the day; a smile from a baby, words of encouragement from a loved one, a simple conversation with a stranger, and insights into decisions I was trying to make.

As Henri Nouwen reminds us, "The presence of God is often subtle, small, quiet, and hidden. ... The Lord, who is the creator of the universe, comes to us in smallness, weakness, and hiddenness. God speaks in subtle ways and that peace and certainty follow when we hear well."[1]

God became my go-to person for pretty much everything. The more I took to God, the more I was reassured, "I got you." And God always did.

Soul Searching:

- Take a moment to look up at the sky and smile.
- Imagine God saying, "I got you."
  - » How does that feel?
- When you're feeling down and troubled, take a moment to stop, close your eyes, feel each breath going in and out, and imagine the place deep within you filled with love, light, and hope. Ask God for a hug.
- If you feel inclined, say the following: *Ask and you shall receive. Seek and you shall find. Knock and it shall be opened.* Trust in the Higher Power above.

Song suggestion:

"I Got You (I Feel Good)," by James Brown & The Famous Flames

Sticky Note #41
Laugh Every Day

"Abraham Lincoln always kept on the corner of his desk a recently published book of jokes and opened its pages to read a passage whenever he felt tired or depressed. Pleasant humor, clever witticism, innocent nonsense, a roar of harmless laughter—these are forms of good natural medicine given to us by heaven. ... They are medicine you should take in an even greater quantity when you are exhausted by the battles of life. ... A person is fortunate who is able at all times to laugh freely and vivaciously, loudly and cheerfully."

—MASAHARU TANIGUCHI

Sister M, the director of the Spiritual Exercises and the Spiritual Director Program, is one of the holiest people I know. She's a woman who prays, discerns, and enjoys a good laugh from time to time. Among the people I know, she's the closest to a person I'd consider a saint. Her lightness, her loving ways, her genuine concern for others, and her peaceful presence are comforting and soothing to be around. She helped me understand the deep desires of my heart, notice where God is in my life, and laugh a little along the way. Psalm 2:4 says, "But the one who rules in heaven laughs."[1] I imagine God has a sense of humor too.

For most of my life, I was disconnected from God and imagined him to be very stern and serious and unapproachable. I now believe God's spirit lives in each of us and that this Divine force created us and gifted us with our personalities, including our ability to laugh.

I love to laugh and often at myself. I pictured God with a sense of humor now within me, in my soul. He has a lot of patience, too, and continued to send little nudges—more than once, if I missed them the first time. I imagined him saying to himself, "There she goes with her request for a sign again. I got it, and I got you. Keep on believing."

The Truth of Life devotes an entire chapter on laughter and living cheerfully. The author, Masaharu Taniguchi, shares the story of a woman who was severely depressed. She made a pact with herself that she would laugh at least three times a day, no matter what circumstances she encountered. She decided to laugh heartily from the bottom of her heart and fully commit to the laughter pact. She intended to do it whole-heartedly. She stood in front of a mirror and looked at herself as she laughed.

This one simple practice, which she was committed to practicing, improved her health and lifted her mood. She actually felt cheerful and lighter. Laughter is also contagious—her husband and her family also became brighter and cheerful. The positive and healing effects of laughter cannot be underestimated.

I decided to give it a try and commit to laughing at least three times each day, even during those times when I'm feeling down or sad and far from wanting to laugh. I am a believer in the power of positivity and have made a promise to myself to add a daily dose of laughter to my toolkit for leading a soul-based life.

Here are my findings thus far from the practice of daily laughter: the dose of laughter truly did shift my perspective and lift my spirits particularly during an extremely anxious moment.

Laughing helped me realize how my thoughts had spiraled out of control about a particular situation. It instantly derailed my negative train of thoughts. Try it now. Pause for a minute and laugh. Just start laughing. Did you notice a shift in your perspective?

Rhonda Byrne was another spiritual teacher who wrote about the healing power of laughter and shared a few stories of others who used laughter to help heal their bodies. Laughter and joy were considered important elements in helping dissolve diseases in the body. Byrne shares the following story, "Norman had been diagnosed with an "incurable" disease. The doctors told him he had just a few months to live. Norman decided to heal himself. For three months all he did was watch funny movies and laugh, laugh, laugh. The disease left his body in those three months, and the doctors proclaimed his recovery a miracle. As he laughed, Norman released all negativity, and he released the disease. Laughter really *is* the best medicine."[2]

As fate would have it, I somehow found myself on the Mayo Clinic's website while writing this chapter reading about "Stress Management." The caption at the top read, "Stress relief from laughter? It's no joke." The article further mentioned, "Laughter is the best medicine."

God seemed to be letting me know the importance of laughing everyday. It seemed as if the celestial faculty were having the last laugh. God knows us better than we know ourselves because he created us. With God's spirit in us, and if we like a good laugh, perhaps God does too.

Soul Searching:

- Take some time today and have a good laugh. Maybe you can stand in front of a mirror and begin to laugh.

Even if you're feeling worried or stressed, try to pause for a minute and laugh.

- Smile at one stranger you encounter in your day.
- Perhaps you can listen to a baby giggle.
  - » A dear friend of mine has two granddaughters who giggle all the time. My friend shared with me that when her granddaughters giggle, she starts laughing and can't stop.
- Laughter is contagious.
- How do you feel after a good laugh? More relaxed?

Song suggestion:

"Happy," by Pharrell Williams

Sticky Note #42
Know Thyself

"God desires for us to be the persons we were created to be: to be simply and purely ourselves, and in this state to love God and to let ourselves be loved by God. It is a double journey, really: finding God means allowing ourselves to be found by God. And finding our true selves means allowing God to find and reveal our true selves to us."

—JAMES MARTIN, SJ

Who are you? When you look in the mirror, do you feel like you recognize the person looking back at you? What excites you? What are you passionate about? Do you know your authentic self? Are you open to the idea that you have a higher self? Those are some heavy questions.

Don't worry if you can't respond immediately and with clarity to them especially the *Who are you* question. It's taken me more than fifty years to even ask myself that question, and if I had posed the question years ago, I would not have been able to answer it succinctly. I would have rattled off roles I played such as mother, daughter, sister, and businesswoman.

After reading more than forty books in Soul School from various spiritual teachers with different beliefs, I am going to refer to a few teachers who seem to be a little more closely aligned with how I might answer the question, *Who am I?* Now.

As a believer in God, I was drawn to Father James Martin, SJ's book, *Becoming Who You Are,* and his reflections upon the writings of Thomas Merton, an American Trappist monk and a Catholic priest. Father Martin discusses the "false self"—the outward persona we present to others. Our job titles and roles we perform would fall under the false self category. The "true self" is rooted in being—it's the person we are before God.

Discernment is about discovering who we are and living our lives true to that. It's about finding one's identity. It's about listening to the little voice of the Spirit within us. It's about finding God in all things and an openness to where God may be leading us. So how do we hear and follow our inner voice?

As Henri Nouwen writes in his book, *Discernment*:

> When certain poems or scripture verses speak to us in a special way, when nature signs and creation reveals its glory, when particular people seem to be placed in our path, when a critical event seems full of meaning, it's time to pay attention to the divine purposes to which they point. Discernment is a way to read the signs and recognize divine messages ... discernment helps us come to know our true identity in creation, vocation in the world, and unique place in history as an expression of divine love.[1]

I was becoming aware of people coming into my path and events that seemed to unfold with complete ease. I felt the difference between going with the current, and struggling against it.

Through my experiences, in order to see the signs and recognize the path to take, a connection with the inner place of love within was necessary. It seemed as if that peaceful place within was where the true essence and true self was. Connection with the channel of the soul was the answer for me to the question Who am I? And the way I could best connect to it was through moments of silence and stillness. Nouwen expresses this beautifully:

> When we are spiritually deaf, we are not aware that anything important is happening in our lives. We keep running away from the present moment, and we try to create experiences that make our lives worthwhile. So we fill our time to avoid the emptiness we otherwise would feel. When we are truly listening, we come to know that God is speaking to us, pointing the way, showing the direction. We simply need to keep our ears open. Discernment is a life of listening to a deeper sound and marching to a different beat, a life in which we become "all ears."[2]

Many other spiritual teachers spoke of their journeys to discovering their true selves. In *The Power of Love*, James Van Praagh writes, "To be discerning, first, you must know yourself. As it says in *Hamlet*, 'To thine own self be true, and it must follow ... thou canst not then be false to any man.' In other words, take care of yourself first so that you will be able to take care of others. Instead of making choices based on other people's opinions, honor who you are."[3]

Deepak Chopra also wrote about our true Self as our spirit, our soul in his book, "*The Seven Spiritual Laws of Success.*" Describing the true Self he writes, "It is immune to criticism, it is unfearful of any challenge, and it feels beneath no one. And yet, it is also humble and feels superior to no one, because it recognizes that everyone else is the same Self, the same spirit in different disguises."[4]

As I was learning about the importance of knowing oneself and loving oneself, I was also discovering my authentic self, my desires, and my intentions through the books I was reading, meditation, writing in my journal, walks in nature, and Divine therapy sessions with God.

James Martin's description of his journey to understanding who he was in *Becoming Who You Are* resonated with me. Martin wrote, "Much of this journey involved letting go of the need to be somebody else. ... For example, I would notice that another novice whom I admired was quiet and soft-spoken and diffident and introspective. I would think, 'I need to be quiet and soft-spoken and diffident and introspective.' My spiritual director kept reminding me that I didn't really need to be like anyone else except me. But it took a while for that to sink in."[5]

That's exactly how I was feeling when I observed what others were doing. Oftentimes, it was in admiration of others' actions and personalities. While there's nothing wrong with admiring others, it can become an issue if we change from who our true self is to try and become someone else. I reminded myself once again to stay in my lane.

To know thyself is a very important message. It is the gateway to leading a fulfilled life in alignment with your principles, values, and purpose. Know your story, embrace your story, and live your story. Believe in yourself and trust yourself because you do know.

Soul Searching:

- Who are you inspired by and why?
- How do you like to relax?
- What does your ideal day look like?
- What excites you?

- Imagine being in your nineties and looking back on your life. What memories do you want to have?

Song suggestion:

"I Got a Name," by Jim Croce

Sticky Note #43
Make Friends with Uncertainty

"Uncertainty, on the other hand, is the fertile ground of pure creativity and freedom. Uncertainty means stepping into the unknown in every moment of our existence. ... Relinquish your attachment to the known, step into the unknown, and you will step into the field of all possibilities. ... When you experience uncertainty, you are on the right path—so don't give up."

—DEEPAK CHOPRA

We all live with uncertainty every day, but uncertainty was at an all-time high during the height of the COVID-19 pandemic. Here's my journal entry from May 2020, during the height of the global pandemic:

Uncertainty

When can we safely leave our houses? When can we safely fly again? Will the pandemic emerge again in the fall? When can I see my family? So many questions during a time of uncertainty. Sadly, nobody knows or has the answers. Each of us has had to embrace a "new norm" of social distancing, sporting face masks, and limiting physical contact with others. Yet, we still ask, "When will this be over? What's going to happen next?"

I too have been guilty of asking these questions daily. I ask these questions as I pray in the mornings. "God, tell me what to do and how I can help." I've reminded myself daily how important it is to practice gratitude for my blessings. I've written positive messages around my house reminding me to smile and to laugh often. I've listened to inspirational podcasts on how to cope with such uncertainty. I've prayed not only for myself, but also for the world to have faith and carry on.

I've tried my best to embrace some positive coping mechanisms, yet the burning question, "What happens next?" creeps into my mind often. That is, until this morning. I was watching mass in my cottage and was struck by a powerful homily. The message, "Be courageous and be confident." Seems so simple and basic, but it resonated with me. If we are courageous and confident in God, we can be untroubled by the unknown. We don't need to know what's going to happen next to be at peace. Have faith, whatever your belief is, and lean into it. For me, my faith is in God. Trust in what you believe!

I reflected on my life and realized that if I had been told in advance certain events were going to unfold, including some very sad and painful moments of losing those I loved, I would have gasped at the idea of being able to go through any of that. I pledged myself and to God that I would try my best to no longer ask, "What happens next?" I will carry on with courage and confidence in God. I believe. I am prepared and ready to do my best to conduct my affairs with humility, honesty, love, and faith.

Pema Chödrön writes about uncertainty in her book, *Comfortable with Uncertainty*, "A warrior accepts that we can never know what will happen next to us. We can try to control the uncontrollable by looking for security and predictability, always hoping to be comfortable and safe. But the truth is that we can never avoid uncertainty. This not-knowing is part of the adventure. It's also what makes us afraid."[2]

Eckhart Tolle also wrote about accepting uncertainty and moving away from an ego-driven life. "If uncertainty is unacceptable to you, it turns into fear. If it is perfectly acceptable, it turns into increased aliveness, alertness, and creativity."[3] I decided to choose the latter.

Despite many moments of uncertainty, I wanted to meet fear head-on armored with some tools—faith being one of them. Sitting in silence, turning to God, and loving affirmations were a few of the tools I incorporated in my days to combat the fear of uncertainty. I was on a mission to love big, and fear was no longer going to get in the way.

Soul Searching:

- In what ways did the pandemic help you make friends with uncertainty?
- What are some questions you could ask yourself when you're facing uncertainty?
- Remind yourself of past moments when you felt uncertain and things worked out in your favor.

- Perhaps you can write the word *believe* on a sticky note and place it somewhere you can see it this week. This may serve as a reminder for you to trust in what you believe in.

Song suggestion:

"Up On The Roof," by James Taylor

Sticky Note #44
We Are All
Connected

*"We're all connected. We just don't see it. There isn't
an 'out there' and an 'in here.' Everything in the
Universe is connected. It is just one energy field."*

—JON ASSARAF

Are there people in your life who you've felt like you've known forever after just meeting them? Have you ever called someone who answered their phone and said they were just thinking of you? Did you ever feel a connection with someone who wasn't physically with you? What are your thoughts that we are all energetically connected to one another?

The cumulative effect of sitting in silence and stillness most days for a few years was that I could feel the powerful force of love deep within me, the force that had been there all along. I looked at everyone and everything in a different way, with the belief they also possessed the same Divine force within them. We are all created in love, connected through love, and each of us has the force of love within us. I don't think there is a right or wrong term for the force of love within us all. It's more about the feeling of love, and less about the label.

After countless hours in Soul School, I unquestionably felt the love of a Divine power in my life whom I call God, and it seems as if this Divine love lives within our spirits or souls. At least that's been my experience. I was in awe that God's spirit and love has been within me, in my soul, since the moment I was born, and I finally connected to the peaceful presence within. We are Divine beings with the powerful force of love within us. I believe we are all connected—both living and deceased—through the soul.

ENCOUNTERING ONENESS

I'm certainly no expert on any of this. I'm simply sharing my experiences of how I've felt that oneness during times when I've allowed myself to be fully present in the moment and aware. That feeling of oneness seemed to be what my son and I experienced on our walk when we encountered the owl. It felt as if we were connected with the owl, nature, and everything. We were all one. I've experienced this oneness feeling at other times in nature. I felt connected with the birds, the squirrels, and even the alligators, as crazy as that may sound. During those moments, it felt that we were all connected through a much higher force—a power of love—which I call God.

In *A New Earth*, Eckhart Tolle describes what I was feeling, "[T]here is an even deeper level to the whole than the interconnectedness of everything in existence. At the deeper level, all things are one. ... The whole is made up of existence and Being, the manifested and unmanifested, the world and God. So when you become aligned with the whole, you become a conscious part of the interconnectedness of the whole and its purpose: the emergence of consciousness into this world. As a result, spontaneous helpful occurrences, chance encounters, coincidences, and synchronistic events happen more frequently."[1] Perhaps this explains the frequent celestial synchronicities I was experiencing.

On a regular basis, I remind myself of the message that we are all created and formed in Divine love. This powerful message has helped me to better understand others when their behavior may have been difficult to understand and reminded me to try my best not to take things personally. The power of love has helped me shift any negative feelings to love.

I look out my window and observe two birds working very diligently, building a nest in a tree right in front of me. I observe their hard work in awe and wonder as they gather large branches that barely fit in their small beaks and somehow fly up to the tree branch and build their house. They work many hours a day in search of the right material for their nest.

I watch them use their beaks not only to gather sticks for the nest but also to secure and tighten the base and outer edges of the nest. They have been working on their home for about a week, all day long. They make sure each twig and branch is secure and tightly in place.

Humans have the same devotion and love for their families. We do things out of love, just as the birds build a safe place for their family out of love. Love is the common bond. Love is the connection. I ask myself how we all got here. I think of the baby birds that are about to be born. I think of a close friend of mine whose daughter is about to give birth to a baby girl. All created out of love—Divine love. It's all about love.

I have also awakened to the awe-inspiring idea that God has been connected to me, and to all souls, through the soul from the moment we arrived on this planet. I just hadn't been connecting with him. I pictured the soul being God's home—a quiet home and a soothing place.

My soul was sending little nudges from this place of peace, but I had been too busy and active to recognize them. It wasn't until I embraced a little space, silence, and stillness that I began to recognize the whispers and the gentle messages from my soul. This was the beginning of my powerful awakening and transformation.

Once again, God was reminding me how important we all are to him. His love is never ending. What do we need to do with this Divine love in us? Give it space to appear, share it with others, love big, and stay connected to others through the channel of the soul.

Soul Searching:

- When have you tuned into the channel of the soul?
- Sit quietly for five minutes. Place your attention on someone you love dearly. Close your eyes as you think of them and imagine sending love to them. Notice how your body feels.
- Where does your energy begin to shift? Can you feel the connection to the person?

Song suggestion:

"Every Kinda People," by Robert Palmer

Sticky Note #45

Keep Your Chin
Up, and Let Your
Spirit Soar

*"Put forth your entire strength and push yourself ahead without
wasting a moment, step by step, through self-improvement and self-
education, so that you might win the one victory that you seek. This
is the way of the winner. This is the road to becoming the winner
always, through utilizing the Infinite Power (God) that dwells
within you. ... Have faith in yourself. Believe in God, who dwells
within you. Believe in the infinite power that dwells within you."*

—MASAHARU TANIGUCHI

As I was reviewing thousands of journal entries from over a de-
cade, I came across one from January, 2017, three months before
my father passed away. I spent as much time as I could with my
dad those last few months of his life and tried my best to savor
each minute. I wanted to capture as much of his spirit and his
wisdom as I could. I would jot down his messages in my journal
as soon as I got into the car at the end of our time together so I
wouldn't forget them.

Here's what I wrote from our time together on January 11,
2017, "Keep your chin held high" and, "Worry and being sad
isn't worth it; it's a waste of time and energy." My dad used to

remind me to keep my chin up quite often, especially during our time together in the office. I had a tendency to take things to heart, and his words often lifted my spirit. He also knew how much of a worrier I was.

I found myself repeating my dad's advice to keep my chin up many times during the day and then physically doing it—I lifted my chin and cast my eyes to the heavens. This one simple practice reminded me to keep my focus on God and stay connected to God's spirit within me.

Perhaps you can take a minute now and try it—close your eyes, lift your chin up, and feel your breath. The movement of tilting my head upward also reminded me to trust and surrender in the power of God. Does that movement evoke a feeling of surrender in you? One of the daily meditations in *The Word Among Us* reminds us, "People ridicule faith and stoke fear with stories that make evil seem greater than God. But rather than being shaken, we can keep our eyes on God, our focal point. … [T]urn your eyes to the Lord."[1]

This practice became my reminder to stay connected to the spirit of love within my soul and to continue to surrender to this Higher Power each day. It kept me connected to my soul. I would lift my chin to the sky, close my eyes, and bask in the Divine power within me.

Perhaps you can give it another try—pause for a second, close your eyes, and tilt your chin towards the sky. What feelings does that evoke in you? Do you feel the peace within you?

In *The Untethered Soul*, Michael Singer writes, "The secret of the ascent is to never look down—always look up. No matter what happens below you, just turn your eyes upward and relax your heart."[2] And yet again, another celestial synchronicity—*The Untethered Soul* reinforcing the importance of my dad's "keep your chin up" message.

Soul Searching:

- Always keep your chin up.
- Try it now—tilt your head back, lift your chin, and feel the Divine power of love from above.
- As you go through your day, be aware of how many times you take the time to pause, close your eyes, and tilt your chin up.
- When you catch yourself worrying, remind yourself that worrying and being sad is a waste of time and energy.

Song suggestion:

"What's Going On," by Michael McDonald

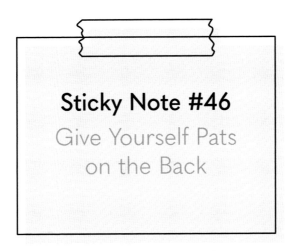

Sticky Note #46
Give Yourself Pats on the Back

"When we become more loving and compassionate with ourselves and we begin to practice shame resilience, we can embrace our imperfections. It is in the process of embracing our imperfections that we find our truest gifts: courage, compassion, and connection. … [E]xploring our fears and changing our self-talk are two critical steps in overcoming perfectionism."

—BRENÉ BROWN

I don't know about you, but I may be my worst critic. I analyze what I say or don't say to others, and I often reprimand myself for not saying or acting differently on many occasions. It's like I have an inner critic sitting in my mind providing a constant commentary on what I'm doing wrong everyday. My self-talk can be harsh and critical at times, yet my others-talk is kind and compassionate.

For others, I feel tremendous compassion as they maneuver through challenging situations and difficulties in their lives, and I console them with kindness every step of the way. But for myself, I am lacking in the self-compassion department. There are very few kind and consoling words for myself. I tell myself to just get on with it and keep moving forward.

More than five years ago, a business colleague helped me notice my self-critical ways. I was downplaying (in a negative way) something positive that happened in our company. My friend said, "Don't be so hard on yourself. Give yourself a pat on the back sometimes." It stopped me in my tracks and I thought about his suggestion. Here, we had something very good happen in our company, and I was dismissing it.

This piece of advice helped me realize the importance of honoring and savoring the little victories and positive moments in life I had been quickly discarding and sweeping away. It also reminded me of the importance of a little self-compassion along the way.

BE KIND TO YOURSELF

Perhaps I had never fully developed self-compassion because I was always striving for some type of perfection. I didn't even know what that perfection looked like or was, most likely because it didn't exist. I had been setting myself up for failure. As Brené Brown says in her book *The Gifts of Imperfection*, "Perfectionism is, at its core, about trying to earn approval and acceptance. ... Perfectionism is other-focused. What will they think?"[1] I had certainly been other-focused for much of my life.

Brené Brown shared Dr. Kristin Neff's research from the Self-Compassion Research Lab, "According to Neff, self-compassion has three elements: self-kindness, common humanity, and mindfulness."[2] Self-kindness would include being kind to ourselves when we stumble or feel insecure. Common humanity recognizes that we all have shared feelings, at times, of "personal inadequacy,"[3] and feeling like we're not good enough at times.

Mindfulness requires staying detached from our emotions and not letting our feelings spiral us down the rabbit hole. I don't know about you, but I have been guilty of not applying any one of these three techniques for most of my life.

TAME THE INNER CRITIC

So here's what I did—I made a pact with myself to start noticing the positive comments from others or events that happened during the day. For example, I would say to myself, *Look at what you got done today*, instead of looking at the tasks I may not have completed. I also cut myself some slack for not completing everything on my to-do list.

I started to talk to myself the way I would to others. If I wouldn't tell a friend, "You'll be fine. Get on with it." I wouldn't tell myself. I began to incorporate some kindness in my self-talk. I reminded myself *I am enough* and I didn't need to keep proving myself to others or striving for some type of perfection.

Just as I accepted others for who they were, and I looked for the positives in others, I wanted to accept myself for who I was and look for the positives in myself (in a humble way). I also relied on a simple affirmation to repeat to myself when my negative self-talk began or I noticed I was identifying with negative thought patterns. This affirmation instantly derailed my unhealthy self-talk train. One of the affirmations was, *I am loved,* when my thoughts might have been telling me otherwise. This became a powerful practice.

In many ways, the inner voice of my soul was my cheerleader and reminded me of the importance of staying positive not only with others but with myself too. I was changing patterns that had been ingrained in me for more than fifty years—patterns of negative self-talk and self-sabotage. I was saying goodbye to my inner critic.

The phrase, "Give yourself a pat on the back," came to me regularly, and I found myself writing down nice things people did or said each day. I imagine we all not only need some pats on the back from others, but we also could benefit from savoring them and remembering them on our journey to a little more self-compassion. My brother recently told me something our dad shared with him about our grandfather. Apparently my grandad told my dad, "We are all doing the best we can."

Soul Searching:

- What are a few positive words others have said to you?
- Ask a friend or family member to share one thing they like about you, then return the favor.
- Offer some pats on the back to others, and notice how you feel.
- Next time you are aware of negative thoughts, repeat a positive and kind affirmation about yourself. Here are a few examples: I am loved, I am enough, or I am worthy.

Song suggestion:

"Love Train," by The O'Jays

Sticky Note #47

Keep It Simple

"*Simplify. Simplify. Simplify your life and you will find the inner peace that the poets and saints of every age have coveted more than any possession. ... Silence. Solitude. Simplicity. Three great friends! They may be the subtlest of our legitimate needs, but when they are honored our spirits soar to unimaginable heights, and we are left only to wonder how or why we ever followed the promptings of all the jeering voices of this world.*"

—MATTHEW KELLY

In many ways, Soul School taught me about the importance of keeping it simple, and I was not only reading the messages, I was being given the opportunity to practice them. In one of my favorite books, *The Jesuit Guide to (Almost) Everything,* James Martin devotes an entire chapter to the simple life. "The mystery is why more people don't choose to live more simply. ... Rather, as de Mello's parable suggests, not being controlled by possessions is a step to spiritual freedom, the kind of freedom that most people say they want."[1]

SPIRITUAL FREEDOM

What does living simply mean to you? The best way I can describe what it means for me is to focus less on material possessions and focus more on living as our best selves tapping into the power of divine love within. What does it mean to live as our best selves? I'm still trying to get there. I suppose it may take an entire lifetime to answer that simple question. Living as our best or our highest selves, according to lessons from Soul School, seems to involve awareness of our thoughts and connection to others and the force of love within us.

I was doing my best to live free of any attachments to material possessions. In fact, I had gotten rid of most of my belongings early in my journey. I found it very liberating to simplify my life to basic necessities. I had not only cleared out a storage unit of furniture and belongings, but I had also gotten rid of most of my business suits and dresses and simplified my wardrobe considerably. I replaced much of the clothing in my closet with books (many of them about the soul).

I felt much lighter and more open to surrendering to where God was leading me. Following the ways of St. Ignatius seemed to be all about detaching from anything that keeps us from getting closer to God. This could represent any attachment to material possessions, attachment to the need of approval from others, or attachment to success and esteem. It seems to be all about openness, awareness, and spiritual freedom.

MORE SPACE FOR DIFFERENT THINGS

Father James Martin described how I felt after getting rid of most of my belongings in the beginning of my adventure, "You find yourself surprised that you can live with so little. ... The less you decide to buy, the more time that you have for the things that matter most."[2] The Ignatian approach to live more simply seemed to be a stepping stone toward greater spiritual freedom.

I certainly felt more lighthearted and freer with fewer possessions. I was also surprised I had been able to live with so little, as Father Martin wrote, after I got rid of the belongings in the storage unit. I had to be very intentional with what I wanted to bring with me at the beginning of my trip because there wasn't much room for anything. I chose to bring a few essential belongings and more sentimental treasures like cards and notes from those I held in my heart. Relationships with loved ones mattered the most to me.

These cards are accessible to me today, and earlier today I reread Mother's Day cards my sons wrote to me when they were teenagers. Those memories are what matter the most—the memories that touch my heart and soul. This past year, I reread a birthday card my mom and dad sent me for my thirty-fifth birthday. Reading it again made me feel like my parents were right there with me, as I believe their spirits are. It felt like time hadn't passed at all. It also helped me reflect on what life may be like for my sons and daughter-in-law and others who are in their thirties.

James Martin offers three suggestions to simplify your life:

1. Get rid of whatever you don't need.
2. Distinguish between wants and needs.
3. Get rid of things you think you need but can actually live without.[3]

Martin also writes, "The turn to a simple lifestyle frees us, reminds us of our reliance on God, makes us more grateful, and leads us to desire 'upward mobility' for everyone, not just for the few. Ultimately, it also moves us closer to the forgotten and outcast."[4]

The fewer possessions we have, the freer we are to turn our attention to God, listen to our inner voices, notice others who may need our help, and surrender to divine love.

Soul Searching:

- What does living simply mean to you?
- What is one step you can take to choose the simple life, the life of your soul?
- Where can you declutter to make room for more important things?
- What thoughts can you clean out of your mind to make space for more inner peace?

Song suggestion:

"Simple Times," by Kacey Musgrave

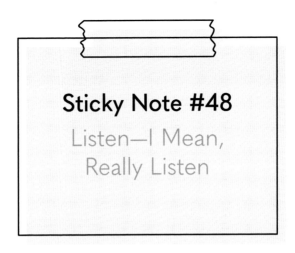

Sticky Note #48
Listen—I Mean,
Really Listen

"Spiritual discernment requires us to put our ears to ground that we may hear the low notes that vibrate for the poor and keep us focused on what is most important—that is, whom God cares most about. ... Whether you turn to the right or to the left, your ears will hear a voice behind you, saying, 'This is the way; walk in it' (Isa.30:21 NIV). In other words, when you come to a fork in your road, you will hear a voice behind you—what Nouwen calls the 'inner voice of love'—that reminds you of God's presence and reveals to you God's will, sometimes specifically which way to turn."

—MICHAEL J. CHRISTENSEN

Have you ever trained for a biking, running, swimming or other sporting event? My son trained for a Half Ironman a year ago. I remember observing his devotion, discipline, and persistence with the utmost admiration and awe. *I don't know how he does it,* I thought to myself. He created a daily workout schedule a year in advance of the race, and consistently stuck to it. He was at the pool before the sun was up every morning, and clocked in thousands of miles on the roads biking and running for a year. He was persistent, consistent, and devoted to his goal. He has true grit. His discipline and persistence paid off, and he not only finished the Half Ironman, but he hit his targeted goal, and wasn't even out of breath at the end of the event. Those of us who cheered him through the finish line were speechless.

Imagine if we incorporated the same discipline, perseverance, and daily practice to train our minds and listen more to others like my son did for his race? Truly listening to another person is an art and something not done often in today's busy world. When was the last time someone truly listened to what you were saying? Was there a time when you felt someone's complete attention while you were speaking with them? How did you feel when that person allowed you to speak honestly and freely at your own pace?

In my experience, many people are preoccupied or distracted and don't seem to listen very well. (I would include myself in that group.) It's not as if we don't want to listen attentively to others, rather our thoughts seem to be elsewhere. Or perhaps we have a short attention span and are not able to concentrate for an extended period of time. Or maybe we're so connected to our phones and social media that we don't even realize when someone we love is trying to communicate and share something important with us.

James Martin devotes an entire chapter on listening in *The Jesuit Guide to (Almost) Everything*. He writes, "Listening is a lost art. We want to listen, we want to think we're listening, but we are often so busy planning what we're going to say in response or what advice we're going to give, that we fail to pay attention."[1] Oftentimes, we are thinking about what we want to say next, preoccupied with something else going on in our lives, or consumed with lots of chatter in our minds. It is a gift to be in the presence of another person who truly listens to what we are saying.

If we can't listen well to what others are saying, how can we listen to our inner voices where the Divine power of love resides? Whether you call that Higher Power of love God or another name, how are you able to connect with it if you're not able to listen? How are you able to sense where that Higher Power may be leading you? The importance of really listening to our inner voices was a big lesson in Soul School. As a student in Soul School, I was committed to leading a soul-based life and learning to listen and connect with the peaceful soul to become aware of prompts or nudges was important. I had been completely disconnected from this peaceful place at the beginning of my journey, but thanks to Soul School I learned that silence, awareness, an open heart, and listening were important practices in order to hear the messages from the soul and follow the path intended for me.

LISTENING IS AN ART

M. Scott Peck, M. D. also emphasized the art of listening in his book, *The Road Less Traveled,* "When we love another we give him or her our attention; we attend to that person's growth. When we love ourselves we attend to our own growth. When we attend to someone we are caring for that person. ... By far the most common and important way in which we can exercise our attention is by listening. ... Listening well is an exercise of attention and by necessity hard work."[2]

He further writes, "For true listening, no matter how brief, requires tremendous effort. First of all, it requires total concentration. You cannot truly listen to anyone and do anything else at the same time. ... If you are not willing to put aside everything, including your own worries and preoccupations for such a time, then you are not willing to truly listen. ... True listening, total concentration on the other, is always a manifestation of love."[3]

Father Thomas Keating also speaks of the importance of being fully present with others in his book, *Divine Therapy and Addiction*. He writes, "The health of any relationship relies on being able to bring one's total presence to the other person or to the group that one is relating to, whether this is God or other people, or even oneself or the rest of creation."[4]

He further mentions getting to the point on our spiritual journeys where we "fine-tune our ability to listen to the Spirit and recognize what it is saying."[5] Listening to the promptings of the Holy Spirit requires improving our listening skills.

ENHANCING MY SPIRITUAL LISTENING PRACTICE

Perhaps it would be helpful if I share how I incorporated spiritual listening in the course of my days. To be clear, it wasn't as if I heard God's powerful voice speaking directly to me saying, "Take this path or do this." Far from it. I actually didn't hear much of anything except a steady stream of thoughts racing in my mind most times when I sat in silence. But, I stayed committed to the practice.

Here's what I did: I set the timer for five minutes and sat in silence. When my mind began to race, I focused my attention on my breathing and directed my thoughts, as best I could, on my heart. I actually moved my attention from my head to my heart. When thoughts appeared, I chose a word to connect me back to my heart. Oftentimes, that word was God. I did my best to teach myself to shift my attention from my thoughts racing in my mind to the peaceful place within the heart and soul—to God.

In many ways, it was similar to training for a physical event like my son did for the Half Ironman, yet I was attempting to train my mind instead of my body. Although I suppose training for a physical race does require training both the mind and the body and they may be more similar than I realized. At the end of five minutes, I wrote down a few insights or ideas in my journal. Sometimes, I had nothing to write down.

After a few months, I noticed that I wanted to sit longer than five minutes, and I gradually increased my time. Another thing that happened was I began to have a few insights and ideas. I wrote them down. For example, when I was struggling with making a decision, I brought it to God and did my best to listen for any insights. I also noticed I felt more peaceful. The effects were cumulative and each session built upon itself over time.

I felt the impact from sitting in silence to truly listen to the voice of my soul. I devoted my full attention to being still and listening and tried to remember to also continue the practice when I was in conversations with others. I wanted to hear the sweet sound of my soul, and I wanted to be fully present with others. I wanted to simply delight in the company of those I loved without words.

One of my mom's messages in a card she wrote me was, "Continue to listen to the voice in your heart." She was onto something many years ago. I was finally beginning to listen.

Soul Searching:

- Perhaps you can sit in silence for five minutes. Are you aware of insights or ideas that arise? Is there a yearning in your heart?
- Try bringing a decision you're struggling to make to a Higher Power. See if any insights or suggestions come to you. Write them down.

- The next time you have a conversation, focus your attention for five minutes on what the other person is saying instead of how you want to respond.

Song suggestion:

"Shower the People," by James Taylor

Sticky Note #49
Embrace the Five-Minute Rule

"We are what we repeatedly do. Excellence, then, is not an act, but a habit."

—WILL DURANT

Do you think you could sit in silence for just five minutes during the course of a day? Five minutes feels like a blip doesn't it? Consider an experience when you were totally engrossed in an activity you completely lost track of time. Did it feel like time flew by too quickly and you would give anything to get back just five minutes from that experience?

I think we've all realized at some point in our lives that time passes quickly, but imagine how your life could change if you allow yourself just five minutes each day to check in with yourself and incorporate a healthy practice of sitting in silence. The cumulative effect of intentionally doing something for five minutes a day over time adds up and can help us form new habits. It certainly helped me create some new habits that were more in line with my soul.

THE GIFT OF TIME

I was first introduced to the concept of the five-minute practice a few Christmases ago when I received a *Five-Minute Journal* from my son's girlfriend. The idea is great—you answer a few questions in the mornings and a few in the evenings—short, simple questions that take approximately five minutes to answer. As an avid journal writer, I loved the idea of spending only five minutes at the beginning of the day setting intentions for the day and five minutes at the end of the day jotting down the highs of the day and lessons learned each day. Five minutes certainly seemed like an attainable goal.

I've also applied the five-minute rule to other mindfulness practices such as meditation and prayer. I experimented with different types of meditation initially—guided ones and meditations with music—but for me, the best way to connect with the peaceful place within me is in silence.

Sitting in complete silence was difficult at first, because like most people, I have a very active mind, and when I'm doing one thing, I am usually thinking of my next task. I reminded myself I only had to sit quietly for five minutes. That's it.

IT'S ONLY FIVE MINUTES

At first, sitting in silence for five minutes felt like a long time, and I probably spent most of those minutes wondering how long I had been sitting and how close I was to the five-minute mark. That was OK, I reminded myself. The most important part was doing it every day. *Just show up and put in the work* I told myself.

Like most things in life, the more I practiced, the easier it became, and I slowly increased the time by one minute. I was teaching myself to sit quietly with myself, my thoughts, and connect within. When the voices in my head started to take over, I would quietly say, "Thinking," and shift my attention back to my breathing and the loving peaceful place deep within me.

I was trying my best to lead a soul-based life and controlling my thoughts was a necessary step in order to connect within. Connection to the soul seemed to be movement away from the mind into the heart space. My soul was now beginning to quiet my thoughts, not the other way around, as had been the case for much of my life. This practice helped me break the bad habit of getting lost in the thoughts in my head, and feel the peaceful love in my heart.

Not only was this a comforting experience, but it also allowed me to observe the many thoughts in my mind and not allow them to control me. I began to feel a sense of peace wash over me at the end of the five minutes, and I actually started to look forward to sitting in silence, connecting to the peaceful place within each morning. It was like hitting a reset button. Although I've actually increased my time to sixteen minutes, I still remind myself I only *need* to do it for five minutes.

I also applied the five-minute rule to incorporating other activities into my life, and this simple rule has helped me create some new and healthy habits. For example, rather than become overwhelmed and having no idea where to begin with reading the Bible, I've decided to read it for five minutes. That's it. I've started with reading a Psalm a day for five minutes.

Breaking activities into small increments of time feels much more manageable and less overwhelming. If there's a fun hobby or project I'm interested in, I've told myself to start it for only five minutes a day. The key is to begin; Take the first step.

For much of my life, I had a tendency to put off activities I was interested in because I told myself I didn't have the time to invest in them. My perfectionistic tendencies created roadblocks for my interests over the years. I now remind myself I can spare five minutes a day to begin something I'm interested in. Can you spare five minutes a day to sit in silence and begin to lead a soul-based life? Perhaps you can give it a try now.

Soul Searching:

- Use the five-minute rule to help you connect to the soul and create new habits in your life.
- Are there new activities or hobbies you would like to incorporate in your life? Perhaps you can begin one for five minutes each day. The key is to take the first step.
- Journal about your experiences—what lasted longer than five minutes, and what made five minutes feel like five hours?
- Choose a five-minute interval in your day to start.

Song suggestion:

"Let Your Love Flow," by The Bellamy Brothers

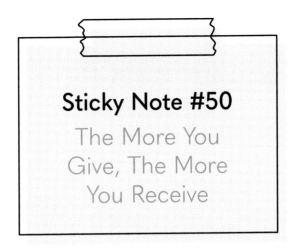

Sticky Note #50
The More You
Give, The More
You Receive

"The more you give, the more you will receive, because you will keep the abundance of the universe circulating in your life. In fact, anything that is of value in life only multiplies when it is given. … It is the intention behind your giving and receiving that is the most important thing. The intention should always be to create happiness for the giver and receiver, because happiness is life-supporting and life-sustaining and therefore generates increase."

—DEEPAK CHOPRA

As a student in Soul School with a mission to love big, giving to others was of the utmost importance. Afterall, love is all about giving without expecting anything in return. Love and giving seem to be one. Here are a few examples of some ways to give to others:

- Your time
- Your attention
- A smile
- A silent blessing or prayer for someone
- An ear to listen

- Encouragement for a friend who's going through a difficult time
- A compliment

THE POWER OF GIVING AND RECEIVING

About six years ago, I met a kind woman who worked at a salon I frequented quite regularly. Over the course of several months, we developed a friendship and shared our beliefs about the power of God's love in our lives and stories about where God had shown up in our lives. During that time, I was working through a difficult situation and was very lucky to be the recipient of her steadfast commitment to leading a life of love and kindness. She gifted me not only with her time and attention, but a wonderful book called *The Truth of Life. Book of Daily Life. Vol. 7* by Masaharu Taniguchi, Ph.D which I included in the Soul School curriculum.

Her note to me in the cover of the book was a gentle reminder of the importance of *discovering the love of God which is present in all things, people and situations that present themselves in our lives.* Her message and her gift were so impactful that I felt inspired to share them with others and include some of the words from "*The Truth of Life.*" Masaharu Taniguchi writes, "The joy of giving is contagious. If we would only let the joy of giving spread from person to person."[1]

Of the seven spiritual laws, The Law of Giving is the second law in Deepak Chopra's book, *The Seven Spiritual Laws of Success.* Chopra reminds us about our relationships with others being one of giving and receiving. Have you ever experienced a desire to give to someone especially after someone has given something to you? I'm speaking more about non-material objects when I speak of giving.

Here's an example: the other night, very much out of the blue, I received a kind note from my brother whom I'm very close with. It was only a few sentences, but his message was one of kindness, encouragement, and love. His message lifted my spirits and propelled me forward in my journey. It left such a positive impact, I found myself wanting to share my enthusiasm and gratitude with someone else so they could experience a feeling of encouragement too. I wrote an uplifting note to someone close to me. It was like the domino effect of spreading kindness and love.

THE POWER OF LOVE

Florence Scovel Shinn was another author who helped me learn more about one of my favorite topics, love, in her book, *The Complete Game of Life and How to Play It*. She writes, "Jesus Christ taught that it was a great game of Giving and Receiving. 'Whatsoever a man soweth that shall he also reap.' This means that whatever man sends out in the word or deed will return to him: what he gives, he will receive … if he gives love, he will receive love."[2]

She further writes, "Real love is selfless and free from fear. It pours itself out upon the object of its affection, without demanding any return. Its joy is in the joy of giving. Love is God in manifestation, and the strongest magnetic force in the universe. Pure, unselfish love draws to itself its own; it does not need to seek or demand."[3] Love and giving seem to be inter-connected.

In his chapter on friendship in *The Jesuit guide to (Almost) Everything*, James Martin states, "You forget that it takes a little effort. And the small things matter: making time to call, staying in touch."[4] He further goes on to say that true friendships are hard to find, "and it also may seem that most people have to spend their lives giving more than receiving."[5]

Rhonda Byrne also writes about the power of giving, "Giving from a heart that is overflowing feels so good … giving from a full heart is one of the most joyous things you can do, and the law of attraction will grab hold of that signal and flood even more into your life. You can feel the difference."[6]

I've experienced the desire to give without any expectation of anything in return. And small acts of kindness truly do matter. Through my experiences, I've found that when I reach out to those I'm close with and care about, it starts magnifying: I keep reaching out to more people, and others reach out to me. Spreading kindness and love help us on our journeys to becoming "lofty souls."

Soul Searching:

- Perhaps you can smile at a stranger today.
- Create a list of ways you can give something little to others.
- Remember, giving your time and attention can be free for you and priceless to someone at the same time.
- Perhaps you can write a note to someone you love and encourage them on their journey.

Song suggestion:

" The Power of Love," by Huey Lewis & The News

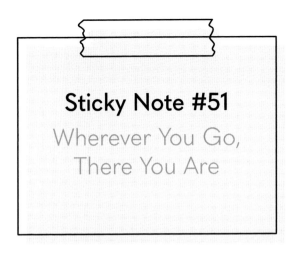

Sticky Note #51

Wherever You Go, There You Are

"Wherever you are, be there totally. If you find your here and now intolerable and it makes you unhappy, you have three options: remove yourself from the situation, change it, or accept it totally. If you want to take responsibility for your life, you must choose one of these three options, and you must choose now. Then accept the consequences. No excuses. No negativity. No psychic pollution. Keep your inner space clear."

—ECKHART TOLLE

My mom was a woman of mantras. "Suffering is optional," she would remind me when I needed a dose of reality. She truly lived that mantra. I always thought she came up with that clever phrase on her own, but my brother recently informed me her mantra was actually a Buddhist saying.

Her actions spoke volumes. I look back with tremendous admiration for her how she cared for her husband, her three children, and her eight grandchildren. She was all about her family. If anyone had the right to complain at times, it certainly was her.

When my dad became paralyzed, my mom was pregnant with my brother, and my oldest brother was only two years old.

My parents moved forward one day at a time with courage, strength, and determination. What my father couldn't do physically he made up for intellectually.

I don't recall my mom ever complaining about anything. She lived her mantra, "Suffering is optional." She once shared with me that she dealt with her difficult emotions through physical activity. When her mother passed away at the young age of sixty-four, my mother came home from the hospital and cut the lawn with a push lawn mower.

She didn't wallow in her emotions or feel sorry for herself; she moved physically through her pain and sadness. I knew she was sad, but she chose to process her emotions through physical activity. I watched her with quiet admiration. We all have our own unique ways of processing various emotions in our lives. For me, it's going for a run, preferably in nature, with more wildlife around than people.

CONTEMPLATING CONTENTMENT

I wish I could go back now and observe my mother's actions more deeply when I was growing up. Back then, my attention and focus were on myself, as is the case with many young people. I could have learned so much more simply from observing how she maneuvered intentionally through her life.

A few years before she passed away, she told me no matter what might happen to her, she had lived a wonderful life and was truly happy. I remember saying, "Mom, don't say that." I wanted her to live forever and didn't want to think about her being gone. Her words came back to me and provided a little bit of comfort years later as I was trying to come to terms with what had happened.

She was a woman of no regrets. She took care of the people and things that were in her life with great love. She didn't compare her life to anyone else's. She stayed in her lane. These are lessons I have worked very hard to live by each day and could have learned much earlier in my life by simply observing my mom's words and actions.

She knew what it meant to be happy, and she lived every day by being fully present in each moment as best she could. She had another mantra that was written on an old rickety plaque hanging in our garage that read, "Wherever you go, there you are." She lived those words to their fullest every day. There were quite a few times she repeated those words to me with a smile, or she simply pointed to the sign when I needed a friendly reminder that we can't escape ourselves. At that time, I was not open to letting the words truly sink in.

My mom had some other mantras which she wrote on a small chalkboard in our kitchen. My brothers and I looked forward to reading her uplifting messages every day. As with most important messages back then, I missed the significance and true meaning behind them. I realize that now when I reflect on my younger years. It was as if I were simply reading the words and not contemplating the deeper meaning beneath them.

FINDING MEANING BEHIND THE MANTRAS

In my younger years, I was always on the move, and if I wasn't moving, I was thinking about where I was headed next. I definitely wasn't living the "Wherever you go there you are" mantra. I had very little concept of what it meant to be present and connect with myself within. I was very social and very busy. One of my nicknames was Chatty Cathy—I was blessed with the gift of gab. I was always looking outward, clueless that an inner world even existed.

I've since learned and experienced that no matter where I was geographically, that inner being—my soul—was always there. Quite frankly, it wasn't until I moved to another state, lived alone, and became a student in Soul School that I began to get a glimpse of the place within—my soul. It's hard to believe it's taken me fifty-six years to begin to learn who I am deep within. I am trying my best every day to live true to that person.

Wherever You Go, There You Are is a book by John Kabat-Zinn about practicing mindfulness meditation in everyday life. I'd forgotten I had read that book with the same title as this sticky note message many years ago. I was reminded of it recently when I was at a coffee shop, and I noticed a young man holding a book. I couldn't help but comment on the title and share with him that I was writing a book and the title of one of the chapters was the title of the book he was reading.

It suddenly dawned on me that I, too, had a copy of that book somewhere in my boxes of books in the attic. I couldn't wait to get home and search through my many boxes of books. And there it was—almost wanting to be found. This seemed like a sign that I was on the right track with including the "*wherever you go, there you are*" as a message for leading a soul-based life.

In his book, Jon Kabat-Zinn writes, "Like it or not, this moment is all we really have to work with. Yet we all too easily conduct our lives as if forgetting momentarily that we are here, where we already are, and that we are in what we are already in … to allow ourselves to be truly in touch with where we already are, no matter where that is, we have got to pause in our experience long enough to let the present moment sink in; long enough to actually feel the present moment, to see it in its fullness, to hold it in awareness and thereby come to know and understand it better. Only then can we accept the truth of this moment of our life, learn from it, and move on."[1]

The present moment is all we have, and focusing on it helps keep us from being stuck in the past or jumping ahead to the future. Awareness in the present moment allows us to not only stay in the moment, but also to connect with ourselves and decide how we would like to move forward.

This moment is all we have—acknowledge it, savor it, and make any changes you wish for the next moment. Wherever you go now and wherever you go next, you are always there. There's no escaping yourself.

Soul Searching:

- Remind yourself to be present in the moment during the course of the day. Accept the moment, change the moment, or remove yourself from the moment. You decide.
- Remember, you can choose how you want to feel in each moment.
- List ways you can live with presence.
- Create a cue you can use as a reminder to come back to the present moment.
  - » Clap your hands.
  - » Tap your leg.
  - » Take a deep breath.
  - » Whatever you'd like.

Song suggestion:

"Into the Mystic," by Van Morrison

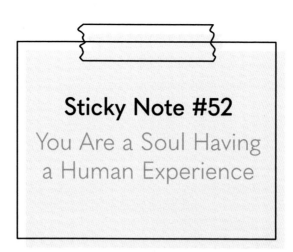

Sticky Note #52

You Are a Soul Having a Human Experience

"When you enter this stage of life (The Spirit), regardless of your age or position, you recognize your truest essence, the highest self. … You know that nothing dies, that everything is an energy that is constantly changing. … As a soul with a body you are passionately drawn to your inner world. … You become an observer of your world and you move into other dimensions of consciousness. … This inner infinite energy is not just in you, it is in all things and all people who are alive now and have ever lived."

—WAYNE DYER

As I sit here today, I realize I am not the only one writing this book. I have relied on a much Higher Power (God) to guide me and give me the words and the messages. I've also relied on my soul, the inner place of peace and love, to steer me in the right direction. I felt the inner light of my soul gently guiding me on my journey, and recognized the many signs I received along the way confirming I was on the right track or steering me in a different direction when I veered off the path. My journey began with a strong longing for space and choosing the road that was less desirable—the path into the unknown. The journey into the unknown has opened up an entirely new way of living for me!

I had no destination when I began my journey, and I learned to rely on guidance from above that is also within. It's my opinion, from what I learned from many of the spiritual writers whose books I read in Soul School, that we all possess this Higher Power of love within us. We are our inner forces of love, our souls. Ponder that for a minute. This means we can connect with the divine presence within us anytime we wish. That is very powerful and freeing—we have nothing to fear.

The more I surrendered to the Higher Power, and stayed connected with it, the more I released any fear and anxiety and better understood the path intended for me. "Have faith in yourself. Believe in God, who dwells within you. Believe in the infinite power that dwells within you. God doesn't exist externally so as to be seen here or over there. He exists within us. When we rely completely on our inner power, infinite power is displayed from within,"[1] writes Masaharu Taniguchi, Ph.D, in his book *The Truth of Life*. It's a powerful feeling to know God's spirit dwells within us!

I've also learned the soul's language is gentle and quiet and can easily be misinterpreted—or worse, unheard. At least in my experience, that's how it felt. The soul isn't loud and stormy; it's gentle and soothing. It isn't chaotic and frenzied; the soul is peaceful and intentional. It doesn't fight to be noticed; it nudges and whispers. I imagine the soul as our spiritual support center of love, peace, and serenity—our inner sanctuary of light.

While our physical bodies are necessary for our time here on this planet, the inner space of the soul is truly who we are. Our physical bodies are merely our shells. As James Van Praagh says, "You are a spiritual being having a human experience."[2] Van Praagh goes on further in his book, *The Power of Love,* to discuss how we are all here to learn from our souls and to let our souls guide us. Take a moment to think about that—you are a soul with a physical body. Can you begin to let your soul guide you?

Imagine how your life might change if you connected with the force of love within your soul and allowed it to guide you. Are you open to the idea that we have an inner light within us and we can connect to that energy, the divine spirit, within us anytime?

BEAUTIFUL GUIDANCE

Connecting to the divine energy within and allowing it to guide me has transformed my life. The more connected I am with my inner sanctuary, the more peaceful I feel and the more celestial synchronicities I notice. The soul is our center of peace and love, and when the soul guides us, we feel immersed in love and peace every step of the way, no matter what challenges or road bumps we may encounter.

I remind myself throughout the day to close my eyes for a few minutes and feel the peace and love within, especially during moments when I'm feeling stressed or anxious. It's like receiving a hug from my soul and being reminded that I'm not alone on my journey. You're not alone either. You have a powerful force of love within you too!

I suppose another way to put it is that leading a soul-based life is like trying to live your life as your highest and your best self. Your best or your highest self would be giving, loving, kind, accepting, non judgmental, considerate, and helpful to others. Your best self would be selfless. Your best self would have faith, hope, and love. Your true self is soul-centered. The ego represents the false self—the self-centered and selfish self. Leading a life from the false self or the ego would be living from our lower selves.

The first inkling of my soul was like a gentle wake-up call, like drops of water landing on a sponge. It wasn't like the loud alarm of a cell phone, that beeps louder if you don't address it. I have since come to recognize the longings that are the language of the soul. Living from your soul is living from love.

Thich Nhât Hanh wrote about the highest spirit within us and says, "When we are in touch with the highest spirit in ourselves, we too are a Buddha, filled with the Holy Spirit, and we become very tolerant, very open, very deep, and very understanding."[3]

In no way do I intend to be an expert on such mysterious matters as the soul and God. My intent is to simply share my experiences with you with the hope that you may also experience the soothing and peaceful nature of your soul and God in your busy and active life. Our world is a noisy one filled with chaos at times, as well as negativity. I hope this book helps you take some space to hear the soft, gentle, soothing, and loving sound of your soul and tune in to your soul's channel.

BEAUTIFUL JOURNEYS

It seems as if we all have our own unique ways of journeying to this greater power that lives within us. Perhaps my father's flying was his way of connecting with his soul. My dad's sense of calm, stillness, and quiet in air space enabled him to access a greater power. That space allowed my father to access his soul.

My journey, although different, started with a similar need for a space that was calm, still, and quiet. Although our journeys were different, our feelings of a greater power were the same.

I believe it's no accident I came across my dad's journals as I was writing the end of this book. I was in search of a winter coat in my attic, and my eyes caught a glimpse of my dad's journals at the bottom of a plastic bin. I suppose my father is in some ways a co-author of this book.

Although his handwriting was hard to decipher, I did my best to understand some of it. I remember that my aunt had given him a journal at his eightieth birthday party. She titled the journal, "The Book of Ben," and wrote a few categories to help him get started. Most of the pages were blank with the exception of one page. Under the category "On Life," my dad wrote, "Never, ever give up!" Apparently, my dad had a mantra too—inspired by Winston Churchill. He lived his mantra to the fullest and truly never gave up!

January 16, 1993

It does take more courage to look at oneself honestly and to act with integrity after disarming the true self. I have shown much courage in facing many adversaries (but perhaps not with much wisdom!) but this challenge—the challenge of self-discovery—which I am beginning and must meet to grow again, I fear will be my biggest test. All that has gone before has been but a preparation for this. What a wonderful opportunity I have been given. I have been granted the chance of a new beginning. I must have the courage to confront myself and others honestly.

* * *

August 13, 1994 (Two days before the birth of his grandson)

My writing has found its metaphor in flying. Flying has changed me. The major challenge was and is my need to focus my attention and have the courage to act—to fly. I have learned something of weather, engines, and most importantly of myself. I have had to shed an old me and reform to openness, youthfulness. My flying experiences will always be with me.

My dad's journal entries describe his journey from the false self (ego-based) to the true self (soul-based), as this book shares my journey from fear (the false self) to love (the true self). My journey which began with no destination, seemed to take me to my inner self, my true self. It was a journey within. Feeling the divine power of love within me helped me dispose of any anxious and fearful thoughts.

With God's spirit within us, what is there to be afraid of? It's interesting that initially my intent was to write a book for future generations in our family to better understand their grandparents, and I am ending it with journal entries from my father. Hopefully, future grandchildren will gain a better sense of what their truly amazing great grandparents were like.

As I perused my dad's journals, I found a wrinkled piece of paper with twenty-six titles of flying incidents my father shared with me. I had completely forgotten I had asked my dad years ago to share some flying stories with me.

We met weekly and I listened intently as he shared his fantastic, humorous, and sometimes frightening flying escapades. He loved a good adventure and a good laugh. I had tremendous admiration and awe for him. I wanted to collect his stories and write a book about him to share with others how amazing this man was who was paralyzed. He didn't let life pull him down—quite the opposite—he drove a car, ran a successful business, and flew planes. He never, ever gave up! Neither did my mom.

As you may have realized by now, I'm a big fan of celestial synchronicities. I'll share a few more with you. A few days ago, as I was writing this chapter, an article appeared in my inbox from my Oprah subscription titled, "What the Happiest People All Have in Common."

The conclusion from the study was "*Love* is actually all you need," and "Happiness is love, full stop."[4] I was stunned. According to the article and study, happiness is *love*. That's it. I had received yet another celestial synchronicity, a pretty big one, as a confirmation that I should finish and publish this book with the simple message to love big. It's all about love. Sounds so simple and basic doesn't it? Love is all we need.

And for the next celestial synchronicity. I smile now as I think of my father. He was a huge fan of Jesuit education and attended a Jesuit high school and college. He always made little comments about the Jesuits and their education being "top notch." He would often jest, "There's nothing like a Jesuit education. Those Jesuits know how to think and learn."

Over the years, he expressed his mild disappointment that neither his sons nor his grandsons attended his all-male high school and that none of his children or grandchildren attended his Jesuit college. The Spiritual Exercises and Rules of Discernment originated from Saint Ignatius of Loyola, the founder of the Jesuits. So I, too, have been lucky to have experienced a bit of the Jesuit education, thanks to St. Ignatius and Soul School, and can honestly say I agree with my dad—it has been quite transformative in my life, just as it was in my dad's.

A FINAL MESSAGE

My dad had a plaque in his office I read hundreds of times when I went in and out of his office. It said simply, "Go forth and set the world on fire," a quote from Saint Ignatius. For the past twenty years, Saint Ignatius had been patiently waiting for me to experience the Spiritual Exercises and discover the wonderful order he founded in 1534—yet another celestial synchronicity.

I hope you also take Saint Ignatius's advice to go forth and set the world on fire. With your soul as your inner spark guiding you, anything and everything is possible. All you have to do is ask, believe, and love big. And remember to stay open for celestial synchronicities.

I can picture my father now smiling down from Heaven, so happy one of his children experienced the power of a Jesuit education under Saint Ignatius of Loyola.

This weekend, my younger son and his girlfriend attended services at a Baptist church, and the pastor gave a sermon on disabilities. My son shared with me that he thought of Chauncey (my sons' nickname for their grandfather) immediately. The pastor told the story of a disabled person whom he knew and said, "He went to Heaven, but the wheelchair went to hell." My son and I agreed that Chauncey would have loved that quote!

PS:

And Dad, I *do* believe in something much bigger than myself. Thank you for inspiring me and nudging me to the soul and closer to you and Mom.

Soul Searching:

- When you look for the beauty in this world, it will appear—be on the lookout.
- Don't let your journey end here—continue to make space and listen to Divine love as your soul whispers to you.

- Co-create your life the Higher Power (God) which lives within you.
- Remember: happiness is an inside job. "True happiness comes from a healthy dependence on a Higher Power."
- Go forth and set the world on fire.
- Never, ever give up!

Song suggestion:

"What a Wonderful World," by Louis Armstrong

Soul School Curriculum

- *A New Earth*, by Eckhart Tolle
- *A Return to Love*, by Marianne Williamson
- *Alcoholics Anonymous: The Big Book of Boundaries,* by Henry Cloud and John Townsend
- *Daring Greatly*, by Brené Brown
- *Discernment,* by Henri Nouwen
- *Discovering Your Personal Vocation,* by Herbert Alphonso, SJ
- *Divine Therapy and Addiction*, by Thomas Keating
- *Grit*, by Angela Duckworth
- *Learning to Pray,* by James Martin, SJ
- *Living Buddha, Living Christ,* by Thich Nhât Hanh
- *Manifest Your Destiny,* by Wayne Dyer
- "Oprah's Super Soul Podcast" (Oprah Winfrey)
- *Permission to Feel,* by Marc Brackett, PhD
- *Reimagining the Ignatian Examen,* by Mark Thibodeaux, SJ
- *Rising Strong,* by Brené Brown
- *The Art of Discernment,* by Stefan Kiechle
- *The Discernment of Spirits,* by Timothy Gallagher, OMV
- *The Four Agreements,* by Don Miguel Ruiz
- *The Gifts of Imperfection,* by Brené Brown
- *The Ignatian Adventure,* by Kevin O'Brien, SJ
- *The Jesuit Guide to (Almost) Everything,* by James Martin, SJ
- *The Mastery of Self,* by Don Miguel Ruiz Jr.

- *The Message,* by Eugene Peterson
- *The Power of Love,* by James Van Praagh
- *The Power of Now,* by Eckhart Tolle
- *The Rhythm of Life,* by Matthew Kelly
- *The Road Less Traveled,* by M. Scott Peck, MD
- *The Seat of the Soul,* by Gary Zukav
- *The Secret,* by Rhonda Byrne
- *The Seven Spiritual Laws of Success,* by Deepak Chopra
- *The Untethered Soul,* by Michael Singer
- *The Word Among Us* (daily meditations)
- *Three Magic Words,* by Uell Stanley Andersen
- *Truth of Life,* by Masaharu Taniguchi, PhD
- *Untamed,* by Glennon Doyle
- *When God Winks at You,* by SQuire Rushnell
- *When God Winks,* by SQuire Rushnell
- *When the Heart Waits,* by Sue Monk Kidd
- *When Things Fall Apart,* by Pema Chödrön
- *Why Did God Make Me?* by Louis M. Savary and Patricia H. Berne
- *Wishes Fulfilled,* by Wayne Dyer

Soul School Playlist

1. "Somewhere Over the Rainbow," by Katharine McPhee
2. "The Boss," by Diana Ross
3. "Philadelphia Freedom," by Elton John
4. "Shackles (Praise You)," by Mary Mary
5. "Carolina in My Mind," by James Taylor
6. "How Can You Mend a Broken Heart," by Al Green
7. "Higher Love," by Steve Winwood
8. "The Light is On," by Christopher Cross
9. "Don't You Worry 'bout a Thing," by Stevie Wonder
10. "Can't Stop the Feeling," by Justin Timberlake
11. "Come Fly With Me," by Frank Sinatra
12. "Don't Blink," by Kenny Chesney
13. "Cold Heart (PNAU Remix)," by Elton John, Dua Lipa, and PNAU
14. "Lean On Me," by Bill Withers
15. "Raindrops Keep Fallin' On My Head," by B.J. Thomas (in honor of Mimi)
16. "Happy Birthday," by Stevie Wonder
17. "Butterflies," by Kacey Musgraves
18. "When You Wish Upon a Star," by Louis Armstrong
19. "Humble and Kind," by Tim McGraw
20. "That's Life," by Frank Sinatra
21. "Unforgettable," by Nat King Cole
22. "The Sound of Silence," by Simon and Garfunkel
23. "What the World Needs Now is Love," by Steve Tyrell, Burt Bacharach, Martina McBride, Rod Stewart, James Taylor, and Dionne Warwick

24. "Love Is the Answer," by Dan England and John Ford Coley
25. "Heartlight," by Neil Diamond
26. "Let It Be," by The Beatles
27. "Call Your Mama," by Seth Ennis
28. "You've Got a Friend in Me," by Randy Newman
29. "The Secret O' Life," by James Taylor
30. "Peace Train," by Yusuf / Cat Stevens
31. "Hold On (Change is Comin')," by Sounds of Blackness
32. "Smile," by Nat King Cole
33. "Magnet and Steel," by Walter Egan
34. "Love's Divine," by Seal
35. "Have a Talk With God," by Stevie Wonder
36. "Shower the People," by James Taylor
37. "I've Got Love on My Mind," by The Beatles
38. "Make Someone Happy," by Jimmy Durante
39. "Yah Mo B There," by James Ingram, Michael McDonald
40. "I Got You (I Feel Good), " by James Brown & The Famous Flames
41. "Happy," by Pharrell Williams
42. "I Got a Name," by Jim Croce
43. "Up On the Roof," by James Taylor
44. "Every Kinda People," by Robert Palmer
45. "What's Going On," by Michael McDonald
46. "Love Train," by The O'Jays
47. "Simple Times," by Kacey Musgraves
48. "Shower the People," by James Taylor
49. "Let Your Love Flow," by The Bellamy Brothers
50. "The Power of Love," by Huey Lewis and The News
51. "Into the Mystic," by Van Morrison
52. "What a Wonderful World," by Louis Armstrong

Soul School Toolkit

Here are some simple practices that have helped me pluck away some bad habits and build new ones aimed at leading a more soul-based life—leading with more love and gratitude, and less fear and worry. Many of these are fairly simple and take no more than five minutes each day to complete. Included are a combination of practices including:

- Mindfulness
- Manifestation
- Meditation
- Prayer
- Self-Love
- Positivity
- Spiritual

Feel free to pick one a day, a week, or whenever you wish. I like to imagine these as little habits, little steps, and little shifts for your days—one day at a time. I hope these tools help you discover the essence within. It's never too late to begin to make changes!

1. Say an I Am Affirmation

Write a simple affirmation of love about yourself and say it aloud twenty times each morning. This helpful practice shifts one to a positive mindset. For example, "I am worthy of great love." or, "I am enough." Really feel the words and let them sink in when saying them.

2. Set a Daily Intention

Journal for at least five minutes in the morning and five minutes in the evening. In the morning, perhaps set a couple of intentions for the day ahead. Perhaps choose a word to take with you during the day to remind you of your intention.

3. Pause for Five Minutes

Sit in silence for at least five minutes a day. Close your eyes and focus on your breathing.

4. Give Yourself a Pat on The Back

Jot down in a journal the nice things people say to you each week. Give yourself pats on the back. I've found that it helps me to reread the positive comments in my journal when I'm having a down day. You may be amazed at how many complementary and appreciative comments others say to you over time. You can also give someone else a pat on the back—write a positive review for someone or give someone a compliment.

5. Write in a Gratitude Journal

Write down at least three things you are grateful for each day in a gratitude journal. My first gratitude entry each morning is: *Thank you for the gift of another day!*

6. Create a New Habit

Write down one habit that you would like to create in your life. Use a habit tracker daily for thirty days to get a sense of your progress. You can make a simple tracker by listing a few activities that you would like to incorporate in your day at the top of a piece of paper, writing the number of each day of the month on the left-hand side of the paper, and placing an "x" under each activity you completed each day.

7. Take a Ten-Minute Walk Outdoors

Take a ten-minute walk outside with full presence and listen to the sounds around you. Maybe you can even disconnect from your phone and tap into your senses. What sounds do you hear? What do you smell? What do you see?

8. Manifest Your Dreams

- What are your dreams?
- What are you passionate about?
- Who inspires you?
- To help you get started, think back to when you were twelve or thirteen years old. What dreams did you have?
- Imagine yourself at the end of your life. What desires and goals would you like to have accomplished?
- Picture each area of your life and what you would like to see in each area (career, relationships).

Create a vision board or journal with pictures of how you would like your life to be. Take one action step a day.

9. Track Moments of Consolation and Desolation

Notice times of consolation versus desolation. In consolation, I see everything with loving eyes. I think about the people I love and pray for them and visualize sending them a hug and wrapping my arms around them. My wish is that I am able to express my love for them. I've written my feelings when in consolation, and often re-read those words when I'm in desolation. It's part of the human condition to have days when we're feeling up and days when we're feeling down. This practice has allowed me to recognize when I'm having a down day, accept it, and attempt to shift my mood by reading what I wrote when I was more upbeat.

10. Do a Spiritual Inventory

Learn about the Twelve Steps program. I always thought that this was only for those struggling with alcohol or some type of substance abuse. The Spiritual Direction Program taught me otherwise. We studied this program and read two books I highly recommend—*The Big Book* and *Divine Therapy*. One of the steps in the program is to do an inventory of yourself. This was a valuable lesson for me and helped me see patterns in my life, focus on my strengths, and change patterns I didn't like. Looking at patterns from the past helped me create new patterns for today and the future.

11. Write a Letter to Yourself

Write a letter to a part of yourself that you want to change. One habit of mine that I became aware of while in soul school was worrying and being anxious. I was amazed after reading my journal from the Spiritual Exercises how much I worried and doubted. During a retreat on growth in midlife, we did a great exercise: we wrote a letter to a part of ourselves that we did not like. That was an easy one for me—I chose fear. Writing a letter to your adversary is quite freeing and powerful. This helps you change the narrative you may tell yourself to a more positive one.

12. Embrace Positivity

Embrace the power of positive thoughts and words. I try my best to speak only positive thoughts and words. This has taken quite a bit of practice, and I've caught myself mid sentence trying to reverse some of what I've already spoken. I've also decided to look at *what is* instead of *what isn't*—another way of focusing on the positive in life.

13. Give Something or Someone Your Complete Attention for Thirty Minutes

Put your complete attention on something you're doing for thirty minutes a day. It can be as simple as a task at work, doing the dishes, or talking with a friend. Think about what you're doing and place your complete attention on what you're doing during those thirty minutes. This helps train the mind to stick to one thing at a time. (This was a suggestion from Father Thomas Keating in a video on Mindfulness.)

14. Come Up With A Mantra

Spend some time each day to discover your mantra, your mission, something you're passionate about. To quote Oprah Winfrey, "There is no greater gift you can give or receive than to honor your calling. It's why you were born. And how you become most truly alive!¹"

15. Tap into Your Feelings

Ask yourself, "How am I feeling?" throughout each day. This one question has helped me stay grounded on my own two feet and not get lost in others' feelings and energy. It's kept me in touch with my inner self. It has reminded me to stay in my lane. Notice any physical sensations in your body when you answer this question. Label how you're feeling and accept them as best you can.

16. Shift to the Present Moment

Ask yourself, "Am I aware?" to be present in each moment.

17. Review the Fourteen Rules for Discernment and Write Them in Your Own Words

Write the fourteen rules for discernment in your own words as they would apply in your life. Review my Rules for Discernment (Sticky Note #26).

18. Ask Yourself Five Simple Questions Each Day

Ask yourself these five questions each day:

- What am I going to learn today?
- Who loves me?
- What decisions am I going to make today?
- What actions am I going to take today?
- How am I going to show my gratitude to someone else today?

These questions were on an index card that my dad carried with him every day. I found this card in his wallet after he passed away. I had no idea he had incorporated this habit in his life.

19. Give Examen a Try

Practice Examen—review your day before going to sleep. Look at the movements of your soul. Where did God show up in your day? Where were you moved towards God and where were you pulled away from God? What were the highs of your day? What were the lows of your day?

Five steps:

- Ask for the light. Ask for the Holy Spirit to help you see where God was.
- Give thanks for things that happened.
- Look for love and joyful moments and those times where you may have been selfish and unkind.
- Ask God for a grace you need for the next day.

This one practice has helped me recognize the patterns of God in my life.

20. Write in a Dream Journal

Write down any dreams you may remember having when you wake up. Keep a dream journal.

21. Find Awe in Your Day

Find one thing in your day that gives you a sense of awe and brings tears to your eyes (not only in a sad way). An example is looking into a baby's eyes.

22. Acknowledge Negative Thoughts with The Welcoming Prayer

Say The Welcoming Prayer when you're caught up in negative thinking. As you say this prayer, feel any resistance and name the feeling. Notice how it feels in your body (gritting of your teeth or a racing heart).

Welcome, welcome, welcome. I welcome everything that comes to me in this moment because I know it is for my healing. I welcome all thoughts, feelings, emotions, persons, situations, and conditions. I give over my desire for belonging and security. I give over my desire for affection and esteem. I give over my desire for power and control. I give over any desire to change any situation, condition, person, or myself. I open myself to the love and presence of God and the healing action and grace within.

This prayer helps shift from the ego and false self and return to our true self.

23. Practice Centering Prayer

Practice Centering Prayer for twenty minutes. Close your eyes and sit in quiet. When thoughts arise, label them as thinking. Notice them and let them go. This practice helps quiet the mind so we can feel the presence of Divine love (God). This Divine love is very healing.

24. Listen to *The Manifestation Sound Meditation* for Fifteen days

Listen to Wayne Dyer's sound manifestation meditation for fifteen days.

25. Review Your Journal Intentions Monthly

Review your journal entries at the end of each month to get a sense of the people and opportunities coming into your path.

26. Shift Worried Thoughts to Gratitude

Shift worried thoughts to gratitude. For example, if your mind is spiraling downward with fearful thoughts, pause and begin to find something to be grateful for. It may simply be that you are still breathing. Focus on your breath. It may be the sun that is shining. It may be someone in your life who is very special to you.

27. Laugh Once a Day

Stand in front of a mirror and laugh. Even if you don't feel like laughing, give it a try. Start laughing for one minute.

28. Come Up with One Sentence to Stop Racing Thoughts

Come up with one simple sentence to quietly say to yourself when your thoughts are racing out of control. This helps train your mind to stay in the present moment. For example, one of my sentences is, *"Out of order—God, take over."*

29. Ask Yourself the Why Question

What's the why behind your dreams and goals? Try to get to the intentions behind what you're doing.

30. Look for a God Moment During the Day

Look for a "God Moment" during the course of a day. Did someone or something get your attention and tug at your heart? Maybe a friend sent you a kind note or helped you in some small way. Jot down any little moments of love in your day.

31. Turn to Your Activity List When Your Mind Is Stuck

Make a list of activities to turn to when your mind is stuck or anxiety is creeping in. A few of my activities to help me shift away from any obsessive and hurtful thoughts are:

- Do a few push-ups
- Go for a walk outside
- Turn on a movie
- Read a book
- Call a friend
- Find three things to be grateful for

Having a list to turn to has given me an action step to take to control my thoughts and not have them control me.

32. Become a Watcher of Your Thoughts

Remind yourself that our thoughts create. Choose your thoughts and your words carefully. Spend five minutes quietly observing your thoughts and detaching from them. See yourself as an observer of your thoughts. Tell yourself, *"I am a master of my thoughts."*

33. Ask Yourself, *"Is What I'm About to Do or Say Going to Bring Me Peace?"*

34. Listen Attentively to Someone for Ten Minutes

Make it a point to listen attentively to someone for ten minutes a day.

35. Schedule a Ten-Minute Worry Session

Set a timer for ten minutes and allow yourself time to ruminate or worry. That's it. Only ten minutes. Maybe write what you're afraid of.

36. Write a Note to a Friend or a Loved One

Reach out to a friend by phone or send a text message and let them know you're thinking about them.

37. Listen to Your Favorite Song to Boost Your Mood

Listen to music for a mood boost.

38. Remind Yourself to Stay in Your Lane

Quietly tell yourself to stay in your lane if you start comparing yourself to what others are doing.

39. Do Something Nice for Someone

Do a simple act of service for someone else. This can be as simple as smiling at a stranger.

40. Look for a Celestial Synchronicity

See if you can notice a sign, a celestial synchronicity from a Higher Power that seems to be guiding you in a certain direction. Perhaps there's a message that keeps being repeated in your life in various ways.

Here are a few prompts to help you get started:

- Do you feel as if you are being guided in a certain direction?
- Do you feel a pull towards a person or a place?
- Are certain things falling into place (ie. moving somewhere, a career change, or a certain relationship?)

Notes

Sticky Note #1

    1.   Dyer, Wayne W. *Manifest Your Destiny: The Nine Spiritual Principles for Getting Everything You Want* (New York, NY: HarperPaperbacks, 1999).

Sticky Note #2

    1.   O'Brien, Kevin F. *The Ignatian Adventure: Experiencing the Spiritual Exercises of Saint Ignatius in Daily Life* (Chicago, IL: Loyola Press, 2011), 3.

Sticky Note #3

    1.   Founder Institute. "What Pivoting Is, When to Pivot, and How to Pivot Effectively." The Founder Institute, April 26, 2023. https://fi.co/insight/ what-pivoting-is-when-to-pivot-and-how-to-pivot-effectively.

Sticky Note #4

    1.   O'Brien, *The Ignatian Adventure,* 57-58

Sticky Note #6

    1.   Andersen, U. S. *Three Magic Words: The Key to Power, Peace, and Plenty* (Novato, CA: New World Library, 2019).

    2.   Brown, Brené. *The Gifts of Imperfection* (New York, NY: Hazelden Information Educational Services, 2022).

    3.   Merton, Thomas, Robert Inchausti, and Thurman Robert A F. *The Pocket Thomas Merton* (Boulder, CO: Shambhala, 2017), 6.

    4.   Stefan Kiechle, *The Art of Discernment: Making Good Decisions in Your World of Choices* (Notre Dame, IN: Ave Maria Press, 2005), 69.

Sticky Note #7

1. Tolle, Eckhart. *The Power of Now: A Guide to Spiritual Enlightenment* (Vancouver, B.C.: Namaste Pub., 2004).
2. Tolle, *The Power of Now,* 22.
3. Dyer, *Manifest Your Destiny,* 4.
4. Dyer, *Manifest Your Destiny*
5. Tolle, Eckhart. *A New Earth: Awakening to Your Life's Purpose* (New York, NY: Life, 2016), 258.

Sticky Note #9

1. Williamson, Marianne. *A Return to Love: Reflections on the Principles of a Course in Miracles* (New York, NY: HarperOne, 2012), 19, 23, 26.
2. Chopra, Deepak, *The Seven Spiritual Laws of Success: A Practical Guide to the Fulfillment of Your Dreams* (Sydney, N.S.W.: Read How You Want, 2008), 11.
3. Chopra, *The Seven Spiritual Laws of Success,* 11-12.
4. Chopra, *The Seven Spiritual Laws of Success,* 55.
5. O'Brien, *The Ignatian Adventure,* 56.
6. Shinn, Florence Scovel. *The Game of Life & How To Play It* (Newburyport, MA: Hampton Roads Publishing, 2014), 8.
7. Shinn, *The Game of Life & How To Play It,* 69.
8. Peterson, Eugene H. *The Message: The Bible in Contemporary Language* (Colorado Springs, CO: NavPress, published in alliance with Tyndale House Publishers, Incc., 2016), 958.
9. Peterson, *The Message,* 957-958.
10. Singer, Michael A. *The Untethered Soul: The Journey Beyond Yourself* (Oakland, CA: New Harbinger Publications, Inc, 2008).
11. Singer, *The Untethered Soul,* 71, 73, 106.

Sticky Note #11

1. Duckworth, Angela. *Grit: The Power of Passion and Perseverance* (New York, NY: Scribner, 2018), 8.

Sticky Note #12

1. DeAngelis, Barbara. *How to Make Love All the Time* (New York, NY: Dell, 1991.
2. DeAngelis, *How to Make Love All the Time.*

Sticky Note #13

1. Dyer, *Manifest Your Destiny,* 20.

Sticky Note #14

1. Martin, James. *Learning to Pray: A Guide for Everyone* (New York, NY: HarperOne, an imprint of HarperCollinsPublishers, 2022).
2. O'Brien, *The Ignatian Adventure,* 48.
3. SQuire D. Rushnell, *When God Winks: How the Power of Coincidence Guides Your Life* (New York, NY: Howard Books, an imprint of Simon &Shuster, Inc., 2001), xxi.
4. O'Brien, *The Ignatian Adventure.*
5. O'Brien, *The Ignatian Adventure.*

Sticky Note #15

1. James Martin, *Learning to Pray: A Guide for Everyone,* 213.
2. Martin, *Learning to Pray,* 223.
3. Martin, *Learning to Pray,* 223.
4. Martin, *Learning to Pray,* 229.

Sticky Note #16

1. John 15:16 Message Version
2. Psalm 139:13-14 Message Version
3. John 15:16 Message Version

Sticky Note #17

1. Nouwen, Henri J, Rebecca Laird, and Michael J. Christensen. *Discernment: Reading the Signs of Daily Life* (New York, NY: HarperOne, an imprint of HarperCollins Publishers), 181.
2. Matthew 7:7-9 Message Version
3. Rushnell, *When God Winks.*
4. Rushnell, *When God Winks.*
5. Rushnell, *When God Winks.*
6. Kidd, Sue Monk. *When the Heart Waits: Spiritual Direction for Life's Sacred Questions* (San Francisco, CA: HarperSanFrancisco, 2006).
7. Nouwen, *Discernment,* vii-viii.

Sticky Note #18

1. Rushnell, *When God Winks.*
2. Rushnell, *When God Winks.*

Sticky Note #19

1. O'Brien, *The Ignatian Adventure*, 14-15.

Sticky Note #20

1. Keating, Thomas, and Tom S. *Divine Therapy & Addiction: Centering Prayer and the Twelve Steps* (Brooklyn, NY: Lantern Publishing & Media, 2020), 136.
2. Keating, *Divine Therapy & Addiction*, 140-141.

Sticky Note #21

1. Chödrön, Pema. *When Things Fall Apart: Heart Advice for Difficult Times (20th Anniversary edition)* (Boston, MA: Shambhala Publications Inc, 2016).
2. Brown, *The Gifts of Imperfection*.
3. Exodus 3:14 Message Version

Sticky Note #22

1. Praagh, James Van. *Power of Love: Connecting to the Oneness* (New York, NY: Hay House INC, 2018), 19.
2. Peck, M. Scott. *The Road Less Traveled: A New Psychology of Love, Traditional Values, and Spiritual Growth* (New York, NY: Simon & Schuster, 2003).
3. Carl Jung Quotes. BrainyQuote.com, BrainyMedia Inc, 2023. https://www.brainyquote.com/quotes/carl_jung_132738, accessed July 24, 2023.
4. Kelly, Matthew. *The Rhythm of Life: Living Every Day with Passion and Purpose* (North Palm Beach, FL: Blue Sparrow Books, 2018).
5. Hanh, Nhât. *Living Buddha, living Christ* (New York, NY: Riverhead Books, 2015).
6. Psalm 46:10 Message Version
7. Kelly, *The Rhythm of Life*, 45.
8. Kidd, *When the Heart Waits*.
9. Keating, *Divine Therapy & Addiction*, 139-140.
10. Nouwen, *Discernment*, 198
11. Tolle, *A New Earth*.

Sticky Note #23

1. 1 Corinthians 13:13 Message Version

Sticky Note #24

1. Brown, *The Gifts of Imperfection,* 26.
2. Brest, Martin, Ron Osborn, Jeff Reno, Kevin Wade, and Bo Goldman. *Meet Joe Black.* United States: Universal Pictures, 1998. https://www.amazon.com/Meet-Joe-Black-Brad-Pitt
3. England, Dan, and Ford Coley, John, Love is the Answer. 1979.

Sticky Note #25

1. Chopra, *The Seven Spiritual Laws of Success.*
2. Nouwen, *Discernment,* 138.
3. Nouwen, *Discernment*

Sticky Note #26

1. Nouwen, *Discernment,* ix.
2. McCartney, Paul, Let it Be. 1970.

Sticky Note #27

1. Martin, James. *The Jesuit Guide to (Almost) Everything: A Spirituality for Real Life* (New York, NY: HarperOne, an imprint of HarperCollins Publishers), 237-238.
2. Ephesians 3:17 Message Version
3. Matthew 19:26 Message Version

Sticky Note #28

1. Martin, *The Jesuit Guide to (Almost) Everything.*
2. Dyer, *Manifest Your Destiny,* 8.
3. Sudeikis, Jason, Bill Lawrence, Brendan Hunt, and Joe Kelly. Whole. *Ted Lasso* 1, no. 1. Apple TV, 2020.

Sticky Note #29

1. Singer, *The Untethered Soul,* 28-29.
2. Carl Jung Quotes. BrainyQuote.com, BrainyMedia Inc, 2023. https://www.brainyquote.com/quotes/carl_jung_132738, accessed July 24, 2023.
3. Singer, *The Untethered Soul,* 13.

Sticky Note #30

1. Byrne, Rhonda. *The Secret* (New York, NY: Atria Books, 2018), 170.
2. Tolle, *The Power of Now,* 79.
3. Tolle, *The Power of Now.*
4. Tolle, *The Power of Now.*
5. Byrne, *The Secret,* 142.
6. Tolle, *The Power of Now,* 65.
7. Kabat-Zinn, Jon. *Wherever You Go, There You are Mindfulness Meditation in Everyday Life* (New York, NY: Hachette Books, 2014), 117.

Sticky Note #31

1. Luke 11:9-10 Message Version
2. Byrne, *The Secret,* 11.
3. Byrne, *The Secret.*

Sticky Note #32

1. The Word Among Us—Daily Meditations for Catholics. Easter, 2022 Issue.
2. Nouwen, *Discernment,* 152.
3. Nouwen, *Discernment.*
4. The Word Among Us—Daily Meditations for Catholics. February 2022 Issue.

Sticky Note #33

1. Byrne, *The Secret,* 4, 9.
2. Byrne, *The Secret,* 55.
3. Byrne, *The Secret.*

Sticky Note #34

1. Marianne Williamson, *A Return to Love: Reflections on the Principles of a Course in Miracles* (New York, NY: HarperPerennial, A Division of HarperCollins Publishers, 1992). 41
2. The Word Among Us—Daily Meditations for Catholics. January 2020 Issue.
3. Ezekiel 26:36 Message Version

Sticky Note #35

1. Keating, *Divine Therapy & Addiction.*
2. Galatians 5:6 Message Version
3. Luke 12:22 Message Version

Sticky Note #36

1. Van Praagh, James. *Power of Love: Connecting to the Oneness* (Carlsbad, CA: Hay House, 2018), 40.

Sticky Note #37

1. Tolle, *A New Earth*, 258.
2. Matthew Kelly, *The Rhythm of Life: Living Every Day with Passion and Purpose* (North Palm Beach, FL: Blue Sparrow, 2015), 30.
3. Kelly, *The Rhythm of Life,* 31.
4. Dr. Martin Luther King, Jr. Quote. QuotePark.com, Wikiquote, 2021. https://quotepark.com/quotes/1941136-martin-luther-king-jr-we-must-discover-the-power-of-love-the-power-the/, accessed July 24, 2023.

Sticky Note #38

1. Martin, *The Jesuit Guide to (Almost) Everything.*
2. O'Brien, *The Ignatian Adventure.*

Sticky Note #39

1. Thibodeaux, Mark E. *Reimagining the Ignatian Examen: Fresh Ways to Pray from Your Day.* (Chicago , IL: Loyola Press, 2015), 1-2.
2. Linn, Dennis, Sheila Fabricant Linn, Matthew Linn, and Francisco Miranda. *Sleeping with Bread: Holding What Gives You Life* (Mahwah, NJ: Paulist Press, 1995).

Sticky Note #40

1. Nouwen, *Discernment.*

Sticky Note #41

1. Psalm 2:4 Message Version
2. Byrne, *The Secret*, 129.

Sticky Note #42

1. Nouwen, *Discernment.*
2. Nouwen, *Discernment.*
3. Van Praagh, *Power of Love.*
4. Chopra, *The Seven Spiritual Laws of Success,* 11-12.
5. James, Martin. *Becoming Who You Are: Insights on the True Self from Thomas Merton and Other Saints* (Boston, MA: HiddenSpring, an imprint of Paulist Press, 2006).

Sticky Note #43

1. Chopra, *The Seven Spiritual Laws of Success.*
2. Chödrön, Pema/ Sell, Emily Hilburn. *Comfortable with Uncertainty: 108 Teachings on Cultivating Fearlessness and Compassion* (New York, NY: Random House Inc, 2018), 3.
3. Tolle, *A New Earth*, 274.

Sticky Note #44

1. Tolle, *A New Earth*, 276-277.

Sticky Note #45

1. The Word Among Us—Daily Meditations for Catholics.
2. Singer, *The Untethered Soul*

Sticky Note #46

1. Brown, *The Gifts of Imperfection,* 56.
2. Brown, *The Gifts of Imperfection,* 59.
3. Brown, *The Gifts of Imperfection,* 60.

Sticky Note #47

1. Martin, *The Jesuit Guide to (Almost) Everything,* 178.
2. Martin, *The Jesuit Guide to (Almost) Everything,* 181.
3. Martin, *The Jesuit Guide to (Almost) Everything,* 204.
4. Martin, *The Jesuit Guide to (Almost) Everything,* 203.

Sticky Note #48

1. Martin, *The Jesuit Guide to (Almost) Everything.*
2. Peck, M. Scott. *The Road Less Traveled: A New Psychology of Love, Traditional Values, and Spiritual Growth* (New York, NY: Touchstone, Simon & Schuster, 2003), 121.
3. Peck, *The Road Less Traveled.*
4. Keating, *Divine Therapy & Addiction.*
5. Keating, *Divine Therapy & Addiction.*

Sticky Note #50

1. Taniguchi, Masaharu. *Truth of Life Volume 7: Book of Daily Life* (New York, NY: Seicho-No-Ie, Inc., 1992) 104
2. Shinn, *The Game of Life & How To Play It.*
3. Shinn, *The Game of Life & How To Play It.*
4. Martin, *The Jesuit Guide to (Almost) Everything.*
5. Martin, *The Jesuit Guide to (Almost) Everything.*
6. Byrne, *The Secret.*

Sticky Note #51

1. Kabat-Zinn, *Wherever You Go, There You Are,* xiii, xiv.

Sticky Note #52

1. Taniguchi, *Truth of Life Volume 7,* 81.
2. Van Praagh, *Power of Love,* 3.
3. Nhât Hanh, *Living Buddha, Living Christ* (New York, NY: Riverhead Books, a division of Penguin Putnam, Inc., 1995), 37-38.
4. Farr, Adrienne. "What the Happiest People All Have in Common." Oprah Daily, October 24, 2022. https://www.oprahdaily.com/life/health/a40622518/happiness-is-love-full-stop/.

Soul School Toolkit

1. Oprah Winfrey Quote. MinimalistQuotes.com, 2020. https://minimalistquotes.com/oprah-winfrey-quote-8789/, accessed August 25, 2023.